In My Sights

G·K
Hall
&C⁰

In My Sights

The Memoir of a P-40 Ace

James B. Morehead

G.K. Hall & Co.
Thorndike, Maine

Published in 1998 by arrangement with Presidio Press.

G.K. Hall Large Print Paperback Series.

The text of this Large Print edition is unabridged.
Other aspects of the book may vary from the original edition.

Set in 16 pt. Plantin by Al Chase.

Printed in the United States on permanent paper.

Library of Congress Cataloging in Publication Data

Morehead, James B. (James Bruce)
    In my sights : the memoir of a P-40 ace / James B. Morehead.
      p. (large print) cm.
    Originally published: Novato, CA : Presidio, c1998.
    ISBN 0-7838-8451-6 (lg. print : sc : alk. paper)
    1. Morehead, James B. (James Bruce) 2. World War, 1939-1945
— Aerial operations, American. 3. World War, 1939-1945 —
Personal narratives, American. 4. United States. Army Air Forces
— Biography. 5. Fighter pilots — United States — Biography.
I. Title.
[D790.M614 1998]
940.54'4973'092—dc21
  [B]   98-10151

I dedicate this book to Ophelia James Morehead.

I dedicate this book to my mother, who saved my skin a hundred times from an abusive father twice her size.

In the defense of her children she fought like a mother tiger.

Ours were like two hearts tied together. I inherited her temperament and the nature of her character, and mine fit hers like a cartridge in its chamber. This made the long days and longer nights sheer agony as she awaited the dreaded knock on the door. The message on the yellow strip of paper would tell her that all her years of toil, of scrubbing dirty diapers, that all the world of guidance and support and the nurturing of her child to productive manhood had been destroyed.

Hers was of the silent service, to wait patiently until the call came for her to deliver unto the service of her country another precious product of her womb, and then another, and yet another.

As a farmer's wife, she knew nothing of tea parties and style shows; she knew toil, and in her fifties in the war years she knew the work of feeding farmhands and harvest crews, and overwork. She knew the need for the physical and spiritual support of a fiercely loyal community engaged in devoted service to its country's war effort. As a teacher and church leader, her remaining energies went toward uniting and advancing her community.

She feared the knock on the door all right, for one day that knock came, to tell her that the war had taken the life of her eldest son, Dr. Jackson Morehead.

James B. Morehead

Preface

Winston Churchill termed that terrible time the "Hinge of Fate." The terrible time was the period of World War II, from 7 December 1941 to mid-1942, when the bulk of the armed forces of the Allied nations lay in defeat and ruins. France and Poland were defeated and occupied, Britain had suffered her greatest defeat since medieval times with the loss of 150,000 men. Its air force and the pride of its navy had gone down to defeat at the hands of the enemy. America had suffered her greatest defeat ever, in the loss of 140,000 men in the Philippine islands and the most powerful ships of her navy lay smoldering at Pearl Harbor. Dozens of countries in Europe and the Far East had been conquered, and Japan occupied millions of square miles of territory in the Pacific. Hitler's armies had killed or captured 5,000,000 Russian soldiers and were deep into Russia and the Crimea.

From the Stone Age forward, human beings have been warring on other human beings. Improvement in weapons and techniques has repeatedly turned the tide of battle. Starting from the stick and the stone, the knife, sword, shield, arrow, gunpowder, jet, and rocket, all have given a decisive edge to the participants.

Genghis Khan and Alexander the Great exploited the use of the horse. Napoleon excelled with artillery. In modern times it has been the aircraft and the rocket.

America was slow to recognize the potential of

aircraft even though she invented it. In World War I she had no modern fighter planes available for service, using British and French fighters. She, shame of shames, refused to provide parachutes for her valiant airmen, who were left with the choice of jumping from their planes or burning to death in the air in case of fire.

Prior to World War II, the fighter plane was being demonstrated to be a decisive factor in battle. In the Spanish Civil War it became a deciding factor.

Again America missed the mark by devoting her major energies to the development of bombers. Successive new bombers were swifter than her fighters. The B-17 and the B-29 were the pride of her aeronautical achievements. Yet they found they could not exist without the fighter. Although one can make the case that fighters became the most important weapon of World War II, America lagged behind in her research and development.

When America entered World War II, her frontline fighter was the P-40, a patchwork of the older P-36 fighter and the Allison in-line engine that the secretary of war Henry Stimson called a "pile of junk."

America's fighter pilots were destined to begin the war in the Pacific, untrained and ill equipped, against an enemy flying an outstanding conventional weapon of World War II, the Japanese Zero fighter plane.

This is my story of the agony of those beginnings.

Acknowledgments

Few books have been written without the valuable contribution of others besides the author. This book would never have been written without the *invaluable* contribution of *many* others. For thirty years I successfully resisted the urging of friends who were aware of my participation in World War II at its most desperate time. Little has been written; indeed, much remains unwritten about that grievous epoch of America's history when she suffered her greatest military defeat at the very beginning of the war and was all but forgotten by the war's end.

There are sound reasons that little is said by a warring nation about its defeats. After the war, stories of its defeats remain unpopular. The Battle of Britain was famous because it was a victory. The battle of Java was all but unknown because it was a defeat.

Some authors in their acknowledgments mention their wives as a matter of obligation, I'm sure. Betty Angerman Morehead's name is not mentioned in that light. She was downright insistent that I write my account, as were author Kay Morgan, and my children, Myrna and Melanie.

Others are:

Lieutenant Colonel Wallace Fields, DFC, flying school classmate, pioneer combat veteran and son, rare patriot Kenneth Fields.

General Joe Foss, MOH, two-term governor

of South Dakota, ranking marine ace, ex-president of the NRA, and ex-commissioner of the NFL.

Colonel Rex Barber, NC, P-38 pilot who shot down Japanese Admiral Isoroku Yamamoto, plotter of "Pearl Harbor," and old hunting buddy.

Lieutenant Colonel Clyde Barnett, combat wing mate, SWP theater

Ralph Thompson, former fighter pilot in England, ex–editor in chief of the *Petaluma Argus-Courier*, and invaluable adviser.

Bill Hess, comrade-in-arms and author of twenty-five military books.

Barrett Tillman, friend, author, and strong supporter.

Colonel Robert Combs, army battlefield surgeon and keen observer of script.

Richard Hoey, friend and valuable critic.

Bill Bartsch, author and donor of photographs and records.

Paul Gambonini, intrepid comrade and wing mate in tough times.

Colonel Gerald Dix, survivor and donor of valuable records.

I am also indebted to Clayton Isaacson, Clyde Barnett, Bruce Harris, David Carey, Royce Priest, Thomas Maloney, Victor Poncik, Dowe Rhoades, Sammy Pierce, Jack Donaldson, Stewart Robb, Thomas Hayes, Francis Harris, Jess Tinsley, Sammy Grashio, Morton Magoffin, and all those old comrades who helped in the increasing chore of recalling.

And to Col. Robert Kane, publisher of Presidio Press, and E. J. McCarthy, executive editor, who read and re-read, revised and re-revised raw, green writings into manuscript; and for their important, real encouragement.

I

Family Moorings

"Moh toup [more soup]," was the plaintive cry of the starving child, bedridden and racked with the burning fever of typhoid. Typhoid fever was a scourge of earlier generations, and it was sweeping the tiny community of Washington, Oklahoma, in the year 1917.

His mother would have given half her life to be able to feed her baby the full pot of soup, but the remedy of the day was to starve a fever patient, and she forced herself to do so.

People in the community were dying. Her brother was stricken, but recovered, his paralyzed arm the only remnant of the disease. Night and day Ophelia James Morehead remained at her infant's bedside guarding him with her every breath. Though death hung like a shroud, life finally prevailed, and the one-year-old, James Bruce, arose from the valley of the shadow.

My father, Clem, came to the Indian Territory at the turn of the century. He was the elder son of an impoverished family of sharecroppers grubbing their meager living from the eroded hills of the Carolinas. The father's parents had migrated from the area of Morehead, North Carolina. They fell on hard times and had to pull Clem from school to help tend the crops. His schooling ended at the third grade.

At an early age he and a brother left home and headed west. They walked, swam rivers, and rode railroad cars as far as the state of Texas. There they found work in a budding oil industry. The work was tough and dangerous. Brother Luke was killed in a fall from an oil derrick.

Clem stayed on in the oil fields, saved his money, and reentered grade school in nearby Humble, Texas. He told of his embarrassment going to class with nine- and ten-year-olds about half his height of six feet four inches.

Clem had visualized a life as a merchant, so he worked and saved toward that end. At age thirty he took his savings and struck out for new country. He decided on Oklahoma, where he found new land on which a railroad branch was planned. He walked ten miles down the new right-of-way now partially cleared, rented a room from a farmer, and staked out a new town, which he named Washington. He built a store and started a hardware business.

My mother, Ophelia, was one of ten children. Her father was a Baptist minister who farmed for sustenance, and was a circuit rider for several small communities on the plains of West Texas. Her mother was one-half Choctaw Indian, from Knoxville, Tennessee. Her parents moved west when she was ten years old, traveling in covered wagons. She walked the entire journey from Tennessee to West Texas beside the wagons.

Later, Reverend James moved his family to Durant, in eastern Oklahoma, where there was a college, which helped to educate his children.

Ophelia obtained a teaching credential and set out to find a school. She heard of a new school being formed at Washington, Oklahoma, went for an interview, and got the job. The "schoolhouse" turned out to be a dugout, a pit covered with logs and earth, a structure used those days by the pioneers for shelter. Water dripped through when it rained.

A short time later she met the leading merchant in town (the only one) and they were married. She continue teaching for many years, for she loved the work.

I started to school in the first grade with my mother as teacher. I graduated from the same school with my mother as teacher.

What a pain that was! She was twice as hard on her own kids as she was on the others. One time, in the ninth grade, a girl in my class and I were cutting up, picking at each other, and giggling. My mother moved us to the front row and told us to behave. Soon we were giggling again. I didn't know she had noticed. She moved slowly over to the row above us, and, wham! She whacked me beside the head and straightened me around with stern instructions. I was a big kid then, and it was one of life's embarrassing moments.

When I was seven my father gave me an air rifle for Christmas. I walked down the railroad track in search of game. A neighbor's chicken walked by — a tempting target. To my surprise, that Daisy air rifle killed that chicken. I had to ditch it and felt guilty.

While I learned to shoot the air rifle, I found I could see the BB at certain angles of light. When I missed, I discovered I could adjust my aim and move onto the target. This fact was later to become an important skill in my life.

When I was eight my father gave me a 410-gauge shotgun. Likewise, on that Christmas day I had to try out the new gun. My brother and I took our dog and the gun for a walk in the cow pasture. A rabbit leapt out of the grass almost at my feet. I jerked the gun high in the air, fired, and yelled, "Get him, Rex!"

In physiological terms this was a classic case of buck fever. And though, apparently, only the instinctive reaction of a child, it was an incident of great significance, particularly in a wartime situation.

Later in this book I cite the study of the Royal Air Force of the reactions of pilots in combat. The cogent conclusion was reached that in most cases fear, adrenaline, and excitement render the average pilot worthless on his first few missions. In short, another case of buck fever. Later we shall understand better the momentous weight of this human reaction in relation to the conduct of war. We shall be able to understand more clearly why America, entering the war as a "cheechako," as they say of greenhorns in Alaska, was able to emerge quickly as a winner.

With the BB gun I was able to watch the

16

trajectory of the projectile as it left the barrel. I could see the effect of gravity as it began its inevitable pull on the missile throughout its travel. And, too, with the little shotgun I was soon shooting moving targets such as rabbits, crows, ducks, doves, and quail. In reality, I was undergoing an early, basic course in ballistics and the all-important art of "leading" in the aerial fighting of World War II.

When I was six years old our own house burned down. We rented a house a quarter mile from town. It was the perfect place to raise a family. There was access to the countryside, a place for a cow, chickens, ducks, and turkeys. We learned the names of all the birds and bugs and bees. We walked the half mile to school and ran chores to town and back for Mom and Dad. My father was a successful merchant, and we were a happy family.

When I was ten my father made a monumental mistake in his business affairs. He sold the prosperous hardware business and bought a large run-down farm. After farming the eroded hills of South Carolina in his boyhood, he had formed some excellent ideas for saving the soil. His plan was to put those ideas into practice and build a run-down farm into a thing of beauty and value.

The sad part of the decision was that he bought the big farm in the prosperous twenties. A couple of years later the stock market crashed, and he was saddled with a big loan and a farm that couldn't produce profit enough to pay the interest on the loan and the taxes.

As the Depression deepened, and the southwestern United States entered an extended devastating drought, the family was stretched to the limit with toil and sacrifice. The task of meeting the loan payments and avoiding bankruptcy and social humiliation made slaves of us all. The demands for labor in an operation that could have employed ten men were absorbed by the parents and children. Twelve- and fourteen-hour workdays, rising at 4:00 A.M. six days a week, ending in toil until well after dark, continued year after year. Drought and the Great Depression increased the strain.

There was no time for school sports, and there was little play of any sort. We three boys grabbed our recreation by riding horseback and fishing at the farm pond, or hunting birds and small game. We learned to love rain and snow, which gave about the only relief from the fieldwork.

Things of interest can be found in the fields and woods even if time and money for other pleasures are not available. We found that if a cottontail rabbit can be headed away from cover and kept in open terrain, we could run it down and catch it. We learned we could imitate the distress cry of the crow, hide, and fling a hat or dead crow in the air when crows were nearby, and shoot birds until the guns got hot. Nearby crows would mob the scene.

After observing the flight of the BB from my air gun, I learned I could see the flight of a .22

rifle bullet. This could be done only when firing against the sky. My being able to see the bullet, when firing at crows, for example, allowed my study of ballistics and trajectory to continue apace. I could see how far out in front of the target my aim had erred, how far it passed behind it or to the right or the left, and thereby could correct my errors and nail the target quickly. That was a skill that would serve well in the coming years of war. Instead of rabbits, it would be men, cars, and locomotives. Instead of winged game, it would be enemy bombers and fighters. It would be adjusting bullets onto the targeting, and target the enemy.

This circumstance, multiplied a million times throughout America, that is, boys with BB guns, rifles, or shotguns, learning ballistics, trajectories, and gun handling at early ages, answers the question as to how America was able to come from so far behind in the war and emerge a winner.

Japan possessed a large cadre of the finest trained pilots in the world. She had a vigorous training program; pilots were given intense training, then large numbers were sent to the front in Mongolia, Manchukuo, Manchuria and China, where they fought against the Russians, Manchurians, Chinese, and mercenaries over a period of ten years. Their pilots were able to learn ballistics and the basics of lead and trajectory in actual combat fighting. This cadre learned those skills only in this manner and was small in number. They had not learned it in the fields and woods in early youth as America's youth had done by the tens of thousands. Hence, when those Japanese veterans were lost to attrition, there was no pool of thousands of youth already endowed with basic hunting skills to draw from. Japan was an urban society, and when her totally unskilled youth were thrown into the fray, they fell, as you might expect them to.

If I had been denied use of a gun in my youth, I would have been as green and helpless in beginning combat as the Japanese were. As it would turn out, I was actually an old pro in some of the important skills from the very start. So were hundreds of others of our pilots, like Joe Foss, Marion Carl, and Dick Bong, all hunters, and tens of thousands of our ground forces like Audie Murphy, Eric Anderson, and Carlos Ogden. In the vernacular, they saved our ass. Perhaps the greatest pilot in the history of fighter pilots was an avid hunter, in both his youth and in maturity. Manfred von Richthofen developed his skills of shooting to the finest art. And actually he was said to be a rather poor pilot.

As the years passed and the children matured and left high school, my older brother, Jackson, set about to work his way through medical school. My sister, Leah, earned a teaching credential and began teaching at age seventeen. My next older brother, Walt, married and found work in Oklahoma City. The monumental task of operating the farm fell to me and one hired hand. There was no time or money for dating or hanging out with buddies. It was a constant grind.

When I graduated from high school I wanted to enter nearby Oklahoma University, but my father demanded that I remain at home. He had grown abusive as the pressures of drought and the Depression weighed upon him. He would whip us mercilessly when something irritated him. We learned to fear him, and I had no stomach to continue the misery.

I had seen enough of farming in a country that had big problems with food surpluses. I had seen enough of prices like four dollars for a two hundred-pound hog that required close to a year of nurturing to produce, or eggs at nine cents a dozen. I had seen the farmer take the dirty end of the stick for years. I loved the outdoor life, but I saw there were less grinding ways to make a living.

I was willing to make sacrifices to attain a different life, and education seemed the way. I left home and spent weeks trying to find work to support myself. I was able to stay with my married brother for only a short time, and my attempt to find employment was unsuccessful. Long lines of men, trained and with years of experience in the jobs sought, left me one among the thousands of unemployed and flat broke.

A friend who had migrated to California had written back saying wages there were double what they were in Oklahoma. I decided to head west, where I would be able to save money twice as fast. Little did I know what lay ahead, probably the least of which were the Rocky Mountains.

I left home wearing only a shirt and overalls. Naive, I didn't realize cooler temperatures came with higher elevations. I caught a freight train going west.

In the Texas Panhandle the train stopped for water at a small town called Canyon. It was late afternoon, and I was growing hungry. Other hoboes climbed off the train and went out in the community to beg for food. I was not yet hungry enough to beg for food. I hunted for a lawn to mow in exchange for a meal and soon located a woolly one and negotiated a deal.

I was just about finished with the lawn when the train whistle blew, and I saw all the hoboes heading back to the train. So as an old quip goes, "I worked all day for my board and lost my appetite!"

The train was moving along when I caught it. Hobo lesson number one: Don't grab the rungs at the rear of the car. The speed wraps you around the end of the car and scuffs you up.

I climbed into a "reefer," a compartment in a boxcar designed for holding ice, with a couple of other hoboes and checked my wounds. One of the men was middle-aged with a weathered face and callused hands. He had a sad face that reflected the disappointments of a farmer mired in the depths of an extended drought and a deep depression.

We appeared to have so much in common that

I engaged Mr. Harmon in conversation.

He had, indeed, suffered disappointment as well as tragedy. He said he had four years of drought, as had I, that each year had left him with shorter crops and deeper in debt. Being a renter farmer, much of his meager profit had gone to lease the land. Hoping to try farming another year, he had persuaded the local banker to back him one more time.

Good luck seemed to be turning his way. Spotty rains had given his desperate farming efforts an apparent blessing. He had arisen well before dawn every day. He had done his chores and taken his meager meal alone by kerosene lamp in a cold house. He had fed and watered and harnessed his team of mules in the dark so he could take advantage of the daylight to nurture his last opportunity to remain independent and pursue the beloved freedom of the farmer's life.

His crops of milo, corn, and cotton had flourished, were knee-high and bursting with vigor, when a violent hailstorm whipped the area.

On the high plains this phenomenon is not rare, and at times storms unleash hailstones as big as baseballs. That particular storm was a bad one, and it literally beat his crops into the ground; only stubs of stems remained showing above the surface of the soil.

A day or two after the storm Mrs. Harmon was busy washing clothes. On a farm during that era, which normally had no hot or cold running water, the method was to heat a large cast-iron pot filled with water over a small fire in the backyard. At the time Mrs. Harmon was tending the fire, but had to go into the house for something.

Their three-year-old daughter and five-year-old son were playing, chasing each other around the house. The three-year-old dashed around the corner of the house and fell into the boiling pot. Mr. Harmon had the heartbreaking task of removing her little body.

Mr. Harmon sold his team and harness, his cow and a few chickens, his farm implements and household goods, and sent his wife and son home to his in-laws. He paid what he could on his debt at the bank and set out to find work.

It was becoming apparent to me that Mr. Harmon was having difficulty talking further. However, with effort he was able to say that he wanted me to know that I should never feel that things were so bad in my life that I could not go on.

I had been feeling sorry for myself — no home, no job, no future, no one to love or love me, no coat (and I was cold!), alone in the world and not one red cent in my pocket. However, when Mr. Harmon finished his tragic story, I felt ashamed for having such thoughts. I was strong, healthy, free, not a single burden, and living in a country filled with boundless opportunity. I was determined I would succeed and fulfill my dreams. I lay my head back on the grit and splinters of the hard boxcar floor and thought of how much harder so many other folks were having it than I.

Sleep did not come easily with the clank of the big iron wheels on the steel rails beneath our heads, and they don't put springs on rail cars. At a 5,000 foot elevation as we approached Denver, temperatures were fifteen degrees colder than at sea level, and I was shivering. It only got worse, for the next night we hooked onto massive steam locomotives double the size of the average ones, and chugged up the mountain grades to a pass at 11,000 feet. It was thirty-five degrees colder there.

The train stopped overnight, and we hoboes sought warmer quarters. Some old hand in the hobo troupe knew of an old vacant "section house" (quarters provided for railroad workers), and we trudged, shivering, in the dark, down the tracks to find it. We lay together on the floor, tightly bunched for warmth, but I was too cold to sleep. I just shivered all night. I covered my face with my arm to avoid getting bitten by the rats that bounced across our prone bodies. The next morning I saw why I had shivered so much. A leaky water spigot out front had built up a mound of ice a foot high beneath it. Even so, I drank from it, as I was thirsty.

We remounted our commodious traveling quarters and soon headed down the western slope of the Rockies.

As our train snaked around the great yawning gorges, sometimes the front end would be going one way, and directly across the canyon our tail would be going the other. To hear a high, shrill whistle today jerks me back in memory to the shrill scream of the steam whistle of the big engines on the slopes of the Rocky Mountains.

Desert warmth was welcome as our steel horse carried us down the big mountains and bolted out across the arid lands of the western states. But all our hope was in vain. At the California line the train stopped for water. At the door of the boxcar a "bull" appeared. We had heard talk of operatives, hired by the state to stop the "Okies" from entering California. Our motley group of eighty-six men was ejected from the train and left out in the sagebrush beside the railroad watering tower. There was one exception. A man had a telegram, he claimed, from his dying mother, and he approached the bull with the yellow copy in his hand to ask to be allowed to continue on the train. The bull pushed his pistol in the man's face and was telling him to stand back, and I saw an opportunity. I dashed to the nearest car and climbed the end ladder to the reefer above. I snaked into the reefer and down inside and waited with bated breath for footsteps, fearing someone had ratted on me. Apparently no one had, but as luck would have it, I was ejected at the next stop. At least it was at a small town with a highway nearby.

This kind of treatment, and the hobo scoop that California would impound you in camps, discouraged me. I walked out to the nearest east-west highway and tried hitchhiking. Hours passed and no one stopped for me. I realized my face and my light-colored shirt were black with soot from the coalburners. I was not an appealing bum. I finally decided to try hitchhiking either way. I would let fortune dictate the direction my life should take.

My first ride was with one of the Lord's angels going east. The kind gentleman was going all the way to Moab, Utah. We talked at length and I'm sure he could see I was a green pea. I was tired and sleepy and dozing off intermittently as we talked. He put his hand on my shoulder, and told me to lie over on his lap. I did so and slept for hours with my head in his lap. He let me out in Grand Junction, Colorado, after buying my lunch and supper.

I found an overpass and slept in the sand beneath the arch. I had found an old coat in a garbage can in Arizona. It was a little short in the sleeves, but it helped. Ants routed me from my first bed, chosen in the dark, but a move of a few yards left me in peace.

I was still trying to find a job, but my lack of experience in anything but farm work was hindering me. I joined a hobo camp in Denver, but it seemed all I was learning there was how to be an effective bum. Who were the easy touches, where to find outdated food and clothes — that was the curriculum. In the Midwest, the wheat harvest was an extra opportunity for farm work. I decided I would head for the "harvest."

I made my way by freight train across the plains of Kansas and found work harvesting wheat. With my first paycheck I was able to buy a penny postcard. I wrote my mother that I was all right.

After the harvest I was homesick, and drifted back down to Oklahoma again. My longest stretch without food had been three days. I wasn't making a very good hobo.

Many years later, in 1991, I saw an ad in a magazine asking that anyone who had experienced the hobo days contact some university in the East. I think it was Duke or Princeton — I've forgotten. I responded. It seemed they were researching the careers that came out of the ranks of the hoboes of the Depression days, and a record was being made of prominent participants.

Now I tell my friends that I have good news and bad news. The good news is I have recently been inducted into the Oklahoma Air Space Museum Hall of Fame. The bad news is I have recently been inducted into the Hobo Hall of Fame.

When I reappeared at my brother's door, everyone was glad to see me. Of course, my mother had been frantic. She had news for me. If I would come home, my father would give me a portion of the farm as my own if I farmed the whole place.

Things were so tight regarding jobs, it seemed my other prospect was just one of surviving as a hobo, so I returned home.

The next year was a repeat of the past; up at 4:00 A.M. six days a week, out in the darkness in bitter wind, horizontal sleet and snow, and howling sandstorms that the drought brought. Milking cows, feeding all the farm animals, separating the cream by manual separator, all before light; then toiling all day, and repeating the routine after dark gave no time for social events or sports. I would lie in bed and dream of ballrooms, dining out, and dating pretty blondes, brunettes, and redheads, but I didn't have a dime, and there was no way to make one, and my folks were broke. It was a poor life for a youth.

My sports were fishing in the farm pond on rainy days, and shooting crows out of the pecan trees and peanut patches. The shooting was an important continuation of my gunnery training; I was polishing the skill of leading. I killed many crows on the wing with the .22 rifle, and Dad willingly provided the ammunition at twenty cents per fifty rounds.

Later that season came the agony of watching the plants shrivel and yellow in the blistering sun, and wither in shreds in the incessant wind. It seemed the drought brought more winds, and strong winds are a scourge to farming.

In early July that year, when the few spring rains had vanished and the growing plants had begun to burn, a small tempest of weather appeared right over the farm. Thunderstorms originate in a given place, but almost all of them appear on the horizon and endure for hours, advancing across the countryside, normally in a single direction. In Oklahoma the prevailing winds in spring and summer blow predominantly from southwest to northeast. In this case the thunderhead formed directly overhead. Currents of wind blew from all directions and wheeled back and forth, dashing the fields with rain for almost an hour. Three inches fell and soaked the growing crops at a critical time. They flourished while the neighbor's crops dried up in the drought.

In October I harvested three hundred dollars worth of corn from the ten-acre patch, which was my compensation for the fourteen months of fourteen hours per day labor, six days a week. My net was approximately sixty-five cents per day, and that was with great good fortune.

With the money I paid for a short course in a business college in Oklahoma City that was having good luck placing its graduates in jobs.

I did get a job with a wholesale drug company at fifteen dollars per week. I did not buy a car and saved about three hundred dollars more for college.

In 1937 I entered Oklahoma University, majoring in biology, and finished three semesters before exhausting my three hundred dollars. By living at home on the farm and commuting the fourteen miles and working part-time at the school, I was able to stretch my funds into forty-four units of college credits.

In the meantime my brother Walton had moved to Los Angeles. He had aspired to be a movie star, and just had to try for it. At that time my money was running low. He asked me to come out and help him make casting appointments. I could enter UCLA in nearby Westwood, live with him, commute, and maybe get a part-time job as well.

With the ninety dollars I had left in the bank I would have enough to pay the nonresident fee of seventy-five dollars and have fifteen dollars to go to school on. However, I still had to get to Los Angeles.

I could hitchhike, but I might not have time enough between semesters to meet the enrollment date.

In those days people in bad straits who owned a car would take passengers from one city to another on what was known as a share-the-ride plan. With five passengers, one could gross twenty-five dollars on a trip to Los Angeles. His time, the wear and tear on the car, and the cost of gasoline at ten cents a gallon meant losing money, but it was a way to get five or ten dollars if a person had to have it. I caught a share-the-ride to Los Angeles, and my savings shrank to eighty-five dollars.

My brother and I had been partners in misery in the bad years — two children, lank with toil and oppression from a father desperate to avoid bankruptcy and social humiliation. We shared the same bed, the same toil, the same tyranny, the same dreams, the same cravings, the same disappointments.

We were elated to see each other, and, of course, visited for hours. Walt had a bed set up for me in the back breezeway of their small apartment.

I went to enroll at UCLA, but found there was a limit of fourteen on the number of credits one could take. I had heard of the Army Air Corps' Flying Cadet program, which required sixty units of college credits. Exemptions did not come easy, and I had to go all the way to the dean's office to finally obtain it. I made good grades; when you have to earn your education, you make sure you get your money's worth. I got a part-time job in the biology lab, and with my seventy-five dollars I had swung an enrollment in a great seat of learning.

In my spare time and between class periods I was able to submit applications for casting trials and interviews for my brother for acting roles. On one, *Golden Boy*, he lost out to William Holden, who later became famous as a leading actor. He was advised to study acting and did so at the Pasadena Playhouse under celebrated actor Victor Jory, but it seemed he couldn't act worth a hoot. After seeing him in one of the plays, I was forced to agree. Walton later changed professions, becoming an airline pilot who flew troops and cargo during the wars and logged over 30,000 hours flying time.

After finishing my fourth semester, I applied for pilot training in the Flying Cadets and was called up for a physical examination. During the examination they dilated my pupils. The doctor was peering into the depths of my eye with a light and an instrument. Another doctor walked by and the first doctor said to the second, "Come over and look at this, Tom." The other doctor complied, and the two of them talked together. I asked "What is the matter; is there something wrong?" "No, no," the one said, "not at all." I said, "Then why the comments between you?" He said, "The orthoscopic muscles have the most accurate alignment I have ever seen." I said, "Is that good?" He said, "That's good." This gift of the Lord would serve me well in coming events.

This gift and the art of leading, added to flying skill, answers the question as to why one man wins a hundred battles and others win none.

I passed the physical exam and was told to stand by for a few weeks until call-up for the next class. This delay was not good news, as it meant I would have to sustain myself for that time and get a job. That wasn't easy. I decided to head for farm work rather than pound the concrete, since it would only be temporary.

Ads were running in the papers for workers in the areas of the Willamette Valley of Oregon and Tacoma, Washington. I called one of the share-the-ride offices and was told they had a car going to Seattle. I took a streetcar downtown to a small office where an attendant set up rides.

He was a young man of about my age and size. His father must have owned the place, and he was arrogant and autocratic. I arrived at about

9:00 A.M., as he had said to come right down. He said he had a car going right away, that the party had gone to pick someone up. I waited an hour or two and no one showed up. While waiting I could hear him tell other callers that he had a car going to wherever the caller inquired about. By noon no one had appeared, so I again asked about the car going to Seattle. He told me not to get ants in my pants, the man would show up soon.

Some people were coming and going and things were quite busy, so I didn't interrupt him until 4:00 P.M. By now my patience was wearing thin. The work slowed, and still he said nothing about the car going to Seattle. I began to suspect that there was no one going to Seattle, that this was a technique being employed whereby he would tell the caller he had someone going, then keep him on the hook until someone called in going to that destination.

I walked over to him and started to ask again about my prospective ride. He seemed irritated at my inquiry. I then said that I thought that he had no one, and that he was just keeping me on the hook. He said something like "Aren't you the smart one?" Anger flared within me, and before I could restrain myself I struck him in the face.

He made no pretense at fighting, but turned and dove into a desk, pulled out a knife, and came for me. I had no weapon whatsoever, so I fled out the door.

I returned to my brother's place and called another share office. The next day I paid a dollar to a share office, and five dollars to a motorist going to Seattle. Three other folks joined the journey, one, a young man about my age, of Hungarian descent. His last name was Baciu. He said, "Just call me Botch."

Botch and I had much in common and became friends. On the trip the driver and I got into an argument about the Okies. I claimed that most were poor folks who had starved out on the dust bowl farms and had no way of making a living. He claimed they were a bunch of bums and no-goods. I made the mistake of saying I was an Okie, for he kept making snide remarks throughout the trip. We weren't making friends.

In Portland the driver said he would take the other two passengers to their homes in Portland, and would then go home and take a shower before taking us on to Seattle. He asked me and Botch to wait on a street corner downtown until he returned in an hour. It was 9:00 A.M. We had traveled all night. During the trip, Botch had said he was visiting farmer friends in Yelm, Washington. He said they truck-farmed and would probably employ both of us in the harvest. He invited me to stop off there with him.

By 10:00 A.M. the driver was not back. At 11:00 he was missing. At 12:00, at 1:00, at 2:00 he still was gone.

Nearly broke on the streets of a big city, Botch and I decided to pursue other plans when the driver drove up. He stopped around the corner, and we got in. I asked, "Where in hell have you been?" He said, "It's none of your business." I said, "You mean to tell me we have waited for you for five hours, dodging foot traffic and worrying about what we were going to do, and you say it's none of our business?" For the second time in two days, I was so furious I could hardly contain myself. The driver had long hair cut in a pompadour. I reached up, grabbed his hair, and jerked it back, then released it. He got out of the car and called me names and told me to get out.

To be arrested for fighting on a downtown street would have meant spending time in jail, as I did not have money for a fine. I said, "No, let's go out of town first." He continued to abuse me and opened the door, but I would not get out. I didn't permit people to call me names like he was using, so I was resolved to settle it later. He finally got back in and we drove out of town and onto the road to Tacoma, Washington. In the countryside I told him to find a wide spot in the road, and we would settle our matter.

He said, "No, it's over."

I said, "It is not over," but he did not stop. After a time on the road, he stopped at a country service station and got out for gas. I got out and invited him to put up his fists. He said the affair was over. I said he was going to pay for his rude, inconsiderate treatment of Botch and me.

I struck him and we started to fight. After a round or two I saw that he had no knowledge of fisticuffs, so he charged me and grabbed me around the waist. I reached down and grabbed his pompadour with my right hand and turned his face up. Then three hard left hooks had blood spurting from his nose and mouth before he could bend me backward. I released my hold and he slumped to the ground.

At that moment a man came rushing at me with a long iron rod in his hand. I turned and fled. At first this was confusing to me. I had done nothing to the second man. Later it became clear. The service station operator was living a peaceful life. Then a car drove up and two men got out. Then, one man jumped on the other and started fighting him. Then the bully beat the other man into the ground. This is how it appeared to the service station man. He helped the oppressed over to the gas pump's curb, got some water and a rag, and washed the man's bloody face.

I climbed back in the car to make sure the driver didn't run off and leave me. I tried to explain to the man the five hours of agony he had put Botch and me through just a little while before, but it wasn't possible. He finally ordered the gas and climbed back in the car, and we continued on.

South of Tacoma, Botch said we would get off at a little town called Yelm. It was dark. I asked how far his friends lived from town. He said a couple of miles. I told the driver that for all the problems he had caused, he could just drive us right to Botch's friend's home, which he did without protest.

At his friend's home we met all the McGregor family — father, mother, and two teenage boys. Botch asked about work and was told there was plenty. We had free room and board at the McGregors' and were paid by the piece. We picked a field of beans every even-numbered day, and a field of cucumbers every odd-numbered day. It was pleasant work, and I saved some money. The second week there I called the army recruiting office in Tacoma. They advised me to come in a week or so later, on 2 August 1940.

II

The World of Flight

Early Monday I thanked the kind farm folk at Yelm, walked to the highway at the edge of town, and hitchhiked to Tacoma. That afternoon six other Washington boys and I took the oath to defend our country against all comers. We were given railroad tickets and boarded a train for Glendale, California, where I entered the military service of the United States of America.

Someone should have informed me of the procedures and accepted practices when entering boot camp or a cadet corps. I was surprised when I stepped inside the camp gate to find eager upperclassmen itching to greet the recruits. One obnoxious little guy, several pounds lighter than I, stormed up and ordered me to stand at attention. I suppose I was a bit casual, and he roared into his best verbal attack.

The necessities of life had molded me into a rather patient young man by then, but I would not take abuse. I said, "Listen, young fellow, I haven't done a thing to you, and you seem to me to be taking great offense nevertheless. Now go away and let me continue being a peace-loving man." *Arrrowwr!* came the reply. I said, "Listen, listen, little guy, bigger fellows don't talk to me this way. Now, bug off before I whack you about the head and shoulders."

Fortunately the enlisted sentry at the gate observed these proceedings and intervened to advise me that I had just stepped into another world, with which I was unfamiliar, and that it was quite acceptable practice for a young man with a bit of pride about him to submit to such tongue-lashings, even in the presence of others, in the interests of God and country. So the little guy escaped a bruising and I escaped having the shortest military career on record.

The little guy was known as "Little Jesus," one of the most obnoxious upperclassmen, who prowled the halls looking for some lowerclassmen to "jump." I still remember his name: Upperclassman Hilyer. Most commanders detest this sort, but are powerless to do what they would often like to do. It turned out that we had a strict, fair, and intelligent West Point–trained captain, to whom my aborted action would probably have gone down as one of the more satisfying incidents of his career.

We were assigned bunks and placed several cadets to each flight. Half the class of around forty cadets had ground school and boot training in the mornings, while the other half took flying training in the PT-13, a biwing, open-cockpit, light training plane built by the Stearman Company.

It might not have been apparent at the time, but these young men as a whole were to prove to be outstanding products. Most had grown up in sound two-parent homes, with a working father and a homemaker mother, and firm discipline and leadership in their family lives. Most had worked part- or full-time to help educate themselves. Most were already productive citizens, and could appreciate the value of the equipment with which they were entrusted.

Our days were a constant struggle for retention as a pilot, for at that time, August 1940, elimination from the program was, we were told, around 50 percent. "Wash rides" were common. If one failed, this was his last flight in the training program. We all tried to help one another avoid the washout, though secretly we each hoped it would be the other fellow rather than ourselves.

We were lucky to have a flying commandant who used common sense, psychology, and a measure of discipline to turn out a sound class of trainees. Everyone respected Lieutenant Carmody, yet he was the major fear in our lives as well, for he was the check pilot.

There was a swimming pool in our compound, and as each cadet soloed, we would seize the fledgling and throw him in the pool with his clothes on. As a budding pilot, it was your first big splash.

My first instructor was impatient, short-tempered, and wasn't getting through to me, and soon I was up for the dreaded ride with Lieutenant Carmody. One was always in suspense after the checkride, but, as it turned out, I was retained and the grumpy civilian instructor was fired.

After the strain of retention subsided, flying became a real thrill. To be able to take off in one of those machines, fly up to the clouds, play in their billows, wheel in any direction, dive, climb, stall, spin, whatever, then bring the plane back down to earth, set it down gently, and guide it back to its parking place was as satisfying for a youth as it was all-consuming.

Our training flying field was an alfalfa patch at Newhall a few miles northwest of Glendale, and our cadet compound was near the Burbank airport, where the planes were hangared.

Some of our ground school instructors were World War I veterans. They all seemed well qualified. One remains in my memory. He was an old submarine captain with great wit and burning loyalty to the United States. His classes were so inspirational that after the war I made a special effort to meet another fiercely loyal submarine commander, the late Adm. Richard O'Kane, MH, former executive officer of the *Wahoo*, and later commander of the USS submarine, *Tang*. O'Kane's books, *Clear the Bridge* and *Wahoo*, are stirring accounts of America's best in fighting men. We became fast friends.

Shortly after soloing I was sent out in the PT-13 to practice stalls. It was my turn to fly afternoons, and the air was bumpy. As the plane stalled, the exhaust would come up in my face, and soon my stomach grew queazy. I became so sick, I just slumped back in the seat and flew straight and level, to give myself time enough to recover and land the plane. When I felt well enough to check my surroundings, I discovered I was far away from the field. I circled back, and after about an hour's searching found it, but I was still sick and groggy and had trouble focusing.

On the final approach I overcontrolled and the plane suddenly dove at the ground. I jerked back on the stick, roughly correcting the error, and by chance made a safe landing, for which I was thankful.

Mine was the last flight scheduled, and I was late when I returned. All the students had either gone home on the bus or flown the ships home to Burbank. Lieutenant Carmody was the only one left on the field. He was so relieved that I was not a casualty that he refrained from censure. He could plainly see that my story was no fabrication.

Our confidence was growing rapidly in handling the sturdy little planes. Practice in stalls and spins was one of the student's first lessons. During one solo mission, practicing steep turns and chandelles, I spotted a crow. As I gave chase I found him to be a worthy opponent. He would cut and dive, then pull up, taking advantage of his maneuverability. On one of his pull-ups I followed in a steep climb and stalled out, and the Stearman flipped into a spin. Remembering my instructions, I held the stick back, then popped it forward and kicked the opposite rudder, and she came right out into level flight. I flew straight and level for an extended period of time, until my nerves calmed from the unsettling experience of facing death, and returned carefully to base. Later, confidence grew so that I could purposely stall the plane, going straight up, off the left or right wing, on its back, or in any position. I found it possible to do any maneuver except, perhaps, dive at terminal speed. I was learning to fly.

Primary training went well, and most of my close friends and I graduated. Then we reported to Moffett Field, Mountain View, California, where we began training in BT-13s (Vultee, low-wing monoplane aircraft). Where the primary trainer, the PT-13, had two wings with an open cockpit, the BT-13 had only one wing and a closed cockpit. This aircraft made training more realistic, and simulated more nearly the war-planes we would be flying in the future. They had two-way radios, which eliminated the procedures of checking the wind sock, green lights, and other visual signals. Ground school became more intense with courses in weather, communications including Morse code, navigation, and cockpit instruments.

The winter of 1940 was extremely wet, and at Moffett fog, low clouds, and heavy rain all but eliminated flying. In a concerted attempt to obtain flying time, we were moved to Bakersfield, where fair skies were more promising.

We cadets were set up in pyramidal tents and operated out of a local airfield at Bakersfield. The wind and rain continued, however, so it was difficult to obtain the required flying time. I remember that we had to sit in our airplanes and hold the controls during one storm to avoid damage by near-hurricane winds.

One of my best friends, Flying Cadet John Bayliss, was killed in a foolish accident. It left me with a feeling of a certain failure on my part for not speaking up when he told me and another cadet what he had previously done. He said that when he was out on a solo hop, he flew down over this large plowed field and bounced his wheels on the ground. I asked, "How fast were you going, John?" and he said, "About one-fifty." I said, "I don't know if I would do that." Being a farm boy, I knew how soft plowed ground is, and that it might catch your wheels, causing the plane to nose over. At high speed this could be disastrous.

We didn't know he was going to do it again, but I should have forcefully told him, "Don't you ever do that again, or you will kill your fool self!" I didn't, and Flying Cadet John Bayliss lost his life. I don't remember that we told the commander, and the cause of the accident remained a mystery.

Regular maintenance facilities at the airfield at Bakersfield were nonexistent, and the ground crew had to maintain the planes in the mud, wind, and rain. As I recall, we had other casualties from engine failures or defective controls. With muddy boots, mud on the rudders, and cold hands working delicate instruments and mechanisms, some accidents were inevitable. Supply, too, must have been a real headache 300 miles from base; it seemed we ate a lot of canned beef.

One of our first night-flying missions remains in my memory. Normally an instructor took a cadet up for an indoctrination hop to get the feel of and see the lighted countryside and the lights of the field. My instructor put me in the cockpit, showed me the landing light switch, and told me to take off. Talk about a case of irresponsibility! I got the plane back on the ground somehow — although it was a hard, sloppy landing.

After our tour at Bakersfield, the administration decided to move us back to Moffett Field, where we scratched out enough flying time to graduate.

Before that occurred, however, I had a career-threatening experience. The upper class had graduated, and two upperclassmen were talking beside my bunk in the dormitory. They were disparaging a close friend of mine, Cadet Charles Finn. I interjected that they just didn't know Cadet Finn, and that if they did, they wouldn't feel that way about him. One said, "Who asked you?"

Well, we had been told that we were now upperclass too, and, knowing little of military ascendancy, I assumed that we were now the equal of the old upperclass. I said, "Nobody. Nobody had to." He then ordered me to stand at attention, and I told him to go to hell. It so happens that the upperclassman did outrank me and would continue to do so because of time in grade. He went to the commandant and reported my infraction.

Lieutenant "Jumpy, Jumped-up" Jumper, a mush-for-brains officer, was commandant of cadets. Big deal! He dealt me 100 demerits and 100 hours on the ramp, full pack. This meant marching 100 hours on off hours and weekends. It rained a lot that winter. Not only that, he tried to get the flight commander to wash me out. He knew me fairly well and knew Lieutenant Jumper better. He blocked Jumper's plan, but it was nervous time for me; all this for a mistaken impression. Tens of thousands of dollars in training already invested in me meant nothing to Jumper. Military discipline had been breached.

Another incident gives an example of Lieutenant Jumper's astuteness. His wife and another young woman were driving on the base in Jumper's convertible. Some of the cadets whistled at them. The girls told Jumper, and he became incensed and called a special meeting of the cadets. He wanted to know which cadets had had the rudeness to whistle at his wife. He should have been complimented, for, as I recall, she wasn't all that good-looking.

After graduation at Moffett, we were moved to Stockton, California, where we began advanced flying training in the AT-6 airplane. This was the largest and sturdiest of the training

47

planes, with retractable flaps and landing gear.

At Stockton the rains continued. Our training field was an auxiliary grass field, and soon became slop in the constant rains. The authorities decided to move us to the old WW I, defunct training base at Mather Field, Sacramento, where there were no buildings or shops, so we were again back in tents.

The rains continued that winter into 1941, and tent living was quite an experience. During one storm our tents were in ten inches of standing water. We waded into the tent carefully to avoid sloshing waves onto the underside of our cots. Charlie Finn and I had a water kick fight and came out with mud, water, and hair in our faces and not a dry stitch on our backs, laughing all the while.

On bad weather days a couple of us would take my .22 rifle and walk out to remote areas of the base and shoot rabbits and crows. On one of those occasions I told my friends they could see the .22 bullet over the end of the gun barrel. I told them where to look to see a dark, diminishing dot over the end of the barrel when they pulled the trigger. I was disappointed that none said he could see it, as I could see it long enough to tell where it went in relation to the target when the target was outlined against the sky. But today I can no longer see it, though eye exams still show twenty-twenty vision.

On one flight a pair of P-40s came over from Hamilton Field, north of San Francisco. They dove on me. I did a steep turn and engaged them. My instructor let me continue, so I fought with them for a few minutes. I found I could outturn the P-40, and they were dumb enough to try to turn with me. I learned there that they should have swept me and kept going, then pulled up and come back at me. Back on the ground my instructor said he thought I did pretty well with the "enemy." That experience made me feel I would like to fly fighters as my assignment.

Advanced training went well and graduation time arrived. Prior to the exercises, our assignments were posted. I was pleasantly surprised when I learned I was assigned to fighters at Hamilton Field, Novato, California, the only one in the class to be assigned fighters. I never learned how that happened.

Wallace Fields, a classmate with extensive combat time and a buddy who flew bombers in the East Indies, claims the Air Corps chose bomber pilots from the calm, level-headed cadets, and fighter pilots from the wild, irresponsible ones. He thinks there is abundant prima facie evidence to prove it.

Many of my fellow graduates went to the Philippines, some to Hickam Field, Hawaii, some to bombers, some to observation squadrons, and many to instructorship.

I reported alone to Hamilton Field on 25 April 1941. My first commander was Maj. Ira C. Eaker, CO of the 20th Pursuit Group. He advanced in the Air Corps to the rank of four star general, and has been credited with being a major influence in the decision to conduct daylight bombing of Germany. He commanded both the Eighth Air Force and the Fifteenth Air Force in the air war over Europe, personally leading a number of daylight raids. His many writings later influenced political support for air power in the United States. He was much admired and respected by his pilots. A few days later my orders were changed, and I was ordered to report to Capt. Thayer S. Olds, commander of the 14th Pursuit Group. Hardly had the orders been printed, when I was again assigned to the 35th Pursuit Group. This time I was further assigned to the 34th Pursuit Squadron, commanded by 1st Lt. Sam Marret.

After graduation, all cadets were given thirty-day leaves, but I had been so excited about being assigned to fighters that I reported directly to my unit.

Sam Marret checked me out in a P-40, the model that blanked airflow from the rudder, causing the pilot to lose directional control of the plane when the tail dropped to the ground. The pilot then had to lift his feet up onto the brakes and steer by using them. Excessive braking here could cause a nose-over and serious accident. Most new pilots ground-looped the plane the first landing or two, and as a result the P-40 had a bad reputation.

Sam, in his gruff manner, said it was "just another damned airplane!" and that there was nothing to it. Just lift your feet on the brakes when landing were his instructions; forget the talk about it being hard to land. It was good psychology for me, taking much of my fear away, so I made a decent landing. It really was a son of a gun to keep straight, since I had no previous experience to guide me on how much brake pressure was required. Sam was proud of my check-out, and after that I was put on the regular schedule.

But, wouldn't you know? I was immediately transferred to the 21st Pursuit Squadron, and instead of P-40s, I was checked out in P-36 fighters. This was the forerunner of the P-40, powered by a radial engine. I really loved the little P-36. It was a dream to fly formation and do aerobatics. I used to do hour after hour of loops, rolls, chandelles, and Immelmans in it.

One day I decided to do an outside loop. I climbed to 16,000 feet and pushed over. I got about two-thirds of the way around in the loop and saw I was not going to make it. I tried to roll out, but the controls were too stiff and the pressure in my head was building. I reversed the stick pressure and came out in a reverse loop, but it was a sloppy one, as I passed out in the down half. During this time I started an extensive dream of being at home with my mother, sitting on the couch in the living room, and visiting with her. After a lengthy visit of what seemed minutes, I awoke and saw the earth coming up rapidly with the plane headed straight down. With very light pressure on the stick I eased the little fighter out of its dive while the snapping sounds of extreme speed and the shudder of compressibility threatened.

Many pilots lost their lives to the phenomenon of compressibility. It means that when an object reaches a velocity of about 740 miles per hour in the air at sea level, it creates a shock wave. This is at the speed of sound and for a long time was a mystery that killed many airmen and baffled scientists who struggled with the barrier it posed. It was this threat that was solved by the brave and daring feat of flying done by Charles Yeager in the X-1, which broke the "sound barrier."

Yeager once told me of a trip he made to Russia at the invitation of Russian military officials to honor "the great American" who broke the sound barrier. On much of the trip, Chuck said, the hosts tried in every conceivable manner to pump him for information on the details of the flight, but their techniques were rather obvious. While they thought they were pumping him, he was shooting pictures from the Russian plane's window of facilities in the Russian countryside.

After recovering from the harrowing dive, I found my face was burning, probably from the blood pressure of the reverse Gs during the outside swing of the maneuver. I returned directly to base in careful flight and concluded that I did not need to perform an outside loop in a high-speed aircraft. I might have made it if I had started in with power off, but I decided it wasn't all that necessary. If I had remained unconscious a few seconds longer, I just might have put a few dings in the plane.

A short time later I had a call from my former flying school classmate, Charlie Finn. We planned to meet in San Francisco for a visit and a kick around town. We were to meet at the corner of Market and Montgomery streets. Finn was a wild Irishman who was habitually late. At the appointed 2:00 P.M. he was not there. An hour later he was not there, so I was furious. At about 3:20 I saw him coming down the street, so I ducked back into a doorway, and when he arrived I leapt on top of him and began jerking him by the neck and yelling I'd kill him the next time he made me dodge pedestrians for an hour and a half on a busy street.

To my surprise, the guy I was beating on wasn't Finn. He was startled out of his wits and started yelling his innocence, but I kept shaking his neck — he was a little guy — and bawling him out. Finally I realized there was something strange about his reaction, and I turned him loose.

As it turned out, Charles Finn had a twin brother, Calvin, who caught a youthful pummeling for his brother's tardiness. He then took me to his brother, who had sent his twin to meet me in his place. I had started to call off my wait and leave, but I was glad I didn't, as later in the evening we went to Charles's girlfriend's house, the Seeger home, where I met her sister, a beautiful high school girl whom I later married.

In the 21st Squadron we had a youthful commander, a handsome, intelligent pilot from Texas, who lived near the Oklahoma line. We had a lot in common. All of his officers and men liked and respected him. First Lieutenant Ed Dyess was a wonderful pilot as well. He used to fly with each of his young pilots in order to learn their capabilities, their strengths and weaknesses. I knew I was soon to fly with him, and was looking forward to it.

The many changes of assignment were a collective strain on a young pilot; switching from one type of plane to another was even greater. The squadrons were equipped with both P-36s and P-40s. One group also had P-35s. It was logical to do this, however, in order to get some training in the P-40 for all the pilots. All the squadrons were to be equipped with the P-40 as soon as possible.

Dyess loved to take his young pilots on cross-country flights. On one we flew between the canyon walls of the great massifs of Yosemite National Park. Flying along those sheer rock cliffs that towered thousands of feet above, then diving down and shooting straight up alongside their bare faces at 300 miles an hour made me feel like I was a special person. On another, we skimmed the limpid waters of Lake Tahoe, then pulled up among the folds of a huge thunderhead and curled around the billowing layers of pearly vapor.

On one of my first flights with Ed, after a beautiful tour of the Sierra Nevada Mountains, I was on his wing with the engines purring. He told the second element leader to pull away and do individual airwork. Then I saw him look around at me to see if I was looking at him, and anticipated a test run, that is, a formation workout to test my flying ability. He then wheeled into a steep diving turn and down, down, down, then hard back and up into a loop and all over the sky in wild maneuvers, and I stuck like a tick. He deliberately tried to lose me, but I was alert to his every move and hung five or six feet off his wing through all his furious moves. We were both sweating profusely when he leveled out to return to base. I was proud when he called on the R/T* and said, "Well done, Jim."

Ed became a prisoner of war on Bataan peninsula after winning a Distinguished Service Cross for ground action there as a foot soldier. He was one of the very few prisoners ever to escape from the Japanese, because the Japanese set the prisoners up in cadres of ten men. If one of the ten attempted to escape, all ten of the cadre were killed.

About this time, August or September 1941, incidents of Japanese brutal military actions in China heated up concerns of war in the Pacific. Just as she ignores the economic concerns and fair play in her business relations with other

---

* R/T: abbreviation for radio telephone.

nations today, she ignored the feelings then of victim China, murdering, looting, and raping. The dead were estimated to be around 20,000,000, mostly civilians.*

Nor did this harsh, inhuman conduct go unnoticed by sister nations, and those with whom she dealt. Such actions created hatred of the perpetrator, but she couldn't have cared less. As a result, America began strengthening her defenses in the Philippines.

Rumors arose that our units would soon be going to a place called "Plum," the code name for an assignment to the Philippines. They proved true, and the 34th Pursuit Squadron was selected to ship out to "Plum" in a few weeks.

The three squadrons continued a sputtering training program with a few hours per month being logged per pilot. Ground loops continued cracking airframes, and bugs in an engine still in development provided minimal flying time per pilot, which in turn caused increased pilot error. My own fortunes figured heavily in the growing problem.

On a mission with an egotistical, inexperienced young pilot leading the two-ship flight, I was determined to do a good job of formation flying, for I knew how mouthy and critical he was of the newer pilots. He was jerky and gave poor signals of his maneuvers. I was determined to give

* *The World at Arms: The Reader's Digest Illustrated History of World War II*, Pleasantville, N.Y.: (Reader's Digest Association, Inc., 1989), p. 465

him little cause to talk. After a while, the engine on my plane began to run rough. I called the leader, but he said, "Aw, get in formation." I tried, but it would not take throttle.

I then turned and headed back toward Hamilton Field. I was losing power so I cut the throttle and began looking for a place to land. Then the engine seemed to punch holes in the cowling and caught fire. I was still looking for a place to land, when smoke started coming into the cockpit. I rolled back the canopy as flames started licking around the instrument panel. Small pieces of molten aluminum began to strike my flying suit and burn through. I had to leave! I rolled the ship over on its back, released my safety belt, and dropped out. With greater presence of mind, I would have been reducing speed. As it was, the wind stream blew me back into the tail surfaces, giving my ankles quite a whack. I grabbed the rip cord and jerked.

To my horror, the rip cord tore loose from the parachute. I had jerked it too hard. Then I knew my time in church was about to pay off. The parachute did not open immediately, but there was a rustling noise at my back that I didn't understand. I was prepared for the gates of pearl to swing open, when, all of a sudden, I was almost jerked senseless.

Unknown to me, a rip cord was supposed to come free, and there was a delay of several seconds before the parachute opened after the cord was pulled. At about that time I heard the fighter plane strike the ground and explode.

As the ground came up, I could see I was drifitng briskly. Then I struck the hard, dry ground of a wheat field and was instantly whipped across it by a strong wind. The parachute was dragging me across the stubble on my stomach so fast that I could not get to my feet. After a couple of minutes my knees and elbows were burning like fire. It finally dawned on me that I could grab the lower risers, the cords that go from the canopy to the harness, and the chute would spill its air, which it did, about the same time it blew into a fence.

Oh, boy! Relief! I rubbed my blistered parts and gathered up my parachute. There was a farmhouse a few hundred yards away, and a man and his small son soon came up and asked if I was all right. I said, "Yes, all but my knees and elbows. This wind was burning me across the stubble blistering my down side." They led me to the house, where I made a phone call to Hamilton Field Operations. I told them briefly what had happened and asked the farmer to give them directions to the farm. In an hour or so an ambulance arrived and took me back to the base where I was hospitalized, more as policy than for injury. My knees and elbows formed scabs, and my ankles swelled, but they soon healed.

One of those "small world" incidents came to light while discussing the history of Hamilton Field at a dinner party there. In 1986 I was an honored guest at the table of a local supporter of an air show being held at the field. I mentioned that I had been stationed at Hamilton and had once bailed out of a burning P-40 north of Santa Rosa. Mister Darrel Sitchel asked when. I replied that it was in 1940. It developed that I landed in my chute on Mr. Sitchel's farm and he and his father helped me gather my parachute and let me use their phone to report to my unit at Hamilton Field.

A few nights later, Lieutenant Stoebe, the flight leader on the day my plane caught fire, was on a scheduled night flight. He was caught in army searchlights by air-defense crews practicing with their lights, and crashed to his death. After that, searchlight crews were banned from spotting "live" targets, because they could blind a pilot if he should look into them.

Once in the military hospital, my elbows and knees healed and the bone bruises on my shins receded and they finally let me out, and back on flying status. The 34th Pursuit Squadron prepared to board a ship for "Plum," and many of my friends left America, never to return. Then the 21st Pursuit Squadron, my squadron, was rumored to be scheduled for departure for "Plum."

At this point I decided I should take the 30-day leave I had postponed when I graduated from flying school. I caught an Air Corps bomber from Hamilton Field to Will Rogers Field, in Oklahoma City, and hitchhiked home.

When I left home nearly two years before, I

had a dog of an unusual nature, a loner, who was friendly only with my mother and me. He would run away from strangers and even close family members. When I walked up the road to the house, he barked at me and would not approach, or let me approach him. I went on in and we all hugged and then visited for hours. I remarked about Duke not recognizing me, and Mother said, "Leave your shirt on the back porch when you go to bed, wait until morning, dress in your old clothes, and walk out back like you used to, and let's see."

Next morning when I walked out the back door Duke jumped all over me, leaping and yipping as of old. Apparently he had thought about it during the night — it looked like he had slept on my shirt — and decided he remembered me.

I helped Dad some on the farm; I fished and hung out with old buddies, walked the fields with Duke, and dated some of the cute gals that used to be hard to get dates with. I had a wonderful time; it made me feel ready to go to distant lands to keep war from our shores if it became necessary.

With leave over I caught a B-18 at Will Rogers Field, flown by a lieutenant colonel and a major, high rank at that time. They treated me as if I were their son on an extended trip of the West. They were making a survey that took us to California via Great Falls, Montana, and McChord Field, Washington, a great tour for me.

Back at Hamilton Field, I logged a little time

in some P-40s that the squadron had acquired. On one flight I flew a few feet over the house where Phoebe Johnson, a girl I was dating at the time, lived, in Corte Madera, fifteen miles from Hamilton, and some old biddy reported me. I was grounded for a week. All pilots were required to perform "officer of the guard" duty regularly. I traded with seven officers and took their guard duty during the seven days of restriction and beat the rap, but lost all my banked time when we shipped overseas.

War talk was growing louder as autumn advanced. True to rumor, in this case my squadron was advised to prepare for shipment to "Plum" around the middle of November 1941.

There were moans and groans, especially among the married troops. For me it seemed rather adventurous, for I had never been outside the ZI*, and foreign travel sounded romantic.

A few days after I was off restriction, an agent for the AVG, the American Volunteer Group** came to Hamilton Field to recruit fighter pilots who were about to be discharged from active duty. Those days your contract required that you serve three years active duty after graduation from Flying Cadets. I think some who were about to be discharged signed up. I, of course, still had more than two years to go, so I was unable to join

---

* Zone of interior.
** The AVG was later to be known as the Flying Tigers, American mercenary fighter pilots who flew P-40s for China against the Japanese invaders.

them, though the pay was far better than ours.

One Monday morning in early November I was scheduled to fly a formation training mission. I was assigned to fly element leader in a flight of four. We took off in trail, and I cut the turn of the lead element sharply and slid into formation and reduced throttle to avoid overrun.

Suddenly I saw my wingman, Lt. Donald Scott, closing the distance between us rapidly, and before I knew it his propeller struck my right wing. There was a blinding crash as the planes lurched together momentarily with pieces flying. We were very low, perhaps at 400 feet, and I knew I had to bail out quickly, or I would strike the ground before the parachute opened. I clawed at the canopy handle and cranked the dozen turns like I never cranked before. I thanked the Lord it wasn't jammed in the collision. I jerked my headset plug, unlatched the safety belt, and kicked out into the wind stream. A few more kicks and I was out of the cockpit and sliding along the fuselage. I jerked the rip cord while I was kicking free, and the chute started opening as I cleared the plane. I swung a time or two, and splat! I hit the mud of San Pablo Bay and sank in up to my waist.

Landing in the old twenty-four-foot-wide parachute gave a 190-pound human a descent rate of so many feet per second, producing a jolt like jumping from a sixteen-foot height. The only nicks I got out of the crash and landing were from sharp clamshells littering the mud of the bay.

The bay was far out on a low tide, so while I was pushing and shoving with my elbows to extract myself from the mud, I knew I had to get out before the tide came rushing back in to fill the flats with three or four feet of water. I was glad the water there wasn't over my head when I went into the mud, or I might have drowned.

The base maintained a crash boat on a canal near the end of the runway. The boat was launched, and after a time I saw it approaching. It came up a tidal gut to a point nearby, then turned and plowed through the viscous goo right up to me. The boatman pulled me into the boat and we made our way back to the boathouse, where an ambulance was waiting. Word was that Lt. Don Scott went into the bay with his plane. My depression was exceeded only by my gratitude that I did not rest there with him.

Again I was hospitalized, and again, thankfully, more from policy than from injury.

The next Sunday, Irene Chida, a Portuguese girl I was dating in San Rafael, came out to see me. She brought me something and wanted to hear about the accident. While she was there, the Seeger family and Aldine Seeger came in. Everyone was embarrassed, and the Seegers said they would wait outside. Visiting hours were limited from 2:00 to 4:00 P.M., and because Irene was jealous, she stayed and stayed.

Irene was not as pretty as Aldine, and I was hoping she would leave before Aldine got huffy and departed with her folks. But when it rains it pours, and sure enough, Phoebe Johnson, an English girl from Corte Madera (Aldine was of German descent) came in. With visitors stacking up, Irene finally left with some remark about this being "Grand Central Station," and Phoebe was the next to get huffy about having to wait. Though I enjoyed having visitors, it wasn't a particularly good day for me.

While in the hospital, the 21st Fighter Squadron boarded ship for "Plum." I wondered what was to become of me after the ship pulled out. Little did I know that the question was what was to become of them?

The inability of the Air Corps to keep the P-40s in commission to fly gave its pilots little flying time. In the six months after graduation I had acquired several hours in the obsolete P-36, but only a smidgin of time in our combat plane, the P-40, and we were restricted from aerobatic maneuvers. A fighter pilot cannot meet the competition if he cannot do skilled aerobatic maneuvers. America should consider such lack of preparation as an indictment.

On Sunday, 7 December 1941, I was visiting in Aldine Seeger's home. Their radio was on and the news of an attack on Pearl Harbor was broadcast. We all looked at one another in amazement. Mr. and Mrs. Seeger said I should probably report to my unit; there were thoughts of an attack on the West Coast. This, of course, meant war for me.

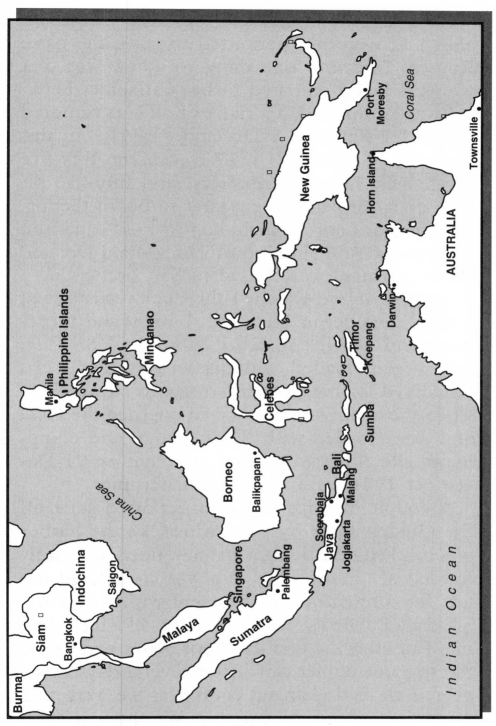

Southwest Pacific Theater of Operations

Back at Hamilton Field we were placed on alert and were not permitted to leave the base. Rumors flew, but one thing we knew was that we were being prepared to be sent somewhere.

I was grouped with a cadre of officers rumored to sail for Plum on 8 December 1941, but this date was postponed. On 17 December, fifty-five mechanics, fifty-five armorers, and fifty-five pilots, many of whom were later to board the aircraft carrier *Langley*, including two old squadron wingmates from Hamilton Field, Gerald Dix and Bill Ackerman, were bused to San Francisco.

At Pier 45 we watched the dockworkers load a large new ocean liner with bombs and torpedoes, and fifty-five crated P-40s. The USS *Polk*, a new ship loaded with passengers, had been scheduled for her maiden voyage to Hong Kong when the enemy struck. We all boarded the *Polk*, and now, loaded with fighting men and equipment, she departed around midnight on 21 December 1941 from a San Francisco pier.

A couple of ships had been reported sunk off the Golden Gate by submarines, so the harbor was blacked out. Being a fast new liner, and badly needed at "Plum," the ship was considered too fast for submarines, so was sent without escort.

Lots of fellows were soon seasick, including me. But after the first day I got better and found the trip not unpleasant. After several days it appeared we had changed course, as we were told we were crossing the equator. We threw a Neptune party and filled the onboard swimming pool.

We threw one another into the pool and later had a swim. From there we sailed the widest part of the world's widest sea.

After almost three weeks, we sighted land low on the horizon, and at 4:00 P.M. we hove into a harbor, stopping beneath a battery of coastal guns pointed at us. We paused there, frantically sending signals back and forth. We later were told that no one had word of our coming and we did not have the proper entry signals. Everyone in the Pacific was trigger-happy at that time, and we were suspected of being a Japanese ship sent to blow up the harbor. We finally obtained permission to enter the harbor and, of course, were welcomed with open arms.

The beautiful city we had arrived at was Wellington, New Zealand. The personnel were given a three-day pass while the ship was refueled and took on food, water, and supplies.

Lieutenant James V. ("Hambone") Hamilton and I walked to the nearest shopping area. We entered a grocery store, and having been without candy, gum, toothpaste, and such, we selected a number of sundry items. When we went to pay for them, I handed the saleslady a five-dollar bill. She drew back and said, "Aiye, Yank, ye cawn't use that kind of money, ye have to have pounds, ye know!" I felt foolish, and said, "Oh, I'm sorry, lady, I didn't think of that." I asked, "Where do you suppose we could change our money?" She said, "I'm afraid it's a bit late for that, as the banks are all closed." Then the dear lady looked me in the face, and said, "Ah, well, here, take this twenty-pound note, and ye can pay me back Monday."

Well, Hambone and I were flabbergasted, and looked at each other in amazement. I said, "Oh, no, we couldn't possibly do that." I added, "Ma'am, you couldn't find one in ten thousand people in my country who would do that for you; I couldn't take your money."

She said, a little hurt by my refusal, "No, no, no, go on, take it. You won't have much fun on the weekend without money." That thought hit home, so I took her approximately fifty-five dollars, a sum equal to about five hundred dollars today, and we left.

As we walked along the street in Wellington, a fine-looking black car rolled up beside us. The driver asked if we were Americans. We replied that we were. He said he would like us to be his guests, and he would show us the town. The gentleman told us that he was the mayor of Wellington, and had heard that an American ship had docked with soldiers aboard. He drove us around the city and to his home near the ocean.

During our conversation I told him of the shock we had when we bought the goods in the store and had no New Zealand money, and the lady lent us the twenty-pound note. I explained to him there was no brotherly love such as that to be found in America.

The mayor said that he considered New Zealand a harsh place now. He said that before 1939, when New Zealand volunteered to accept four boatloads of refugees from Nazi tyranny in Europe, New Zealand was, indeed, a land of brotherly love, and such acts were commonplace. Now, he said, things were all claws and elbows. He said it was a terrible thing to have to say that about desperate, struggling waifs without a home, but, since their arrival, they had, in just two years, upset their way of life with old world distrust and grasping. He said the islands would never accept more refugees. He said it was a saddening experience for the people of New Zealand, both in their feelings for the homeless refugees and for the social structure of his nation, which had suffered.

The mayor's wife served us crumpets and tea with milk, and later the mayor himself returned us to the dockside, where we thanked him profusely, inviting him to visit America after we cleared up this little mess in the Southwest Pacific.

Hambone and I enjoyed the city and a couple of pubs, and on Monday we hastened back to the lady's grocery store and repaid her generous loan. She said, "I knew you would be back; I wasn't worried." We had to say, "Don't do it too often, dear."

Since New Zealand was a British satellite, as we were at one time, and English-speaking, and Caucasian, we had much in common, and we got on well together. We liked them. Back on board ship we were off across the "roaring forties."

Famous for their winds and seas, they fulfilled the promise. Mountainous seas arose that completely hid the 10,000 ton ship. We would slide down one huge wave, then turn to climb the other side.

Each day I would go topside to do my regular exercise, usually by myself. Alone, and in the howling wind and salty spray, the sea seemed so lonely and distant, yet it attracted me. Big albatrosses would hang in the wind just above the ship. They would turn their heads to look down at you and flick an eyelid over a sloe-black eye.

On the rear of the ship there was an exercise bar, about six inches above my reach. When the ship hit the bottom trough of a wave and started up, if I jumped as high as I could, I couldn't go over three inches off the deck. If I jumped when the ship hit the top of the wave, and dropped down the far side, I would fly up past the bar as the stern dropped away beneath me.

Since we were so far from our intended destination, we concluded that the war must be going badly. Our original destination was "Plum," as had been the destination of the 34th and 21st squadrons.

A few days later we encountered ships coming and going, and we soon sighted land, and began that seemingly inevitable wait for a harbor pilot. The port was Brisbane, Australia. With Japan roaring down in a seemingly irresistible charge from the north, Australia was making every port available for permanent call to any ships crammed with military equipment and soldiers. After a day or two in the harbor, we pulled into the docks.

III

Big Change of Plans

At Brisbane we were offloaded right where we were. Hasty plans were made and we were all marched off the ship onto the docks, where we boarded military trucks that took us to an Australian racetrack, the Ascot. The horses were taken elsewhere, and we were provided cots and bedded down in the barns.

Our crated P-40s were also offloaded and trucked to Amberly field, where we pilots joined the ground crews in twelve-hour shifts assembling them. As they came off the line, they were test-flown and given a break-in period for the engines, with careful use of throttle and RPMs. This was a dangerous time for our young pilots, as many had only a few hours in the tricky airplanes, if any at all. For example, I had not flown for many weeks, having been in the hospital prior to the time on the ship.

In digging through some of my old military records to verify names and dates, I came across some torn pages of Lt. William Day's diary that I had acquired. Day later became a member of the 49th Fighter Group and a member of my flight. The impressions of a lad on the scene and facing combat in an uneven war are interesting to read today. Day was later to become an ace in the war.

Jan. 13. (1942) The remainder of the pursuit squadrons at Hamilton Field arrived here today. They are all set for action, they think. Nothing seems to please them. When they are over here for a month they won't be so anxious. Some of the stories from the Philippines will take some of that out of them. The Japs were certainly under rated.

Some of the boys from Manila are down here. 1st Lt. Buzz Wagner, America's first Ace of World War No. 2, and some more of the boys are down here trying to get planes to take back. They've been giving us some instructions on combat flying. From their stories they let us gather that the Jap Zero is no toy, but they try to make us believe the American planes with experienced pilots are a match for them, but where are the experienced pilots? The ones we have here are kids just out of flying school . . . kids just like me. Speaking for myself it sort of gives us an empty feeling in our guts.

"Buzz" tells us the story of his flying around some low mountains with a couple of Japs on his tail. He is as low as he can fly trying to out run them. As he comes around this hill he runs into another Zero coming around to meet him. It scares him so bad he jams the throttle to the firewall. The added soup put him way out front of the Japs. When he finally feels safe enough to look at his instruments he finds he is pulling over 70 inches of mercury. It scares him so he pulled her back to 55 inches. Forty-six inches is the maximum for take-off. Another few seconds and the engine would have blown up in his lap.

I haven't been in an airplane since I landed here. It would seem good to be in one again. I need some time in something in order to draw my flying pay for December and January.

Jan. 20. I have at last gotten an airplane ride. This young Lt. and I went up to test hop this A-24[*] . . . an Army dive-bomber. I rode in the back seat. We flew around the city of Ipswich for half an hour, and then went out near the field for a practice dive, and we did. . . .

The next day Lt. Kitchen[**] took me up with him. We flew on the right wing of a three-ship element. I don't think I ever had such a rough ride in any formation. The air was bumpy, and he wasn't accustomed to flying formation in this type ship. We climbed up to about ten thousand feet and cruised out over the ocean. The leader found a target and signaled the formation into string (in-line flight). We were the second ship in the string. As we came toward the target . . . the shallow entrance to the bay at Southport . . . the plane is slowed down to around 140 miles per hour. We're over the target now. The pilot signals to open the canopy. The wind rushes to fill the cockpit. I feel the

[*] The A-24 was a single-engine dive-bomber manufactured by Douglas Aircraft and used by both the army and the navy. It was a two-seater providing for a pilot and rear gunner.
[**] All-American football player at Oklahoma University, shot

airplane rise suddenly and look out just in time to see the diving flaps being spread. These flaps help to slow the plane down in a dive . . . to around 360 miles per hour . . . and also help to keep the plane going straight down. The stick is pushed forward. The inlet is now directly below . . . right over the nose of the diving plane. The earth rushes up to meet us. The wind is pouring into the cockpit with such force we can hardly breathe. The whine of the propeller and the air is terrific. We begin to pull out. The inlet is coming too close for comfort. The hands on the altimeter are spinning so fast I am unable to read them. The diving flaps close instantaneously, causing us to lurch forward. At this time on actual bombing missions the bombs would have been dropped. We begin to pull out. The forces are several times that of gravity. My jaw drops and my head lolls to one side. My whole body is trying to go through the bottom of the seat. My vision becomes dim. When I can see clearly again we are skimming the tree tops. Blood is pouring from my nose. My head feels as though a small charge of explosive has been set loose in it. We dive several more times, and then they have to take me back. The hospital says I'll be all right, but that I wasn't built for a dive bomber.

---

down over New Guinea and murdered for troop entertainment by the Japanese. Australian intelligence sources reported to the American forces that native tribesmen had observed the execution of two Americans.

Jan. 23. The assembly line here is beginning to show results. Whether it means anything toward ending the war, it is hard to say. All that can be said now is we're turning out airplanes that fly . . . some of them not so far, but they do fly. The first one took over two weeks to put together. Lots of the tools had to be made here. The ground crews were train[ed] on B-17s and all of their tools were for that type of work. None of them had ever worked on P-40s before, but they're doing good jobs taking this fact into consideration, and adding a lie here and there.

We have managed to get enough assembled to send two squadrons up the line to the north. Captain Spregg [Sprague] and Captain "Shady" Lane have led the boys to Java. The first outfit to leave tried for several days to get off. Each time the weather held them up. The rainy season is starting. Twice they have taken off and twice they have returned. Now the other outfit is ready to go. They have both gone . . .

A B-17 has arrived here from the Philippines. How an airplane can fly with so many holes shot in it will always remain a matter of amazement to me. It sums up this way. We have the world's best bombers. We've developed them in conjunction with our development of the best airline service on earth. We're peaceful people and have never had the desire nor the reason for developing good fighter planes. From where we sit in the western hemisphere, fighter planes are about as useful as tits on a boar pig. They are purely defensive weapons, and here-to-fore have had no prominent place in our grand strategy.

Jan. 27. Today we had a sad accident. About five o'clock this afternoon I was standing outside Headquarters talking to some of the men. Two planes buzzed very low in formation. They roared low over the field. Then they zoomed up and prepared to land. The [first] plane piloted by Lt. Hamilton landed. It had almost completed its roll when the landing gear seemed to fold up. Lt. Hamilton climbed out onto the wing to observe the damage. The second plane with Lt. Moorehead as pilot came in on a long low approach. Moorehead didn't see the grounded plane until it was too late. Lt. Hamilton never knew what struck him. He was so bent on what had just happened he forgot about the plane behind him. The wing of the second plane caught him in the middle of the back and side. Such losses are hard to take.

I suppose, though, it's like Colonel Johnson . . . CO of Base Section . . . said in my presence the other day, "Second Lieutenants are expendable." I replied with, "Everything is expendable in time of war, Colonel." And, I gave him a look that implied more than I actually said. He didn't seem to care a great deal for the quick return. He has planned a big party to celebrate his promotion to General, but he hasn't gotten it yet. And I hope he won't. I have never seen such a conglomeration of stupid, ignorant nonentities as he and his staff are.

There are three interesting coincidences in the young man's diary. The first is that he happened to make a flight with Lt. Gus Kitchen of Purcell, Oklahoma, county seat of my home county, McClain, only ten miles from my hometown. His mother pursued me when I returned home from the war in an effort to learn what happened to her son. I eluded her; I couldn't tell her the Japanese cut off her son's head after they captured him.

The other is his reference to Colonel Johnson, who almost certainly must have been the officer our flight of P-40 pilots reported to when we flew from Darwin to Townsville when we were transferred to New Guinea, and whose secretary I dated, as I describe later.

And the third in his coverage of the accident where Lieutenant Hamilton was killed. As mentioned in the diary, we began flying formation missions. Captain "Shady" Lane, also mentioned, was placed in command of our headless unit, although he did little to give it a head.

On that day Lane briefed our flight of twelve pilots that we were to practice rapid takeoffs and landings. This was not illogical, but it was poor policy to be doing stressful exercises that required skill, when we were just getting back into the flying game. None of us had flown for weeks, and our desperate need was time to fly alone and reacquaint ourselves with both the plane and flying itself. Lane, however, threw us right into close formation flying and fast takeoffs and landings. "When you get into combat," he blustered in his posed, knowledgeable stance, "you'll find out. You have to get off the ground and back on the ground in seconds." Everyone knew he had seen no more combat than any of the rest of us, and pressured flying was a strain.

Most people assume that once you learn to fly, it is like learning to drive a car; That is, you can step in and fly a plane like driving a car ten years later, with little adjustment. Not so. Hours of time in the air are necessary to once again feel at ease and confident and erase nervousness and an inherent fear of the third dimension.

We were scheduled for rapid formation takeoff, which is a real sweat on dusty ground where you roar down the field at full throttle twenty feet from your lead plane, and soon can see nothing whatsoever in the dust cloud. Then you pray that none of the planes on your right or left veer into your path, or you chew into one another and burn to death in a tangle of ships loaded with gasoline. A collision did happen, but fortunately there was little gasoline aboard, so the wreckage did not catch fire.

After the hairy takeoff and two or so hours of nervous up and down, back and forth formation flying with Lane leading, he announced on the R/T that he wanted to see us all on the ground in fifty-foot intervals.

The P-40 has a long twelve-cylinder Allison engine for a power unit. It was patched onto the Curtiss P-36 fighter in order to save money, and as a result the beast possessed serious faults. Throughout the war, corrective measures were taken at the factory and test fields, so that improvements were made. Pilots even said the P-40 model, which came much later in the war, was a worthy fighter plane with high-altitude capability as well as improved maneuverability and cockpit comfort.

This evolution occurred in the cases of both the British Spitfire and the German Me-109. The end-of-the-war models of those planes were not recognizable from their beginnings.

It is too bad that our deciding sages did not recognize the incomparable superiority of the North American P-51 when it was offered them for acquisition! The Philippines might not have been lost. But that is water over the dam, as are the lives of so many of my dear friends.

Anyway, the instructions were to land in trail on the runway, one right behind the other in rapid succession. This program not only subjected the pilots to the stress of landing almost on top of the plane in front of you, it forced them to fly in the wake of the powerful thrust of the twelve-cylinder engine. Strong air currents generated can flip a light airplane upside down. They can rock heavier planes severely.

Though I was apprehensive, I did as ordered and pushed right up to fifty or so feet behind the plane ahead. As a pilot makes his flare-out in the P-40, the long nose comes up and he is unable to see directly ahead. I disliked the circumstances so much that I thought of giving it the gun and going around, but knowing the loudmouth would be barking at debriefing, I hung in and landed. One reason I didn't go around was that just before I flared out, I saw Lieutenant Hamilton touch down and start his roll.

I made a pretty fair landing and rolled ahead a few yards, when suddenly ahead I saw the two wingtips of an airplane out both sides of my cockpit. They were stationary. Hambone (Hamilton) had nosed up on the runway and raked off his landing gear. He was flat on his belly. This was one of the hazards of having to use brakes to control the landing. I jammed full left rudder as hard as I could, and my ship veered hard left, barely avoiding running up the fuselage of the other plane. If that had happened, my propeller would likely have chopped into the fuselage tank of Hambone's plane and caused a fire or explosion.

As it was, Hamilton was quickly exiting the left side of the cockpit. My right wing slashed through the tail of his plane, and the propeller, not the wing, caught my dear friend and cut him in half.

In a terrible tangle of wings, tails, and engines, flying parts, sparks, and grinding metal, the skidding planes finally stopped. I released my safety belt, leapt out, and dashed around to see what could be done, only to find Hambone's body in pieces, spurting blood and jerking convulsively. I turned away, shaken and remorseful that I had not gone around for another approach.

Back in the hospital for bumps and bruises, I was alone with my thoughts. Hambone was a Texas boy who had grown up, much as I had, on a farm under severe drought conditions, in the depths of the Great Depression. He had known hardship and toil, and minimal luxuries. His family was poor, and now, somewhere in East Texas, an American mother would be greeted at the door with a yellow slip of paper, announcing that her son had been killed in the service of his country.

Lieutenant Hamilton had had a severe distaste for the brutality of the merciless Japanese, and was eager, as was I, to make them pay for their heartless barbarity. He had said that though he had almost no flying time in fighter planes, it wouldn't matter once we built up combat time. Then the older pilots could talk all the flying they wanted to, but it wouldn't have the weight of combat experience. I would have felt so much better about it if my dear friend had died in combat. (We all seemed to have a deep-seated desire, if we were going to die, that we die in action rather than by accident — I know I did.)

Flying, for such green pilots under those circumstances was far more dangerous than flying normal combat. Pilots with no experience in their planes were often pressed into service. A friend of mine, 2nd Lt. Jay Robbins (later Major General Robbins) finished cadet training and was sent immediately to Australia. He was put up in bachelor officers' quarters, where he was sleeping soundly around 0400 and was awakened by a knock at the door. An officer and a sergeant entered. The officer asked if he was a pilot. He said he was. The officer asked if he was a multiengine pilot. Robbins replied that he had flown only trainers. The officer said, "Well, you will do." Robbins dressed and was taken to a B-17 on the base and placed in the first pilot's seat. With the sergeant manning the cockpit switches and controls, Robbins flew the B-17 to Port Moresby, New Guinea, where it was needed for some critical mission like that flown by my flying school classmate Wallace Field's B-17 that made the initial contact with the Japanese fleet in the battle of the Coral Sea.

At Hamilton Field I had made friends with many of the young pilots. Lieutenant Paul May was there, and we had come over together on the USS *Polk*. We had lived in the same tent.

Being a hunter and fisherman, I had brought with me from the States my little pump .22-caliber rifle and my fishing rod and reel. One Sunday afternoon May and I took my .22 and fishing rod down to a lagoon on the back side of the air base. I needed bait to fish with, so I shot a small bird and stuck the breast of the bird on my hook and cast out into the lagoon. A few minutes passed and then I got a bite. I set the hook and it felt like

83

I hooked something big. Then, to our great surprise, a school of large mottled eels, four or five feet long, came to the surface and seemed to be looking for the cause of the distress to their buddy.

I hated to drop my rod and run, but we both felt like doing just that. We stuck it out, and finally they all submerged, and I fought the big critter and dragged him out on the bank, although we were half expecting the other monsters to come out of the water with him and attack us — a strange experience in a strange land.

As we continued to grab a few flying hours, two other separate flights of P-40s departed for . . . the Philippines? We heard they would fly up the chain of islands in the Indies to reinforce the air units on Luzon and Mindanao.

Word came back that they had had misfortune with both the weather and the enemy, and had lost many planes and pilots. Word also came back that things were going increasingly badly in the Philippines. The ability of our P-36s, P-35s, and P-40s to match the Japanese AGM Zero fighter seemed to be dropping to zero. The only success the Allies seemed to be having against the Japanese fighters lay with General Chennault's AVG, the American Volunteer Group. They were not pitted against the AGM, the navy "Zero," but instead fought less capable Japanese Army fighter types.

It can be said that Japan's whirlwind conquest of millions of square miles and dozens of countries and islands of the Pacific was in large measure due to her superior fighter plane, the Zero.

The rapid conquest of the British and Anzac troops in Malaya, and the retreat of the Americans in the Philippines, was giving the aura of invincibility to the Japanese forces. The Zero was beginning to be held in awe. This was starting to give us in the flying business a feeling of apprehension.

On 20 January, 1942, the commanding general of the Far East Air Force ended plans to ferry P-40s to the Philippines. Staging points were along the ferry route throughout the Dutch East Indies. Many locations were either captured or were about to be. The 17th Provisional Pursuit Squadron had been formed with a group of seventeen escaped fighter pilots from the Philippines plus mostly green replacements from the States. Their orders had been to proceed to Java "to delay the Japanese offensive."

The enemy had followed an efficient military plan against the Allies since the beginning of the war. Japan's armed forces had spread across the Far East and the broad expanses of the Pacific like a large ink blot, piling up astonishing successes. Japan's strategy of interdiction of air and naval reinforcement of the Philippines and Malaya was brilliant. Yamamoto kept the Allied military command off balance. During Australia's "Pearl Harbor" on 19 February 1942, he launched 240 carrier- and land-based planes that sank or damaged 21 ships, bombed the city of Darwin, killed or injured 540 people, and decimated the air defenders. With the occupation of Timor, the fall of Singapore and surrender of 150,000 troops, the rout of 140,000 Americans and Filipinos on Luzon, the attack on New Guinea, and the destruction of the Allied fleet in the Java Sea, Java was isolated. All the Allied fighter units were trapped without an escape route. The few P-40s of the 17th Provisional Pursuit Squadron were seen as easy meat for the eager naval pilots of the Japanese air forces. Three enemy aircraft carriers were roaming the Java Sea, steadily eliminating the meager air forces of the Dutch, British, Australians, New Zealanders, and Americans.

On 29 January 1942, I was part of a flight of about a dozen P-40s from Amberly Field, Brisbane, at 1:30 that landed at Charleville, around six hundred miles to the west, at 4:30 P.M. For the land down under, it was midsummer and blistering hot, about 110 degrees F in the shade. After parking my plane, I stood on the line and watched the rest of the flight land.

Heated air makes flight in aircraft with high-wing loading mushy and difficult for landing. Watching each touchdown by our green pilots kept my heart in my throat. They would slam down hard in the thin air. Two planes cracked up. One damaged a wing, the other caught fire; but the pilot escaped.

We spent the night in Charleville, then turned

north toward Darwin. Next stop was Cloncurry, but before landing we all tested our guns over the jungle.

Next stop brought us in to Daly Waters, a lonely outback cattle station with stored barrels of gas for refueling. The long refueling stop gave Bill Turner and me a chance to dig my little .22 pump out of the baggage compartment behind the cockpit and go for a short hunt in this strange land with all the long-leafed, slick-barked eucalyptus trees. We hardly knew what to expect, but there was good cover for some kind of game with scattered big trees and plenty of underbrush. Suddenly something large leapt out and bounded rapidly away. I led the target a couple of feet and thud, I heard the bullet hit and the animal collapsed. We went over and looked down on my first bagged wallaby, a kind of kangaroo.

Back at the dirt airfield we had seen large black men working with the Australians, gassing the planes. We recognized them as the native Australians, the Aborigines. We had no way to cook the game, so we dragged the forty- or fifty-pound animal back to the airfield and gave it to them, and they seemed very happy to receive it.

Our next takeoff was a hairy one. Captain Lane ordered four-ship takeoffs. Rolling forward on the dusty airfield, with the lead plane stirring up a huge cloud of red dust, the pilots following on were caught in a blur of confusion, unable to see in any direction. To veer right or left could mean a grinding collision; to slow or stop might place you in the path of a plane approaching from the rear. You just had to keep boring ahead at a steady speed and hope for the best. It was a terror-filled situation, but somehow we all made it through without accident.

As we neared Darwin around 7:00 P.M., a dark bank of clouds preceded by an ominous roll cloud appeared to be trying to beat us to the airport, Bachelor Field. On the ground and taxiing back, the tempest struck. Torrents of rain with drops as big as plums struck the field. It was easy to see why other flights that had gone ahead of us had lost their way and crashed. Flying fast, short-range aircraft in unknown territory and unknown weather was proving as much an enemy as the enemy.

At Darwin we met other fighter pilots, some old friends, escaping the Philippines. Lieutenant Stewart "Rattlesnake" Robb, who had been with me in the 34th Pursuit Squadron at Hamilton Field, was there. He had come out on a B-17 after serving as an infantryman on Bataan. "Rattlesnake" was not a tall person. In one of his stories, he told of a night battle on Bataan, where the enemy had infiltrated American lines. He said he was having it doubly tough, for he was short and the Americans were shooting at every form that was short in stature, concluding they were Japanese. Rattlesnake's stories about the Zeros were not reassuring.

The next morning we tried to continue our journey with a B-17 as a guide ship, but a bank of monsoon clouds stopped us an hour out in the Timor Sea.

The next day we tried again to complete the leg from Darwin to Koepang, Timor, a large island some six hundred miles north of Australia. This time we were being led by a B-17 and we flew close formation on his wing. A bomber with a navigator aboard had a much better chance of locating an island in a typhoon. After finding the island came the chore of finding a rain-lashed airfield in a sea of tropical jungle. About halfway across we encountered unstable air; in the distance darkened skies filled the horizon.

Had the scene that loomed ahead through the bent glass of the pursuit plane's canopy confronted me on the plains of Oklahoma as a child in bare feet and overalls, I would have run for my life. For the uninitiated who have never stood in the path of the oncoming fury of a tornado in an open field, my description won't do much for you. But to those who have, I wouldn't have to urge you to join me in fleeing in the other direction at God's speed. Through the clear windshield there appeared a phenomenon that often accompanies violent storms, a white roll cloud, like the ermine ruff of a young girl's strapless evening gown. It is often a precursor of a lashing of the earth by the elements.[*]

[*] In Walter D. Edmond's book, *They Fought With What They Had* (p. 177), he states: "There were Mae Wests for the pilots, and no flying boats or rescue craft to follow up the flight. If a plane went down at sea, it would be for keeps."

If I had been the leader of the group, I would have turned around and followed the clear path back to Darwin. But Captain Lane was the leader. He struck me as being a city boy who had done more talking in his life than anything else. His mouth was going constantly with simple talk, and his flight scheduling, like the quick landing mission that killed Lieutenant Hamilton, was just dumb. I mistrusted his judgment.

Flying in clear air on the wing of a slow (comparatively) bomber, cruising sixty to eighty miles per hour slower than the pursuit plane, is stressful, as the controls are mushy and plane responses are sluggish. Flying with a rain-blurred canopy in violent turbulence just off the waves of a storm-tossed ocean, in danger of colliding with another plane, is a constant terror. While we flew in tight echelon off the wing of the big plane, the B-17 pilot entered the base of the storm clouds and soon was becoming hard to see. One moment we could make out the big ship, the next, he would disappear. Then it began to rain. With no windshield wipers, rain obviously makes formation flying more difficult because of poor visibility. Torrential rain reduces visibility to a solid blur. Hanging on to the wing of your leader, bouncing up and down and lurching through the air, becomes a struggle to survive.

The bomber pilot began lowering toward the surface of the sea, searching for clear air as the storm became an inferno and visibility seemed to become even worse. Fortunately he was able to find a clearer area just above the waves. But that brought new terrors.

The bomber would bounce in the air above us for one moment, then we would be flung above it like a hellish device in an amusement park. Rain became so intense, I feared that it would extinguish my engine. It appeared that the tumultuous waves were reaching for us. At one point I thought I had hit a wave when a splash of water and spray came off my propeller, but it may have been the crest of a whitecap.

The desperate, grueling grind seemed to go on for hours. Then we broke into the clear with a sigh of relief. As the rain slowed and cleared from our windshields, just ahead another tempest bore down upon us. We had brief relief in what must have been the eye of the storm. So we had seen only the half of it.

The bomber pilot bored into the other side of the mighty storm, and again we were thrown about the sky in a seemingly endless struggle to keep from striking the waves, the big ship leading us, or we one another. The blurred objects flying past our wingtips, glimpses of the windblown crests of the mountainous waves only feet beneath our wings, and the mental picture of one's plight if he erred only slightly were mentally and physically exhausting.

Finally the violent gusts subsided, and the rain let up a bit. Although rain had leaked through the canopy where it joined overhead and my arms were wet, the rest of me was soaking with sweat.

Almost surprisingly the Allison engine had not coughed a beat. Although low scud clouds hung over the landscape as we came onto the tropical island, the big bomber climbed to flight-pattern height and headed for a jungle airfield he had homed in on. We got down on the ground at last with five or ten gallons of fuel remaining. Whew!

Of many years of flying in many kinds of weather and flying conditions, the flight from Darwin to Timor led by the B-17 that day in early February 1942 was the worst flight of my life.

We had water buffalo stew for supper, spent the night in thatched-roof huts, and although it rained all night, we awoke dry and refreshed the next morning. After a short briefing we went to our planes for the next leg of our flight. As I was wiping the raindrops from my canopy, I heard aircraft revving their engines.

The field at Koepang had crossing strips cut in the jungle. On one of the strips an Australian Hudson bomber was revving his engines for take-off. On the end of the other strip was an Air Corps C-47 starting his roll to do the same thing, so both planes were approaching the runway crossing. The C-47 saw the Hudson approaching on the other runway and pulled back on the yoke. The ship lifted off and hung in the air. The Hudson ran beneath as the C-47 appeared to bounce its wheels off the bomber's wing. We who were looking on felt our hearts in our throats, but it was only a near miss, thank the Lord. With that out of the way, we all fired up and took off for Bali.

The air was calm and formation flying was a joy. The smooth flying permitted one to look around. The large island of Timor passed beneath, and over the horizon lay Sumba, Sumbawa, and the accompanying islands on the route to Bali and Java. It was a comfort to have the 600-mile-long string of islands lying beneath our path. Flying over open ocean in a single-engine plane has never been comfortable for me. I have been on too many searches for fliers down in the ocean, and it always seemed I never was able to find the poor souls. Air-sea rescue provisions were, of course, unknown in the entire area at this time.

These islands were the most beautiful I have ever seen, lush and green with coconut palms, banana plantations, terraced rice fields, white beaches, blue-green lagoons, and grass huts. My thought was: Why couldn't I just be here without a war going on?

Into view there came perhaps the most beautiful isle of all — Bali. We landed our fuel-thirsty winged chariots by the city of Denpasar. People were everywhere. Any direction one looked, there were people, and the women were beautiful. In their topless dress and regal bearing, they were deserving of our attention.

The airfield was lined with palm trees, only a short distance from the beach. It was a sod field and there was a large stack of fuel drums with hand pumps for our refueling. This landing placed us well within the active war zone, so we kept our planes spread out on the field and taxied up to the gas drums one after the other as soon as each plane was refueled by the hand pump.

While waiting my turn, I suddenly saw a lone airplane turning away from the airfield. I hollered at Captain Lane that there was a plane overhead. Lane yelled that all refueled planes were to take off immediately.

Five or six planes became airborne and while climbing out were hit by about fifteen Zeros. Two of our planes were shot down, two were damaged, and two force-landed, one on a beach and the other in a rice paddy. We were not sure of any Japanese losses.

We have the good fortune of being able to refer to the diary of Lt. Paul Gambonini of Petaluma, California. Paul and I went over on the USS *Polk* after training together at Hamilton Field. We bunked together, worked together, played together, and flew the route from Australia to Java, where we fought together in the 17th Pursuit Squadron.

Paul's diary records:

Four hours in a P-40, even with a belly tank, is stretching it. There is a lot of water between Darwin and Timor. Here we first saw the results of Jap bombing and strafing by their planes. The field was quite a mess. We gassed up our planes, with the help of some natives, and dispersed them. Then we ate supper, had native fruit, water buffalo steak and hard tack. This place is really in a jungle, black natives all over. We slept on a hard bench with a blanket over us and with our clothes on.

Feb. 5th. Got up this morning, ate breakfast, preflighted or [our] planes and were off to Bali at 6:00 A.M. Lt. McWherter had trouble with his plane and couldn't take off. Twelve of us followed a B-24 to Bali. We saw two ships, but were not sure of their identity. Lt. Muckley reported an unidentified plane following us. My radio was not working, so I did not know about it until we arrived in Bali at about 9:30 A.M. The ground personnel at the field started to gas up our planes, a little before ten o'clock we had an alert, Jap planes were reported approaching, the flight leader ordered all planes that were gassed up to patrol over the field, we had five or six planes airborne when about 15 Jap fighters attacked them. I was only partially gassed up, but took off, as I was climbing I had to dodge a falling belly tank from the melee above, planes were going in all directions, I got a few bursts at a Zero that was on the tail of a P-40. I think I hit him but another Zero got on my tail and I had to dive to the ground to get away from him. When I climbed back up I could not see any planes. It was all over in a few minutes. Lt. Landry had been shot down, Lt. Bound was hit and had to bail out, he was picked up OK but injured his arm some way in the chute or when landing. Lane, Muckley, Hague, and Galliene flew to Soerabaja to lose the pursuing Japs. Reagan had his hydraulic system shot out and landed wheels up on the beach. Turner's and my plane had been hit. Turner landed with a flat tire. I came in about ten minutes later about out of gas.

My own plane had not been refueled, so Lt. Marion Fuchs and I ran away from the field, diving into an old rock basin nearby, to avoid the bombs and strafing if any came.

After the skirmish and the departure of the Zeros, thirty-one bombers descended on the field and began a number of bomb runs, trying to destroy the parked fighters there and the fuel dump at one end of the field. After their third pass, we figured they were through. We got up and started to return to the field and suddenly someone started shooting at us from the beach. Some Balinese soldiers charged up and held us at gunpoint with our arms in the air. We convinced them we were their allies, and they finally released us. We concluded that they had seen us running and thought we were invaders. A very few days later they were to see a real enemy invasion, and were all killed or captured.

Fuchs and I made our way back to the airfield just in time to undergo another bombing run.

This time the bombers came in low and surprised us. We dashed over to some palm trees, feeling some protection by putting them between us and the field. But we felt that we were kind of on the receiving end of a bank shot on a pool table. The bomb fragments cut the coconuts down and they were falling all around us.

After a second pass, the bombers turned for another run on the field. Lying on my stomach behind a large palm, I waited until all bomb shards and debris stopped falling. Then I jumped to my feet and dashed out on the field near the exploding gas drums and climbed into the cockpit of my P-40, got it started, and jammed on the throttle. The twelve cylinders roared, kicking up dust and grass. At about fifty miles per hour I taxied off the runway across a meadow a hundred yards or so off the field and cut the switches on its far side. As it slowed, I jumped out and headed back to see if I could find another sound ship to disperse, but, looking up, I could see I would never have time, so I jumped into a shallow ditch.

Wow! The bombs were straddling me only feet away. One to my left just off the runway raised me off the ground. Showers of dirt and debris covered my body as I lay there. More smoke and fires belched from the stricken planes and gas dump. The bombers began another turn as I searched for a sound plane to save.

I dusted myself off and stood up, but I could see only one intact plane. The ammunition was cooking off in the burning P-40s, causing bullets and shell casings to whiz about. A carton of 500 bullets for my .22 rifle in Lt. Marion Fuchs's plane was burning. He carried some of my gear for me and half my precious supply of .22 cartridges in his baggage compartment, and the sound of the .50s firing and the .22 bullets firing off and whizzing in all directions sounded like a battle was going on, so we all thought about an invasion.

After trying to reach the one sound-appearing plane, it was obvious the runway was too pock-marked with craters to taxi. Then I noticed the plane had a gaping hole in the propeller hub.

About the time of the fourth bombing run we had run farther from the field, so as the bombers withdrew, I got Lieutenant Fuchs and Lieutenant Turner to help me push my plane back under some trees and cover it with palm fronds.

A Dutch officer drove up in a jeep and I asked if they could get to work on the runway and fill the craters in a strip wide enough for one plane to take off. Dozens of natives with hand shovels and shoulder baskets set to work. As they did their repairs, we worked through the night to take a good propeller from a burned-out plane and install it on Turner's damaged P-40.

A little after dawn a C-45, a small administrative Air Corps plane, came in with Dutch and American officers aboard. Captain Frank Kurtz and a civilian pilot introduced as "Pappy" Gunn asked if we had any pursuit planes that could escort them to Java. I mentioned my one P-40, so Captain Kurtz ordered me to escort the C-45 to Soerabaja. They took off down the strip narrowed by craters, and I followed. "Pappy" Gunn, we later learned, was an airline pilot based in the Philippines whose family was made prisoners of the Japanese. At that time he was giving valuable information to our forces and helping in matters of intelligence and liaison with the Filipinos. Later he was inducted into the Air Corps and worked tirelessly on important developments like skip bombing and the installation of multiple guns in the nose of the B-25. We understood they were slipping in and out of the southern islands of the Philippines doing undercover work.

The takeoff for me was a real sweat, as little can be seen directly over the long nose of a P-40 until you get the tail up and the nose down. A couple of soggy fills made me feel I had run into a crater, but I managed to get it into the air. No sooner had I cleaned up the cockpit, which means I had retracted the wheels and flaps, reduced the pitch and throttle, adjusted the trim control, shut off the booster pump, and closed the canopy, than I saw an enemy plane at ten o'clock high at about 5,000 feet. I tried to call Captain Kurtz, but the C-45 had different radio equipment, another situation that plagued many soldiers, sailors, and airmen throughout the war.

Our P-40s were camouflaged, but the C-45 was unpainted, bright aluminum. The C-45 was spotted immediately, and he dove on the small transport. I rammed full throttle and pulled up into his path. It appeared that he suddenly saw me and jerked away to the left. He swung out, flew parallel a bit, then began another approach.

Most Japanese reconnaissance planes I had studied carried nose guns, and each two-seater had a gun in the rear seat. This pilot appeared to be trying to use his nose gun, so I turned back into him and again he pulled away.

About that time a formation of twin-engine bombers escorted by about fifteen single-seat fighters crossed over high above at about 20,000 feet. I could see that the pilots in the C-45 had seen them, so I pulled closer to it for an imagined morale purpose. Fifteen Zeros would not have even been able to get warmed up on us, but it appeared that they had not been contacted by the recon. In fact, he seemed intent on aggrandizing himself with a C-45 kill. He eased in on a parallel course with the transport to perhaps give his rear gunner a crack at it.

Again I turned into him, but I never got close enough to fire, as he seemed to be fast. I knew Kurtz would greatly disapprove if I gave chase, because he had told me to stick close to him all the way in to Java. The flight to Soerabaja was not long. What worried me most were the fifteen Zeros heading in the same direction toward Soerabaja, our destination.

Then another chill ran up my spine. Nine single-engine planes, very near, seemed to be strafing coastal assets near Soerabaja. Earlier, Dutch officers had said that three enemy aircraft carriers were prowling off the Java coast. To be caught at this altitude with no room to dive would have meant disaster for both of us.

The single Japanese plane was still trying to figure out an approach on the C-45, when the Soerabaja airport came into view. And wouldn't you know, a damned friendly antiaircraft gunner would start firing on us!

Captain Kurtz dropped down almost to house-top level and bored into the airport as bombs started falling on it. The high-level bombers had beaten us there. As the bombs danced across the airdrome, Kurtz ignored them and set up a low traffic pattern. I covered his landing as he put the small plane down in a clear area just as the Zeros started breaking up overhead and diving on us. I turned to face them head-on, but they pulled up, preferring to come around on my tail. This gave Kurtz time to complete his landing roll, and I bent the throttle, scurrying away inland, where I hoped my overspeeding engine would hold together long enough to stay ahead of my persistent pursuers.

No one caught up to me, and after some time away I returned to the airport and landed between bomb craters. I was given a revetment to park in and went into the city for an overnight hotel.

For these two days' action, I was awarded my first Distinguished Service Cross.

IV

Bloody Java

I stayed in Soerabaja overnight. The next morning we had another air raid, so I got underneath the table where we were having breakfast. Later I went to the airfield to find that my plane had escaped damage. There I was met by Lieutenant Kiser, who led me to our secret airfield at Blimbing, Java, where I joined the reorganized 17th Provisional Pursuit Squadron, which had escaped the Philippines.

It was some time before the scattered remnants of our fighters arrived at Blimbing. At Blimbing we learned from those there that our opponents were indeed formidable, both in number and in ability as fighter pilots.

We later learned that indeed, some of the enemy pilots had been engaged in aerial combat for ten years with thousands of hours flying time over China and Manchuria, and that some were multiple aces with as many as fifty Russian planes to their credit. It was rumored that in order to humiliate America, a special unit, the Tainan Kokutai [group], all aces, had been selected individually to oppose us. In contrast, the most experienced pilot in our squadron had, at the most, twenty hours of combat time.

We were housed in an old sugar cane mill. Our operations were conducted from the lush green grass field, allocated by the Dutch to the 17th Squadron. Our operations shack was hidden in a coconut grove, with our planes scattered about under the coconut palms.

Java is a land of greenery and, from above, the field was almost impossible to distinguish from the rest of the countryside. Almost every time I returned from a flight, I had to search and search to find it. One time, low on fuel, I was reduced to looking for a long rice paddy to land on, gear up, when much relieved I spotted the field a short distance away. We used triangulation off a certain high line to find the place. That feature was not all bad by any means, however, as the enemy also were unable to find it. No doubt the intelligence department of the Japanese navy was poring over stereo maps to pick out one green spot from another that held a few American fighter planes that they just had to erase. Later on they did, and followed up with a good strafing.

Shortly after arriving at Blimbing, surrounded by large sugar cane fields and copra orchards, I was scheduled for an indoctrination hop. I was flying the wing of Lt. George Kiser, who put us in string formation in order to look over the terrain. In string, you fly several dozen yards behind one another in order to take a look around without risking running into one another. That way you can relax and absorb the terrain features, and indoctrinate yourself by use of the compass so you can find your home base when alone. This proved less simple than said, however. Java is a beautiful emerald isle with a string of volcanoes running down its length. As we flew over them you could see the red, boiling pot of fire inside their cones. Then Kiser waggled his wings and we rejoined formation to return to base. Having had a midair collision previously, I received quite a scare. Kiser decided to dive down to a lower altitude from where we were flying at about five thousand feet. One of the easiest ways to lose altitude in a fighter is to simply roll over on your back, pull back on the stick until your nose is pointing straight down, and dive to the altitude you wish. That is what Kiser did, without signaling his intent. I jammed a hard right skid and missed hitting his tail surfaces by inches. It was one of those close shaves that fighter pilots dread, and its memory scares me to this day.

The Dutch were our hosts, and they put us up in some workers' quarters at a rubber plantation. Lieutenant Paul Gambonini, a dear friend and flying mate, records an amusing incident in his diary:

February 10. We are staying at an old rubber plantation near the field, it is staffed by several Javanese, who help with the cooking and housekeeping. We had chicken to eat tonight, the Javanese who was cooking our chicken was standing on top of the stove with his bare feet, walking back and forth while he was turning the chicken.

For me personally, Java was a sad affair. I had seen the movie *The Rape of China* just before Pearl Harbor. I had seen, read of, and heard of the details of Pearl Harbor. We heard the first-hand accounts of the murderous Japanese forces from our personal friends who had been exposed to them.

I was eager to employ my own skills against the brutal forces who conducted themselves like animals. But now we were up against pilots with all the advantages. Old hands using tried and true tactics with one of the outstanding weapons of WW II were our enemies. We were the green-horns; we were the unproved; we were the ones flying around in dogs that the secretary of war, Henry Stimson himself, had called "a pile of junk."

Yes, I was eager to fire into their ranks, to riddle their bodies and watch them spurt blood and clutch at their throats. I wanted to wrap it up with the best of them, but now I could not do so. For to do so would have been doing exactly what they desired. With their superior plane they could outmaneuver us every time. That way they could eliminate us in one battle, then have the skies to themselves, facing no opposition. By now, and later, even experienced British and An-zac pilots who flew against the Zeros were essentially vanquished. Trying to maneuver with them was their downfall.

For me this meant the worst. If engaged in combat with a Zero pilot, and he was gaining the advantage on me, I would have to run away. This was galling. But we were later to see what happens when logic is ignored. Brave Australian pilots, led by "Killer" Caldwell, a most able twenty-two–victory ace, overeager to avenge *their* "Pearl Harbor" at Darwin, equipped with the famed British Spitfires, suffered the loss of fourteen planes on one mission early in 1943, with only a small number of enemy kills.

On 17 February 1942, my first official combat mission came on a scramble when Lt. Jack Dale was leading four of us on an intercept. It had rained and the field was wet. As he taxied to the end of the field for takeoff, his wheel dug into the mud and he was stuck. He called to me to take over the flight. I felt like saying "Who, me?" I had never even led a flight in peacetime, much less in combat. I had never fired the guns of a P-40, I had never fired at an aerial target — talk about the blind leading the blind!

After takeoff I made a shallow turn to let my wingmen join up, and then contacted fighter control, who directed me to take a certain compass heading, which I did, but which, I will add, was a mistake. This left us flying up under the intruders. We should have flown away from the scene until reaching at least equal altitude, then returned to intercept. As it was, a string of five Zeros came diving down on our three P-40s. I turned into them and started to aim at the cowling of the lead plane, when he pulled up. I jerked the nose of the P-40 up with lots of lead, and he flew through my fire. Since four others were coming at me, I dove beneath them, giving them a poor shot.

Pushing over in a lead mode is difficult; as a result not a single one of them hit me. At this point I had to dive away, because I knew that those who had passed over me would soon come around to latch on to my tail. I pushed over in a maneuver that would be like the beginning of an outside loop, which is difficult to coordinate and difficult to use to bring accurate lead on your target. I then jinked and continued the dive to the ground, leveling off among the trees, and ascertained that I had lost my pursuers.

I have mentioned the term *leading*. Due to its importance in aerial warfare, perhaps I should explain it.

In the art of wing shooting, the judgment of distance and angle off is extremely important. These skills depend on eyesight. When a game bird is fired on, it is flying at a speed of, say, sixty miles per hour. That equals one mile per minute, or eighty-eight feet per second, or about eight and one-half feet per one-tenth of a second. If you fire at a bird at a ninety-degree angle off target, that is, if it is flying straight across in front of you, the bird travels eight and one-half feet between the time you shoot, from the average range of forty-four yards, and the time your pellet reaches the bird. This means that to have your bullet strike the bird, you must fire at a spot eight and one-half feet in front of the bird.

It is probably close to fact that one-tenth of a second is consumed between the time a hunter decides to fire and the time the pellet reaches the target. The brain must pass the signal to the hand. The signal travels from the brain down the spinal cord, branches at the arm, and travels down the arm to the finger. The nerve message tells the finger to pull the trigger. Muscles contract, and the trigger slides back, releasing the hammer. The hammer springs forward, traveling perhaps an inch, and strikes the firing pin. The firing pin travels forward perhaps one-quarter inch and pierces the cap. The cap ignites and burns forward into the powder chamber. The powder ignites, expands, and forces the bullet forward down the barrel of the gun. The bullet travels down the barrel, out the barrel, and through the air some forty yards to the correct spot in front of the bird if he expects a duck for dinner that night.

To shoot at blank space several feet forward of your target is not a natural thing to do. The natural thing to do is to shoot *at* the bird. You see it; it is there; it is flying right before your eyes; then you shoot *it*. You shoot at *it*, yet your effort will bag you nothing.

This is wing shooting, whether at birds or airplanes in the air; and it takes years of training for the human being to accept, on a regular and instant basis, the requirement to shoot at blank space. In case of an airplane, the problem is magnified, for the requirement is to shoot at a spot in space more like eighty feet forward of the target instead of eight feet. There are other variables that figure potentially into the art of wing shooting, such as varying angles and varying distances, but they would tend to confuse rather than clarify. Suffice it to say, the precious judgment of distance is an overwhelming element of importance.

Back on the ground I was to learn that my wingman had made it home, but our number three man had been shot down. At that time I resolved to use my own judgment in choosing the approach and attack instead of blindly following orders from fighter control, or whomever. Of course, I had no opportunity to observe what results I had obtained with my fire, though one Zero was reported shot down. My wingman quickly claimed it, and I did not wish to be arguing over claims. A major mistake was made when we were directed to approach an invader from beneath, and I was a fool to follow directions that placed us beneath the enemy.

On 19 February another raid came in on Soerabaja. We put up our best effort of eight planes. The British scrambled a number of Hurricanes, and the Dutch put up a good number of P-36s and Brewster Buffalos. Japanese records show their effort to be a sweep of twenty-three Zero fighters. From our ranks Lieutenants Blanton, Gilmore, and Fields were shot down. An account from the Japanese side was given by Saburo Sakai, author of *Samurai*, and a leading Japanese fighter ace with sixty-three victories.

Lieutenant Paul Gambonini's diary records on 19 February 1942:

There was an air raid about 11:00 A.M. Our pilots ran into about sixteen Zeros. Japs bombed Bandeun [Bandung], we lost three planes, Blanton and Gilmore bailed out and Fields was shot down.

Sakai tells of flying the mission at a sixteen-thousand-foot altitude, when they encountered a large force of Allied fighters at ten thousand feet. This, of course, gave the Japanese fighters a distinct advantage over our planes. On sighting the Allies, the Japanese pilots bored into their formation, creating a swirling dogfight.

A P-36 flew toward him, which he evaded with a swift left roll, but the P-36 foolishly maintained its course. Sakai "snapped around into a sharp right turn, standing the Zero on her wing, and came out directly on the tail of the startled P-36 pilot."

Insuring that he was safe from attack, Sakai maneuvered into position and fired his guns and cannon, causing the P-36's right wing to snap away, followed by the left wing. The pilot was killed with his plane.

Not content with one kill, Sakai turned his sleek fighter back toward the battle, where he saw six planes falling in flames. He tried to protect a Zero being menaced by a P-40, trying to draw off his enemy, but the other Japanese pilot had the situation under control, whipping his Zero . . . "in a tight loop which ended exactly above and behind the P-40. The guns and cannon hammered and the P-40 burst into flames."

Sakai said he saw another P-40 in flames with a streamer much longer than the plane and another P-36 as it "flipped crazily through the air, its pilot dead at the controls."[*]

Before the one-sided affair was finished, Sakai reports having seen a wingman shoot down two more Allied fighters, and he himself downed another. These enemy pilots claimed a total of forty Allied planes shot down that day. The impressive successes of the Japanese fighters rolled on.

The next day we lost our squadron commander, and five others were shot down. Paul Gambonini gives us a record of that action in his diary:

> 20 February. We went on a mission to Bali today. We escorted A-24s to attack a Jap landing party. We strafed the field there. My prop went out of commission and I had to land at Malady [Malang] on the way back to have it fixed. Major Sprague and Lt. Galliene were shot down at Bali, Lt. Stauter and Lt. Johnson crash landed on the coast of Java. Lt. Hayes crash landed on landing at our

---

[*] Saburo Sakai, et al., *Samurai* (New York: Time-Life Books), 1990, pp. 64–65.

field, quite shot up. Just after I left Malang they had a strafing raid by Zeros that destroyed about five B-17s. Hope we get some reinforcements soon.

Nothing worse can happen to a unit than to have it lose its commander, especially if he is well qualified, skillful, and well respected. The morale of the 17th Pursuit Squadron was not high when I joined it. It was bouncing on bottom after the Bali raid.

Whereas youth is normally optimistic about fate, forever feeling that if bad things happen, they will never happen to me, now there was a reversal. Unlike any combat circumstance I was ever exposed to, it switched. The attitude changed to: "I am a goner, the next one lost will be me, I know it will be me." Many times I heard "We're just flying tow targets. We are all on suicide missions!" Such conclusions were only logical. Anyone's arithmetic can figure out how many missions you are likely to last if ten go out and only five come back. Where an alert stack normally is boisterous with laughter and wise-cracks, silent anxiety was the mood in those days.

In the other theaters of war that I had the honor to serve in, I fortunately was never exposed to such losses. On two different occasions in Europe, I lost four tentmates and was left alone in a five-man tent until other replacements were brought in. On one mission over the Ploesti oil fields in 1944, my squadron lost nine out of twelve planes put up.

As an interesting physiological sidelight to the latter mission — after that dive-bomb/strafing mission over Ploesti, the hair on one of the young pilot's head turned snow white in two-by-four-inch splotches. However, nothing I experienced later in two other theaters of war would compare with the despondency we all felt here so far from home, isolated on a Pacific island, sinking in the conflict of war.

By now, the operational readiness of the 17th Provisional Pursuit Squadron was down to a very few planes.

On 21 February, Gambonini's diary records:

> I was sick today, had a high fever, Dengue fever the Doc thought. Lt. Hynes took my place. Planes went up on an alert at 9:30 A.M. Hoskyns and Hines were shot down. Hoskyns got a bomber and Morehead got a fighter.

Again I was not credited with the victory. One of the other flight members claimed the kill when the Dutch reported that it went down on Java. I did not see the results of my fire as I flashed by, although I had raked my guns through him at point-blank range.

In this instance our flight was on an intercept mission when we were cut off from our attack on a flight of eighteen bombers. After a skirmish in which we were outnumbered, it was mostly another frustrated interception where we had to dive away.

Our Allies were suffering even more than we. With their outdated planes like the British Wildebeest, Curtiss Hawks, Brewster Buffalos, Curtiss Falcons, and tired old Hurricanes, all were being slaughtered by the fast, maneuverable, high-altitude Zeros of the Japanese navy.

I drew officer-of-the-guard duty one day. On my rounds checking the guard around the field, I drove up to one post late that evening. Two half-caste Dutch soldiers were squatting beside a tiny fire, cooking some kind of meat wrapped around a split bamboo stick. They were dipping the little shish-kabobs in a small dish of sauce and eating them. One politely offered me one. I thanked him, took it, and ate it. When I finished, the soldier again asked me in broken English if I would care for another. I finished the second kabob, and before driving on to the next post I asked what kind of meat it was. He replied in his best form, "Chickenentrails." I was engaged in interpreting his reply, when I thought I encountered a little grit.

A day or two before Major Sprague was shot down, I was scheduled to go on a mission with him. I wanted to fly with him because he was a terrific pilot and I wanted to learn from him. After the mission we returned to the field in string formation. I was number two man in a flight of four, and when we came over the field the major did a slow roll at about a one hundred-foot altitude. I had never done a slow roll in a P-40, and I didn't realize that with the long nose on the beast, little rudder was necessary. Excessive use of rudder thrusts the nose and fuselage into the slipstream, throws the craft out of line, and it snaps. Snapping means that airflow over flight surfaces is interrupted, and a violent reaction takes place, with the craft out of control momentarily, until normal airflow is reestablished as the plane windcocks into the line of flight. I was later to learn that in order to slow-roll properly, one should use about one-third rudder and two-thirds stick.

I followed my leader into a slow roll, but used too much rudder and went out of control at 100 feet. Before the plane had windcocked back into normal flight, I had lost the 100 feet and was upside down just above the grass. The only thing I could do was push forward on the stick to make the plane climb. This put me in negative Gs with all the maps, pliers, pencils, dirt, and gravel cascading down around my head, making it hard to see. I knew I had to hold the climbing altitude until I had room to turn right side up, which I did. Then, because of the negative Gs, the engine quit. Luckily it started up before I struck the ground. It was one of my life's closest calls.

Little was funny those days, but I do remember one incident we got a laugh from. I enjoyed the flesh and juice of young coconuts, and they were plentiful in the big grove where we were hidden. I would shoot them off the tree with my .22 rifle that I kept close all the time. (I had plans to go guerrilla with it as my protector and food supplier, with the ammunition I had brought, if it came to that.) We carried our canteens on our belts and I would fill mine with coconut milk.

One of the pilots was a bit obnoxious, bumming cigarettes or candy, reading over your shoulder, or asking for a drink from your canteen. That day he asked for a drink from my canteen, and I winked at a couple of my companions there, standing alert.

He took the canteen, unscrewed the cap, and took a big swig, then immediately spat it out. "Ptaw! What the hell have you got in that canteen?" he cried. He was expecting water and got the milky fluid instead, and we got a laugh.

That day we were swatting flies and listening for the tom-toms. Those drums were our alert system telling us of the approach of the enemy and probably our death notices.[*] Every mile or two on the tropical island, natives with a small bole of some tree, hollowed and covered with rawhide, would send signals throughout the island. They would sound before an air raid and we would get ready. Then we would probably get an alert from Ground Control to scramble.

[*] In his book *They Fought With What They Had*, Walter D. Edmonds records: "The last two squadrons [that formed the 17th] — the 33rd and 13th — were both wiped out. When, therefore, the 17th was disbanded on March 1, just fifty days after it had been formed, not one of these units remained and a large proportion of the men were dead."

The Allies' air raid warning system was not effective as yet, which left us in danger of being caught on takeoff by fighters sneaking through the net.

The enemy was closing in on Java. Indonesia was the great oil prize of the Far East, and her war machine was slavering for its fruits. A regatta of aircraft carriers was prowling the seas off Java, and land-based bombers and fighters were already occupying the recently conquered air bases in Sumatra, Borneo, and the Celebes. Competition among the Zero pilots to find a worn-out, run-down, shot-up Allied fighter pilot was at a feverish pitch.

America has always placed great value on life. As stated earlier, Japan considered taking the life of subjugated populations as no more than killing a carp. In addition, the Japanese pilot had the advantage of considering it an honor and privilege to give his life for his god, the emperor.

I personally was well aware that I had been cheated of my childhood and late youth by misfortune. I very much wanted to live and experience the normal activities and pleasures of the average youth of my era. I did not want to die! My country had really not given me much so far. Members of the poorest nations on earth had not worked as hard as I had helping tend the farm in my youth. Nowhere on earth have I observed general laborers toiling like my family did; now it looked like my death was quite probable. At least I was experienced at bailing out. I figured

117

I could free fall and make it harder for the murderous bastards to hit me during the descent. It is interesting to note that the Germans never practiced shooting men in parachutes.

Lieutenant Caldwell, son of missionaries to China, who was born there, had done interpreting for the government before Pearl Harbor. He had a burning desire to prepare himself to fight against an attack by the Japanese, which he said he had predicted. He left a good-paying job to join the Air Corps to learn to fly.

I felt bad because I had flown with him, and observed that I didn't believe that he had good instinctive piloting skills. To add to our morale problem, this fine, brave man had ignored fighter defenses on one of our missions and had bored on in, and was shot down. He was rather seriously burned, but refused to go to the hospital and continued to fly. I remember that he showed me where he was burned on the inside calf of his right leg. It was solid blisters from the ankle to his knee, and weeping. I don't know what the other leg looked like.

That same day Caldwell went on another mission, and again bored in to face a hundred or so guns on a score of bombers, and this time they got him. I was told that he attacked from the rear, which gave him the best opportunity to make hits with his guns, as there is no lead requirement involved; but the same applies, unfortunately, for the opponent. So Morris Caldwell gave his life for freedom.

The pilots of the Battle of Britain are remembered. The pilots at the Battle of the Coral Sea, at Guadalcanal, at Midway are remembered. Praise be! In his book, *Luck to the Fighters*, the author, George Weller, advances his opinion on the subject of the service of the American pilots in the Java campaign:

He, this nameless American pilot, was the American boy whose two slim hands — he must have been hardly twenty, not yet grown — were thrust into the Dutch dike at Java and held long enough for the American and British High Commands to get away, held long enough for Soerabaja to be destroyed by the Dutch themselves with fire, ax, and explosive and thus denied to the Japanese navy, held long enough for Australia to get sufficient additional American aircraft to stop the Jap on the Java-Solomon line after the battle of the Coral Sea.

The boys at the Java dike were members of the Seventeenth Pursuit Squadron. We can name it now, because now it is only a name. It is gone forever, scattered and dispersed. Everyone knows the work of the Flying Tigers in Burma and China. None were more gallant than Patwing Ten in the Philippines, Java, and Australia. But few have ever heard of the Seventeenth Pursuit.

After serving in Java, we who served there

would ever wonder at America's awe at Japanese kamikazes. Some said, "Just what the heck do they think we have been doing?"

I was later to experience what our flight leaders were going through at the time and can now appreciate their gallant conduct. Few planes and little time had been available to them in their struggle in the Philippines, and their combat experience had been so limited and sporadic that there was little continuity of effort. Although they were expected to lead us younger pilots, it was the blind leading the blind. Major Charles "Bud" Sprague was an excellent pilot, and his demeanor and bearing gave his men confidence. But, on 20 February he was shot down and killed. We had lost eleven planes in the last week, and the squadron's morale hit bottom.

The fortunes of the 17th Provisional Pursuit Squadron were fading. We were all aware that we were being thrown into the path of the on-rushing military juggernaut of Japan to honor a commitment to our Allies, and I suppose it had to be done, although just a few weeks of training together would have helped make us a military unit instead of the conglomerate that we were. Like the title of Bill Bartsch's book about the struggle in the Philippines, *Doomed from the Start*, our meager effort was, indeed, doomed from the start.

We parked our P-40s under the coconut palms, which made them hard to find from the air. We used the old army field telephones for scrambles, those in the square leather containers, but most of our air raid alerts came via jungle tom-toms that you could hear coming for leagues in the still, tropical air. We would dash to our planes and wait for the confirming call on the phone. That way we got into the air quicker. Many of our scrambles were unsuccessful due to poor radar and flight control facilities, and we were often in proximity of the enemy but unable to make contact.

About this time Borneo and Sumatra were being invaded and we were scheduled for a mission to attack airfields around Balikpapan, Borneo. I asked to go, as I was eager to get into action and this mission promised just that, but I missed out because it was already scheduled. Sure enough, when the pilots returned, they reported engaging a good number of Japanese Army fighters and bagged several without loss.

At a symposium at McClellan Air Force Base in 1995, former members of the Flying Tigers, the American volunteer group of fighter pilots who flew for China at the beginning of World War II, were honored. The AVG was commanded by Gen. Claire Chennault, who worked with Chiang Kai-shek, of China, providing air support in their war with Japan.

David L. "Tex" Hill, one of the P-40 pilots, was the squadron commander. Since they had had greater success than we in the 17th Squadron had, I was eager to learn how they had managed to do so.

Tex explained that they were not up against the navy Mitsubishi Zero, which was thrust against Java and the Philippines, but lesser, army fighters, which gave the Tigers opportunity to develop successful tactics. Because of the importance of this information, General Chennault sent a résumé to headquarters. He assumed that this vital data would be passed on to all units in the field, but, Tex added, they never were.

This oversight cost the lives of many of our fliers, for we desperately needed this knowledge. The fighters in the Philippines had few victorious experiences, and were essentially decimated, both on the ground and in the air. All the British, Dutch, and Australian contacts in India, Burma, Malaya, and Sumatra had been, in terms of one British author, a "bloody shambles."

Greenhorn pilots like myself, who didn't even know their own plane yet, were just groping. That night, with rain coming down on the sheet-iron roof of the Dutch-provided quarters, tucked beneath a mosquito net, what sleep I got was fitful. I realized that my death was an imminent probability, and as more and more of the pilots were exposed to the Zero, and more went down, the morale dropped lower and lower.

I had ridiculed my wing mates for their pessimism and had garnered resentment. But by now I was having to be a realist. With losses of 50 percent and 75 percent per mission, how many can you expect to fly?

My thoughts ran to: How will I die? Will it be

quick? Will I plow into the ground? Will both arms be shattered by bullets with the plane on fire? Will I bail out and then be machine-gunned in my chute or on the ground? Will I blow up? When there are just one or two of us left in the middle of all of them, will we be able to help one another at all? Is my morale going too?

One day a Dutch pilot landed on our field in a Brewster Buffalo. The Buffalo was a short, fat, radial-engine fighter that couldn't outmaneuver, outclimb, or outrun the Zero, and was slow to dive. We really felt sorry for those men, as there was no escape. At least we had one chance if we had enough altitude for a long dive, but all strafing missions and missions of interdiction were at low altitude with no opportunity to dive. His visit did our morale no good. Their missions were pure suicide, and ours were very nearly so.

It required true grit to take to the air and present your life on the chopping block of an unequal war. America should be proud to have had men who faced those circumstances and offered their lives in order to slow the onrush of Japanese military power, to buy a little time to prepare, and to bolster the last great Southwest Pacific outpost, Australia.

Back at Blimbing the enemy was growing impatient at the stubborn resistance of the Allied air forces. Even the old biplane Wildebeests, along with the Hudsons, Brewster Buffalos, Hurricanes, and P-40s, were posing a threat to the planned invasion of Java.

On one of our last missions from Blimbing, thirty-six twin-engine bombers with fighter escort were bombing our B-17 base at Malang. Four of us were scrambled to intercept. Lieutenant Kiser was leading. I had a dog of an old P-40 that could not keep up. Kiser was eager to gain as much altitude as possible, because the P-40 couldn't hold a candle to the climb of a Zero. He should have circled to give me a chance to catch up with the flight, but I didn't blame him too much. Soon I could see the bomber formation and a gaggle of Zeros with them. Kiser bravely led the three P-40s into enemy territory. Immediately the Zeros descended upon them. The P-40s met them head-on, then dived away as the Zeros followed on their tails.

Fortunately the Zeros had not seen me and I was able to approach the bombers at their own level. From my previous observation of bombers of many models, and the results of my friends' and late friends' attacks on bomber formations from the rear, I had formed in my mind the best approach for an attack on them. Most defensive gun turrets on bomber aircraft face the rear. In a thirty-plane formation, a fighter can face as many as 120 machine guns firing on him at one time. I decided to fly forward of the formation and turn and fly in on a forty-five-degree angle for a frontal attack. After completing my turn, I fired a burst at the lead bomber. My bullets fell behind the entire formation and I felt like a fool. But I learned two things; I learned that I was obviously way out of range, and my lead was in great error.

I pulled the nose forward and fired another burst. Somewhat better, as this time the tracers caught the rear of the group. I pulled farther forward, and this time tracers seemed to enter my target, the lead bomber, and I was very close. I had to dive beneath him to miss hitting him. For the next pass I decided to fly out front and turn to make a head-on pass. Flying out in front of the bombers for position, I suddenly saw a Zero bearing down on me from ahead. I decided I would pretend to dive away, then turn back into the bombers and try to get one before the Zero got me. A lot was riding on the efforts of our meager air forces at this time, and I wanted to make a showing.

My country had spent thousands of dollars on my selection and training; it had likewise spent thousands on procuring and maintaining the finicky, expensive fighter plane. It had shipped us both thousands of miles overseas to do this job before me. My feeling was: If this Zero's job is to shoot me, then he is just going to have to shoot, for I am not missing this opportunity to do my job. I did a split S, which put the Zero on my tail; then I hauled back hard on the stick, coming up under the bombers in a loop, winding up beneath the lead bomber. I opened up at close range, coming so close to him that I scared myself, but there was little time for that. I had still another problem. I didn't know how many Zeros were around, so I dove straight down, skidding and yawing and jinking all the way to the ground, hoping they couldn't hit me, but they did — with one bullet in the tail surfaces.

Near the ground my canopy fogged over so I couldn't tell if I still had pursuers. I rolled back the canopy, turned back and forth to clear my tail, and looked around.

I found that I was right over a large airfield. Since this old dog of a plane had used up most of the gas, I decided to land and try to get some fuel. I cleared the sky, did a steep turn, put down my wheels, and landed. Strangely there were no planes in sight, not even a human being. I taxied off the runway and down to a big hangar, trying to find somebody.

About thirty yards from the hangar two American soldiers rose up out of foxholes and stood there. I then realized this base was a target. I shut down the engine, and when the prop stopped turning, one of the men yelled and asked if they could help me. I said I needed gas and ammunition. They looked all about the skies and then cautiously approached and directed me to start up and taxi to a nearby gas pit. I asked them what outfit they were with and they said the 19th Bomb Group, that this was Malang and was their headquarters.

I asked if they had seen any of the skirmish overhead. They said they had seen three fighters tangle with a bunch of Japanese escort fighters, and that some of them had dived down. Then a lone fighter had attacked the leader of one formation on one pass, had made another pass on the leader of a following group, and was then attacked by Zeros and dove away. The first bomber attacked spun into the earth, and that the second bomber had gone down in smoke. The enemy had dropped their bombs before reaching the target. This was joy to me, of course, as I had seen absolutely nothing in the way of results and I had no wing mates to confirm my victories.

Now at least I had confirmation on one of them. Then one of the men went to the hangar and brought out a belt of ammunition. He asked my name, and we talked of the worsening situation.

They filled my tanks and rearmed my guns, and I thanked them kindly. I was touched when they in turn thanked me. And I must confess I had pangs of conscience that I was unable to stay up there in the sky and fight it out with the beasts who had thrust them and me into this war. It graveled me much that I had to run from those bastards when they got on my tail, but that is what they wanted most. The fact that we ran away and returned to fight other days instead of being blown out of the sky by the superior Zero was an irritation and a deterrence to them.

An interesting incident developed years later from the contact with these 19th Bomb Group men. Many of the ground personnel did not escape from Java and the Philippines. My brother

Walt flew for TWA for many years. Toward the end of the war, TWA flew former prisoners of war home from the Far East. They were litter cases, and he used to go back and talk with the men about their experiences. On one such occasion, one of the men stopped him in the aisle and asked him if he had a brother in the war, if the brother was ever in the SWF, and if he had been in Java. He said he noticed on Walt's airline uniform the name Morehead, which prompted the question. Then the patient told the story I told. He had been one of the 19th Bomb Group men who had been in the foxhole and later obviously was taken prisoner.

Before being taken prisoner, these men must have told this same story to their squadron mates — and mentioned that the pilot was only in his skivvies. I learned of this over fifty years later, when one of my flying school classmates, a pilot with the 19th Group in Java, told the story while attending a 41-C flying school class reunion. I don't remember what I was wearing; it may have been shorts, but I don't think it was only underwear, although on some scrambles we may have not been fully clothed.

When I landed back at Blimbing, they had crossed me off. I told them firmly to give me back my personal belongings. This was jest, for it was common practice that we divvied up the belongings of our downed mates post haste. Someone said, "Now we have to put up with you again!" Thanks, fellows! The truth was they were damned glad to have me back to share the scrambles with them.

My flight leader, George Kiser, assembled the flight and asked which of us had attacked the bombers. I described my actions and he said that the Dutch had word that an enemy bomber had gone down on Java, and that the Javanese had killed the crew. Since no one else had attacked the bombers, I was given credit for the one the airmen of the 19th Bomb Group had reported spinning in, and also the one they said had gone down smoking, which was concluded to be the one that had crash-landed on Java. For attacking the large formation alone, I was awarded the DFC.

My return to the field has been described by author George Weller in his book *Luck to the Fighters*: "They remembered the day when Morehead came burning in over the field, did a victory roll straight down the middle of the runway, and then did another. They remembered how he landed — how he threw back his canopy before his wheels stopped rolling, stood up with two fingers in the air and shook them grinning, and how he yelled, "Hell, you guys are crazy! Those Japs can't shoot . . ." He had run into nine bombers over Malang and shot down two.

On 27 February, for a special duty, three of us pilots were given train tickets and driven to a nearby town, where we caught a little, narrow-gauge passenger train. It was pulled by a small steam locomotive about seven feet high. It chugged along about twenty or thirty miles per hour. This was an experience in itself. I spoke no Dutch or Javanese, and the other passengers spoke no English. We in the train were packed like sardines, and I had no seat. The girls felt pretty soft. I guess today they would call my trip "hanging out," as I hung out the side most of the time.

Incidentally, the Balinese and Javanese girls were knockouts. They had long hair, dark eyes, soft brown skin, and fabulous figures. In Bali they wore no blouses — they were exceedingly distracting. In Mauldin's war cartoon, I suppose Willie would have said to Joe, "Why couldn't we have been assigned to Java when there weren't no war goin' on?" I got hungry on the train, and at a stop I took some bananas and mangosteens from a peddler and shoved a guilder in his hand. The guilder probably would have bought a bushel of fruit.

Finally the little puffer arrived at the port of Tjilatjap, a port city on the south Java coast. We had been instructed to contact the port authority there and lead thirty-two P-40s back to Blimbing. They were to arrive aboard the old aircraft carrier *Langley*. We got off the train and walked down to the port area, where I spotted a Caucasian. I walked over to him and greeted him. He was a reporter for a Chicago newspaper.[*] He asked my

---

[*] The reporter was probably George Weller, a correspondent for the *Chicago News*, who later wrote the book *Luck to the Fighters*.

purpose for being there, and when I explained, he informed me that the *Langley* had just been reported sunk. What a blow! Many of my friends were on the ship and no information was available on survivors. We caught the little puffer back to Blimbing with a sad report.

Later I heard from Col. Jerry Dix, a friend and pilot aboard the *Langley*, about the terrible time they suffered through.

Jerry happened to drop by my station of assignment at St. Paul, Minnesota, in 1948. He spent the night with us in our home there, and the dear boy, as one of the two survivors of the thirty-three pilots aboard the *Langley*, told the terrible story of their ordeal. Later he recorded it in his memoirs.

It seems that around 9:00 A.M. on 27 February 1942, not far out of the port of Jogjakarta, a Japanese reconnaissance aircraft flew overhead. A couple of hours later they were attacked by a flight of six high-level bombers from about thirty thousand feet. The bombers dropped their bomb load, but fortunately the captain made a sharp turn and their bombs missed.

A short time later they were attacked by a formation of nine high-level bombers. On their first run they did not bomb, but made a wide turn and made a second run at a lower altitude of around fifteen thousand feet.

It appears the enemy bombardier guessed the captain's next maneuver, for five bombs hit the ship. There was much damage, and fires broke out among the aircraft on deck. Some of the men and aircraft were blown overboard, and many were left injured on board. Jerry himself suffered a serious wound: A fragment broke his left jaw and another sliced through his left arm. As the bombers turned away, a number of Zero fighters dove down and strafed the remains until they had expended their ammunition.

Then the big ship began to list to port and began sinking by the bow. It lost power, the engine room was flooded, and it began settling in the water. The captain gave the order to abandon ship and all the people, including the wounded, were taken off the ship and put on two escorting destroyers, the USS *Whipple* and the USS *Edsall*. One of the destroyers then fired their heavy guns into the *Langley* to make sure it sank, but this proved to be ineffective, and they departed.

The destroyers that picked up the survivors of the *Langley* made their way to Christmas Island some two hundred miles south of Java. There they transferred the injured personnel to the USS *Pecos*, a tanker, and the uninjured were placed on the destroyer *Edsall*. The *Pecos* was to return to Australia and the *Edsall* received orders to escort a convoy to India. Both of these ships were sunk by Japanese dive-bombers and the survivors were again strafed by the escorting fighters. The remaining victims, including Lieutenants Dix and Ackerman, clung to timbers and debris throughout the night, and around 0900 the following morning the oil-soaked, famished few were rescued by the destroyer *Whipple*. The destroyer *Edsall* sank with all aboard.

The USS *Whipple* made it to Australia with her cargo of war victims, but thirty-one of the *Langley*'s thirty-three P-40 pilots were not present. Two survived.

With Major Sprague gone, and loss percentages climbing, the morale of the unit was descending further. Captain "Shady" Lane was now squadron commander, and his nickname quickly changed to "Shaky." As leader, his morale was lowest, and he was heard to say that he would "rather step in front of a truck than face those Zeros."

When I was off duty I would take my little rifle and shoot the doves that frequented the coconut palms near our alert shack. We would then clean them and roast them over an outside fire and they were delicious. Also, in Java, there was a beautiful wild pigeon that was good eating. Once in a while a .22 bullet would ricochet off a coconut or something, and "Shaky" would jump out of his skin when he heard it. He promptly put a stop to my shooting.

There was no mail, of course. I had not heard from home for over two months. I had written often, but we weren't sure the letters ever got into the hands of the mail service.

The weather in Java was different from weather in temperate climes. It was soft and warm. There was little wind; no cover was necessary at night.

In fact, it appeared the natives had no bedclothes at all, and slept on wooden mats on stakes or on the floor. It rained almost every afternoon, usually in the form of thundershowers, and there appeared to be little air-mass-type weather. Most were fleeting clouds and sunshine. Unlike in many theaters, weather was not a big problem for us at that time of the year. One of our biggest problems was finding that doggone field.

In our desperate circumstances in Java, we failed to develop any real fighter tactics. The Mitsubishi Zero fighter was so light — the Japanese even took their radios out of the plane to lighten it — maneuverable, and climbed so high and fast that to remain engaged with it for any time at all meant that it was soon around on your tail and shooting at you. So we made as many passes as our altitude advantage — which we almost never had — permitted, and then departed as rapidly as possible. We had not learned to designate the element's wingman as protector of the element leader while he did the shooting; there were never enough planes to develop a weave of flights or box-defense formations. We were just up there helping one another as much as we could, meeting Zeros head-on, or attacking as much as possible, then diving away. Good advice might have helped occasionally, but usually there was no opportunity to employ it. Later, in Australia and New Guinea, where more than three or four planes were available at a time, tips from seasoned pilots like the Flying Tigers would have helped immensely.

By the beginning of March, we heard the enemy was invading Java with a giant sea armada in three different places. We were alerted to expect multiple missions. Paul Gambonini's diary records from 6 February 1942 to 1 March 1942:

Took off on an alert at 8:00 A.M., didn't see any Japs, took off again at 11:00, didn't run into any enemy planes, took off a third time at 2:30 P.M., saw six Jap bombers and about twelve fighters, they were above us and dove down on us. One of the Dutch pilots was shot down but bailed out.

The following morning we were scheduled to strafe enemy ships and landing craft. I was not on the mission. I asked Lane to go, but he said the roster was already made up. I was eager to rip into bunches of them with six .50-caliber machine guns. Damn! They had a ripping good mission all right, but three of the nine were shot down. Lieutenant Atkins bailed out and landed in sight of the enemy, but grabbed a bicycle from a native and outdistanced them. He made it back to Blimbing before we closed shop and burned all our planes and records. All the other six P-40s were shot up. Lieutenant Fuchs's controls were shot out, but he got her down on the ground safely.

I have repeatedly stressed the losses we suffered and the dismal outlook for our pilots, but I don't think anyone will call us crybabies. James Parton, in his book *Air Force Spoken Here*,[*] discusses the relative casualties of our different armed forces. Parton says: "This [issue] when boiled down to the final essence, merely means that a Ground Commander who gets the same percentage of casualties that we in the Air Force take as a matter of course, might be criticized and might be called a butcher."

I have heard many pilots claim they never lost a wingman. God bless them. It is a most admirable accomplishment, but I can say their experiences are limited. In some encounters over Java, they could have lost their entire flight.

By the end of the Java campaign, my own spirits were so low that I wasn't sure I would have a career as a fighter pilot. The B-17s and B-24s were suffering far fewer casualties than we fighters were, and they seemed to be shooting down more Zeros than we fighters were. I had never yearned to be a bomber pilot, but the thought was becoming more appealing as the superiority of both the enemy fighter pilot and his machine was becoming more obvious at each engagement.

The condition may have been apparent to others as well. Author George Weller states in his book *Luck to the Fighters*:

The planes had brakes that were worn out:

[*] James Parton, *Air Force Spoken Here*, Adler and Adler, 1986, p.376

the tachometers were gone or broken. "Wild-man" Morehead, wild no longer, was the thrifty armament officer who kept reminding the armorers as he walked in the sun from revetment to revetment: "Save every loose round. We might not get any more. The ammo isn't coming through from Australia. Keep looking around the grass and pick up any lost rounds you can see. Never let a round get corroded. We need every round. We might never get any more."

His opinion, also expressed in the book, would have been a morale booster for me at that time, for he wrote:

As the Seventeenth was disbanded and scattered, their fortunes became different. Andy Reynolds and Jim Morehead became two of the finest fighter pilots in Darwin, where the pickings were poor because the Zeros didn't like to fight after the long, fuel-exhausting run from Koepang. R. S. "Big" Johnson crashed in Moresby and "Toughey" Hague was lost in August on a raid in north-ern Papua.

With the Dutch, the British, the Anzac, and the American fighter planes decimated, air supe-riority by the enemy was assured. Java would soon be added to the list of whirlwind conquests by the storming Japanese forces. And no modern army or navy can propose to stand up against an enemy that possesses air supremacy.

At this time — 1 March 1942 — Captain Lane instructed me and five other pilots to take one of the staff cars and drive to the B-17 base at Tjilatjap. It seemed there was a chance we might be able to escape Java on a B-17. The Battle of the Java Sea had been a disaster with near-total destruction of the Allied naval force there. So escape by boat appeared to be unlikely. I remember the dirt and gravel road was steep and winding, and we cut across a range of hills to save time. Tension grew as fear increased that we might not make it in time. Our fears were well justified.

As we approached the base we saw it was being hit by a bomb raid. At the edge of the field we found Captain Lane was there with other pilots and some of our enlisted men. About that time a Zero flew by at about forty feet from us, some thirty feet high. Some of the enlisted men started firing at him, and "Shaky," typical Lane, yelled, "Stop that firing, he might come back here and strafe all of us!" His timidity embarrassed me to the core.

As we drove on toward the parking ramp, the only planes we could see were on fire. With Japanese planes in the air above the field, our hopes of finding a sound one were sinking. We raced around the corner of the operations hangar in desperation. Fortunately at that time we did not know that the Japanese forces treated captives like vermin, often simply killing enemy troops as they entered. Had we known, our terror would have burgeoned. Later accounts of the conduct of those advancing troops in Java were enough to curdle the blood.

As we swung to the front of the hangar, one lone B-17 stood with its engines running. We dashed to the port side of the plane and rushed to the aft entrance. The plane was piloted by the commanding officer of the 19th Bomb Group, Col. Eugene Eubank. We were told to climb aboard. Again I was disappointed in leadership. The big plane was not overloaded and could have carried several more men. The remaining pilots of the 17th Pursuit Squadron escaped the island on a B-24 bomber.

As we were about to taxi out, someone knocked at the rear access door. I opened it and found Lt. Les Johnsen there, asking if it would take any more. I reached down and grabbed his hand and pulled him aboard. No one told him to leave, so we took one more. At that moment the plane began to roll. After we got in the air we could see Zeros strafing the field below. They set a B-24 on fire and I grieved that the Japanese would take thirty more American prisoners of war.

We set course away from the bloody skies of Java, and thus ended my participation in its sad struggle.

All who participated in action in the islands and waters of Indonesia were awarded the Philippine Defense Ribbon.

V

Lick Your Wounds
and Try Again

Our four-engine angel of mercy pierced the night skies to span the fourteen hundred miles of ocean to deliver its militarily precious cargo of surviving combat airmen to the shores of Australia. Colonel Eubank set the big ship down on the red clay soil of northwestern Australia. A quick refueling stop saw us back in the air again, heading south, with the next stop Perth, a port city on the southwest coast of Australia.

A few minutes after our takeoff, en route to Perth, further devastating news came. Broome had been attacked by Japanese fighters, with heavy loss of life, plus twenty-nine aircraft. Sadly, twenty-four American airmen were killed, many of whom were the very men Captain Lane had chastised for shooting at the Zero, our own P-40 mechanics.

Volume Two of *Air War Chronology, 1939–1945, 1942: The Decisive Year, Part I, January–June*, by Myron J. Smith gives a brief account of the event:[*]

2488) In combat over Pameungpeuk, Java,

---

[*] Manhattan, Kan.: Kansas State University, p. 63.

140

4 RNAF Buffalos of 3.VI.G.V. and an RAF Hurricane of No. 232 Squadron are downed by 9 JNAF Zeros of the Kaohsiung Fighter Wing.

2489) The 5 AAFSWPA B-17's and 3 LB-30's, which evacuated Allied air personnel from Jogiakarta the previous afternoon and evening, arrive at Broome, Australia.

2490) Shortly after the US bombers land at Broome, 11 JNAF Zeros of the Tainan Fighter Wing attack that airfield, now being evacuated by women and children; in a 15 minute sweep, the Rising Sun fighters destroy 2 LB-30's, 2 B-17's, 6 RNAF B-10's, an RAF Blenheim and a Hudson of No. 225 Group, on the ground, 16 Catalina, Dornier, and Empire flying boats at anchor off shore, and 1 LB-30 attempting to take off. Some 45 Dutch civilians and 24 US airmen are killed in the raid.

Returning to base from this mission, the victorious Zeros meet and down a RNAF C-47 evacuating Java with a valuable shipment of diamonds.

Of course, this represented a close shave for Eubank's plane and its cargo of pilots. To the Japanese this plane would have been a richer prize to have bagged than the plane they had downed carrying its treasure of gold and diamonds.

From Perth we headed east across the Great

Victoria Desert for the city of Adelaide, with a stop at Woomera, a lonely windswept dirt strip where no trees were visible as far as one could see in any direction.

After a partial refueling with primitive facilities and a few barrels of gas to help finish the two-thousand-mile journey, we were back in the air to complete the task of delivering to safety a large share of the only existing combat-experienced fighter pilots America possessed.

At Adelaide five of us were ordered to drive a staff car some seven hundred miles to Canberra, where we were to join a new unit fresh from the States, the 49th Fighter Group.

The automobile trip crossed inland from the southern coast to the national capital. It was an interesting tour.

I remember how many rabbits there were, and later learned what a real problem they were in Australia. The rolling hills and countryside were beautiful; so were the girls with their dry Aussie accents. At one stop along the way we entered a shop to buy some snacks. A pretty girl attended us. We bought candy and gum and lingered to ogle her. When I went to pay, I asked the price. She said, "Tuppence 'aypunny." I asked again, and she said, "Tuppence 'aypunny." I was embarrassed to ask again, so I put down a five-pound note. I learned later she had said "Two pence and one-half pence." My problem was like that of the Aussie nurse and the wounded American soldier who was brought into the field hospital. The soldier came to and looked up at the nurse and said, "Oh, nurse, did they bring me here to die?" and the Australian nurse said, "Aye, no Yaink, they brought ye here yesterdaiye!"

After 700 miles of travel and education in a foreign land, and wonderful peace, we arrived at the capital city of Canberra. What a paradise! A modern city with beautiful modern homes, shops, paved streets, automobiles, trains, buses, and beautiful girls, and beautiful girls, and beautiful girls! With the ratio of ten girls to one man, lost time was about to be made up on the double.

We five officers reported into the Canberra air base, and to headquarters, 49th Fighter Group. We reported to a Maj. Paul "Squeeze" Wurtsmith, commanding officer. Major Wurtsmith was a kind, friendly man of around forty years of age. He explained that the 49th had been a bomb group, but, due to wartime expediency, was renamed a fighter group. Oh, me! From the frying pan into the fire! Instead of what was needed, a unit of fighter pilots with experience flying fighter planes, with men who had flown together a few hundred hours in tactical fighter formations and training in ground and aerial gunnery and dive-bombing, we are assigned to a bomb group! Now the pressure is on again; the blind are again leading the blind.

Most of the pilots were youngsters just out of flying school. Most had no time in a P-40 and had had no tactical training of any sort.

The 49th was activated 16 January 1941 with

a cadre of pilots from the 31st Fighter Group that had been in existence for only one year. The experienced pilots became its command and staff. Flight positions awaited graduating flying cadets. The ground echelon was filled mainly from drafted civilians.

Organization progressed slowly at their first base at Selfridge Field, Michigan. It then moved to West Palm Beach, Florida, where better flying weather could be found. Their first assigned aircraft were P-35s.

The group received its overseas commander in November. On Christmas Day 1941 the group was told it would be departing for overseas in two weeks.

On 2 January 1942 the group departed Morrison Field, Florida, by troop train. Arriving in San Francisco, they were quartered in the Cow Palace, awaiting sea transport. On 11 January 1942 they boarded the USAT *Mariposa*, a Matson liner–converted troopship. The shipment included nineteen P-40s.

By the time they arrived in Australia, the Japanese were on the offensive. Britain's, France's, Holland's , and America's holdings in the Pacific were being invaded, and within weeks they were fighting delaying actions against hopeless odds. Of the 102 pilots arriving in Australia in February 1942, eighty-nine of them had no flying time in fighter aircraft.

That this unit became the leading American fighter group in aerial victories in WW II is noteworthy, for at the time they were little more than civilians in military clothing.

In an incident during the Battle of the Coral Sea, Admiral Leary explains the deficiencies of the crews of the Army Air Corps planes as:[*]

> Their pilots are civilians who had three months training at an airport, and are then sent out here to be entrusted with important missions, which they are in no sense qualified, but it is all they have.

At this point one might question the sanity of military commanders — and junior officers forever do — but to themselves. Yet in reality what would *you* do? The rampaging forces of an aggressor nation were charging down on the very land you stood upon. Those savage forces were fresh from total victory on land, at sea, and in the air — especially in the air, for that air superiority was what had produced total victory on land and sea.

Quoting *Bloody Shambles* by Shores, Cull, and Izawa:[**]

> What had been surprising perhaps, was the speed and completeness of the collapse [of the Allied forces] . . . What else arose [re-

[*] Coulthard Clark, *Action Stations, Coral Sea*, p. 136.
[**] Christopher Shores and Brian Cull with Yashuho Izawa, Bloody Shambles, Volume Two London: Grub Street, 1992, p. 442.

sulted from the devastating victories of the Japanese in the Pacific] was the pervading awe of the A6M Zero fighter, which was perceived as the epitome of the Japanese victory in Allied eyes, in much the way that the Spitfire had been seen as the victor of the Battle of Britain. Note, however, that it was the aircraft — the machine — which stuck in the Allied psyche rather than the remarkable skill of its pilots, which was in fact every bit as important. The superior performance of the aircraft was credited with all its dashing successes.

So, here you are, in the path of hundreds of land-based planes, and six aircraft carriers flushed with total victory down from the Java Sea, all charged with the chore of clearing the skies and securing air superiority for the final minor task of cleaning up the Pacific once and for all. (They probably would have remained in the possession of the Japanese for as long as one could foresee, had she won the war.)

Imagine, then, that you are the general in charge of the defense of the theater. Would you send those raw green kids, just able to keep their planes aloft, off into battle with an enemy superior in every respect, and feel guilty the rest of your life? Or would you leave the coastline unprotected and hold the kids back until they had received time and training sufficient to equalize the playing field to some degree?

The latter course could mean immediate invasion, as you would have given the enemy clear skies, and probably an open road for its army to a continent depleted of its military strength. The decision is obvious, you send them in, training or no training, and hope, somehow, they can pull it off.

Bad as the P-40 (the "pile of junk"* the secretary of war had described) and the P-39 were, through God's deliverance they were planes a greenhorn could survive in if he was extremely alert and made the proper moves in time. To do so and become an effective striking force at the same time was another matter. The fighter units' very presence was of value, though, for it meant the beaches, the troopships, the landing barges, the thousands of troops on foot and in the water, were exposed to six heavy machine guns on each of forty to fifty fighter planes of a group like the 49th. If they could exist and pose such a threat, they would be of inestimable value irrespective of their air-to-air abilities. This being the case, you, as commanding general, could sleep a little better, for some of those planes with the .50-caliber armor-piercing and incendiary bullets would get through to the beaches. Japan had lost several ships already after strafing by Allied fighters. My old squadron commander, Sam Marret, died while strafing a Japanese ship that exploded. This was part of the landing force

---

* The assistant secretary of war for air, Robert Lovett, had no

on Luzon two days after Pearl Harbor.

So the flying school graduates were to receive two weeks' training in P-40s and then rush north to try to discourage the Japanese conqueror. My job was to try to keep these young folks from getting killed and still pose as a force to threaten a Japanese invasion. I had learned from the men who had braved the first baptism in the Philippines never to try to outmaneuver the Zero. Never hang on in the area alone if you had no target, as the visibility from the P-40 cockpit was too poor, and the enemy could slip up on you. Constantly clear your tail of your executioner, as that is what he will be if he gets there without your knowing it. Keep an eye toward the sun, as that is the favored quadrant of the attackers. These were some of the things I taught my flight while going through rigorous flying exercises and maneuvers, simulated dogfighting, close and string formation, and so on.

We were given ammunition and worked over offshore rock promontories for ground gunnery, and bird flocks for aerial targets. I once downed two birds from a flock of pelicans in echelon (angled-line formation) on one pass with the six fifties. I found that the lead on a pelican at max range was about ten feet; on a Zero, about one hundred feet. We had no tow rig for aerial targets,

---

more respect for the P-40 either. In the book *Air Force Spoken Here*, in remarks referring to General Eaker, he stated: "We talked about the P-40 for a long time. How the hell he ever got that plane to fly I don't know. Worst pile of junk."

so the lads just had to learn the hard way, that is using the enemy for targets. That often got them killed too.

In the social arena there were patriotic families in Canberra that extended their hospitality to American soldiers with parties, teas, and frequent dinner invitations. One young lady of about thirty who I met in a cocktail lounge invited me to her apartment for dinner. In the government office town of Canberra, the lounges were crammed with girls. This particular girl was slender and attractive. She had jet-black hair, long, sweeping lashes, dark eyes, and a faint tint to her skin that suggested one distant ancestor may have come from India. She was also a little mysterious.

Ericka served curried chicken for dinner, and it was delightful. During the dinner I learned that she was married and that her husband was overseas. My moral code did not permit me to date married women, so I thanked her for the evening meal, shook her hand, and returned to base.

While the 8th Squadron of the 49th was training at Canberra, the other two squadrons were doing the same thing in southern Australia. The 7th Squadron was stationed at Bankstown near Sydney. It was commanded by Capt. Robert Morrissey, another native of Oklahoma.

Because of the Japanese threat to an important RAAF air base on Horn Island at the tip of Cape York peninsula, the northernmost point of Australia, on 12 March Captain Morrissey was ordered to take a detachment of P-40s there for its defense. While there, Morrissey was alerted by the RAAF that a large formation of enemy bombers was en route to attack the base. He scrambled his unit and intercepted them though they were accompanied by a number of Zeros.

Morrissey attacked the Zeros, shooting one down, but was himself attacked by them, one of which was riding him mercilessly. His wingman, 2d Lt. A. T. House, came to his aid, but, as was common in the early days of the war, he found none of his guns working. He continued his attack on the pursuing Zero in great frustration until he was within inches of the other plane. Finding himself on top of the other ship, he dipped his wing into the Zero's cockpit and fuselage, ripping it apart. The collision raked off three feet of the outer wing of his own plane, sending it into uncontrolled cartwheels. House thought he had been blinded when his oxygen mask was jerked up over his eyes by the force of the collision, but he soon realized the cause. He was able to straighten up his ship and with great caution landed it safely back at the airfield.

Soon the time of peace was cut short, and on 8 March 1942 we were ordered to the front. My little brood had made good progress, and I felt they were accomplished enough in the P-40 to avoid killing themselves at least. One of the kind ladies with a home near the airfield gave us a party, and we danced and laughed the night away, and finally filtered home about 0200.

The next morning we were up early, and Kingsley, Dennis, Davis, and I were scheduled to fly four P-40s north to Darwin. The first leg of the flight was to Brisbane, with a refueling stop at familiar Amberly Field. The next leg of the two-thousand-mile flight was from Brisbane to Charleville.

About halfway between the two stops, flying at about five thousand feet in cool air, the sun shone down, pleasantly warming the cockpit. As the engine droned on with a steady beat, the short night began to tell. My eyelids were growing heavy, and the next thing I knew I was dreaming. An odd yawing feeling interrupted my dream, and I was jolted wide awake as my plane was headed straight down toward the ground. As I yanked back on the stick to bring the ship out of its dive, I saw three other P-40s go sailing by me. They had stayed in formation as I eased over into the dive, and they followed closely until I jerked back on the stick and we came screaming out of the dive. When we landed at Charleville they all asked, "What the hell are you trying to do, get us all killed?" I sheepishly explained I had fallen asleep.

From Charleville we pressed on westward into the true "out back" of Australia. Mile after mile of eucalyptus scrub, short grass, and red soil of the Northern Territory met the eye. Now the opal capital of the world, Alice Springs was then a dusty village. The small hotels had verandas for cooling off, warm beer, and only a few hundred residents. On our departure, much time was consumed by waiting for the boiling red dust to settle. Each takeoff stirred up the dust and each pilot had to wait until he could see the runway through the swirls of it. I circled the field until the last of my lads were airborne and then set course for Daly Waters.

It is surprising how small the maps were that I used for navigating in a fighter plane. Navigators on bombers and transport planes apparently used large maps of small scale and could distinguish each road, railroad, stream, and power line, whereas most fighter pilots then used small large-scale maps like Australia superimposed on an eight-and-a-half-by-eleven inch sheet of paper. We did not have time to follow a map closely, but looked for large landmarks like seas, big rivers, big cities, and so on. Occasionally the bomber boys would call and ask if we had a handle on the target, or destination, and we usually could tell them. The old adage "too close to the forest to see the trees" prevailed, I suppose.

Daly Waters was a watering hole for large ranches. It had no dwellings that I remember. So while we were being refueled, Dennis and I walked out into the woodland to hunt. We didn't know what to expect, but soon we flushed several wallabies and I bagged one on the run, or the "hop," I should say. Their long, leaping bounds made them difficult targets.

By now it was the dry season in Australia and the heat was oppressive, perhaps 115 degrees in the shade during the day, and the world's most persistent flies were in full hatch. They would land on your face and start a march for the corner of your eye. Accustomed as one is to the ordinary fly, we would wave our hands close to our faces expecting the pest to flee, but no, the cheeky little bugger simply continued his march toward the eye. At this point the eye is becoming nervous and implores the rest of the body to do something about the steady march of this damned, infernal critter that is bent on plunging into the corner of your eye. It's your eye, you know! I'm you, part of you, we're together. Now, stop this damn beast!

So you draw back, and wham! You slam your cheek a hefty blow, and here one of two things occurs. The fly has just departed of his own volition, or you slam the bugger, and roll him viciously all the way down your cheek with the pressure that should squash a case-hardened BB. He rolls off your jaw, falls halfway to the ground, then unfurls his wings, catches himself, buzzes back alongside your ear while adding a few extra rpms just for spite, lands on the other cheek, and begins his advance on the other eyeball. They are probably the world's most annoying insects.

Dennis and I returned to the dirt field and soon our flight was airborne, heading for a temporary field at an outback station called Adelaide River some sixty miles south of Darwin. A camp site had been set up for the 8th Squadron. The 7th and 9th Squadrons were to arrive by 19 March. A flight strip was being prepared for each squadron beside the highway running south from Darwin to Alice Springs. This location of the strips right on the road facilitated supply of the units to be stationed there.

At Adelaide River we began standing alert for scrambles against the increasing bombing raids on Darwin and the port of Darwin. For the first month or so our scrambles were ineffective, as the air raid warning system was a bummer, and the communications we received from them were too late, or too early, or vectors were off the mark, and I was extremely cautious of leading our inept unit into combat with any disadvantage.

But in late April, two weeks after the fall of Bataan, the capture of Java, the fall of Sumatra, the capture of Rangoon, the Japanese invasion of New Guinea, and the capture of the southern end of the Burma Road to China, Allied morale was at its lowest point of the war. The British had lost one hundred and fifty thousand men in Malaya and suffered the worst defeat in her entire history. She had lost the pride of her battle fleet, the thirty-five-thousand-ton *Prince of Wales*, which had played a leading role in the sinking of the German battleship *Bismarck*, and the super battlecruiser *Repulse* was lost off Malaya to Japanese air attack with the loss of only three enemy planes.

America's loss in the Philippines was her greatest land defeat with the loss of one hundred forty thousand troops, plus her entire air force there. As further humiliation, the Death March had just ended and the siege of Corregidor begun. The Germans were preparing their summer offensive in the Crimea; two hundred thousand Russians were facing encirclement at Kharkov, the line before Moscow was facing a precarious stalemate; and Rommel was preparing an offensive on the Gazala line in the North African desert.

The U.S. Navy had lost ten capital ships and had not sunk a Japanese naval ship larger than a destroyer. Its air arm had shot down only thirty-four Japanese planes. True, most of the ships were sunk by the sneak attack at Pearl Harbor; sneak or not, the backbone of the battle fleet was lying on the bottom of Pearl Harbor. In short, the Allies could find no victories to shore up their morale, and the most critical battles of the war were only days away.

Japanese air raids on Darwin were increasing daily, and, of course, the greenhorn group was doing little to stop them. With the war going badly for the Allies around the globe, it was going equally badly for the 8th Squadron, 49th Fighter Group.

At Darwin another fine pilot and respected officer, Capt. Allison Strauss, was in command of the 8th Fighter Squadron. On a scramble one day, a large group of enemy bombers and fighters raided Darwin and the port. Captain Strauss led the squadron in an attack on the bomber formation. On his wing was Lt. Earl Kingsley. Strauss was cut off on his approach by a Zero about the time Strauss started firing. This is a critical time for a fighter pilot, that is, at the moment he is coordinating all elements of flight: gun sight, stick, and rudder, and judging the important aspects of distance, angle off, and lead. He did not observe the enemy's approach, and before Kingsley could bring fire on the Zero, it had raked Strauss's plane and set him on fire. He failed to get out.

Strauss was an "oldie." That is, he was commissioned in 1940 and had many hours in the P-40. His loss was another feather in the cap for the reputation of the vaunted Zero, but was another minus for the morale of the 49th Fighter Group as well as the morale of all the Allied forces, air, land, and sea, opposing the Japanese. The continuing domination of the skies, and suppression of Allied opposition, simply increased the "pervading awe of the A6M Zero fighter, which was perceived as the epitome of the Japanese victory in Allied eyes," as Shores, Cull, and Izawa stated in their book *Bloody Shambles*. As with the other air units that had opposed the Zero, the 49th Fighter Group was off to a bad start.

But we had learned a few things in the Philippines and Java, and by applying those lessons, the 49th was reducing the death rate and beginning to strike back.

VI

Execution Date Has Arrived

You execute or be executed!

The morning of 25 April 1942 dawned bright and clear. Since the Japanese had been stepping up their attacks, the pilots on alert duty at the 8th Squadron alert shack were apprehensive. Two flights were standing by with their pilots in full flight gear, engines preflighted, and cockpits at the ready. Captain Sims, who had taken Captain Strauss's place as commander, was holding duty with one flight of four; I with wingmen 2d Lt. Richard Dennis, 2d Lt. Edward Miller, and 2d Lt. William Herbert, had the other scramble flight of four. Around noon the telephone rang. Captain Sims took the call. Scramble!

We were finally airborne and climbing hard. Takeoff had been a sweat. Sims was slow in revving the engine and checking his magnetos. This requires a few moments to flip the magneto switches while the engine is at high rpms. The ground surface temperature was probably 120 degrees there in Darwin and the metal throttle handle was so hot it would blister your hand if you tried to hold it. We adjusted throttle by tapping it forward or backward, that is, touching it for only a split second. We always left the canopies open on the ground and in the air, climbing to a cooler altitude before trying to grasp the crank to close the canopy. The in-line engine was liquid-cooled, and on hot days, if the takeoff were delayed, it would overheat, and if it got too hot on takeoff, it could freeze up, leaving you to crash into trees, rocks, or whatever else was in front of you.

Sims headed the eight P-40s on a vector of zero degrees as ground control took over direction of the flight. As we crossed the coast, we were pretty bunched, as he had not given the signal to spread out. Tight formations make the defense of spotting the enemy difficult, so I eased my flight away to the east a few hundred yards. We were learning that planes flying abreast can better protect one another from attack.

At this time of the war, the warning our radar could give was still little better than a fly striking a spider's web. Something had pierced the perimeter but you didn't know just where.

Some thirty to forty miles at sea we were coming up on the northern tip of Bathurst Island, approaching the service ceiling of the P-40 — the altitude at which the craft will no longer climb at a rate of one hundred feet per minute. None of the new pilots had sighted the enemy. Several missions were required before the novice pilot attained the knack of spotting aircraft at great distances.

To the east I discovered a large formation of enemy planes in close formation. Bomber formations look much like flocks of wild geese. There were also tiny specks weaving above the bombers, which represented the usual protective formation of Zero fighters.

At first I said nothing while I struggled with my over-speeding heart. I wanted to sound calm and confident and in control when I spoke into the mike to warn Captain Sims of their presence.

It was normal for the Japanese to provide an ample escort of Zeros for their land-based bombers. If it were a flight of nine bombers, fifteen or so Zeros were provided as escort. If it were eighteen bombers, twenty-five or thirty fighters were sent. This raid consisted of thirty-one bombers. I don't know how many Zeros were present, as my target was the big boys.

We were on a converging course when I called Sims and said, "Bogies three o'clock, Captain." Sims came back, "Roger."

My own flight started bobbing up and down, trying to fly formation and get a glimpse of their first enemy aircraft. The bogies were on my right, to the east, as we bore out to sea away from the Australian mainland.

The enemy formation appeared to be letting down (losing altitude). They must not have seen us yet, for they continued letting down as we drew nearer.

Captain Sims had never been in combat before, and since my flight was nearer them than his, I called him and asked if he wanted to make the attack or should I go ahead. I was greatly relieved when he gave me the job.

The point at which an attack is begun is extremely important because the firepower of a bomber formation is concentrated at its sides and rear. As a result, I always tried to initiate a frontal attack and avoid being sucked back into the deadly cone of fire to the sides and rear, where, with a formation of thirty-one Betty bombers, one hundred and eighty machine guns could bear upon an attacker. With Sims's inexperience, that is what probably would have happened, for the IP — initial point — of a frontal attack takes delicate positioning.

I immediately started a shallow dive to place us out front of the big ships, a kind I had never seen before. They looked huge. We later learned they were their new Bettys, the heaviest bombers the Japanese built during the war. I was holding my breath, for as yet no Zeros were entering our airspace and it looked like we were, for once, going to catch the Japanese at our working altitude.

Our luck was holding and still no escort fighters seemed to be alerted. They had swung to the starboard side of their charges and away from our approach. I could see that their sweep to starboard would carry them too far out for them to ever make it back for an intercept of our attack from the port.

A week or two before, a formation of Zeros had flown over the Fifth Air Force base at Port Moresby and put on an aerial display of the aerobatic abilities of the Zero. I had resented their arrogance and with the thought of raising

Tough times at the old farmhouse, Oklahoma, 1928. I am on the extreme right. My mother is to my left resting on the porch.

I have just graduated from pilot training, a proud and brand new second lieutenant, U.S. Army Air Corps, 1941. In the Seeger rose garden, San Francisco.

Eighth Squadron pilots, RAAF Base, Canberra, February 1942. Top row: Eisenberg, Galatka, Morehead, Kingsley. Bottom row: Dennis, Martin, Davis. (Jack Ilfrey)

Captain Kiser, 8th Squadron, Darwin, 1942. A truly brave man. (Jack Ilfrey)

Seventh Squadron in formation at awards ceremony, New Guinea, 23 March 1943. P-40 number 24 is "Nick Nichols Nip Nippers." (Ernie McDowell)

My P-40 after crash landing at Adelaide River. Blown tires and forty-two bullet and cannon holes after engaging enemy bombers and fighters, 25 April 1942. Note wing tip is blown off.

As a new first lieutenant, I'm shown standing beside my P-40 at RAAF Bachelor Field, Australia, June 1942. This was the nose art chosen by my crew chief. (Australian War Memorial)

Two fighter pilots congratulate themselves (probably on each other's survival). I am on the right with Capt. W. J. Hennon. This great American was later lost in action. (Australian War Memorial)

Morehead, Kiser, Reynolds, unknown, and Hennen, posing for photograph. (Australian War Memorial)

Squadron P-40s preparing for takeoff, Bachelor Field, 1942. Here dexterity is crucial. (Australian War Memorial)

Alford, Barnett, Martin, Keator; seated: Harris and Kiser. Kiser and Keator were experienced pilots, the others with maybe 100 fighter hours time between them. (Australian War Memorial)

Eighth Fighter Squadron over Darwin, 1942, form big US in the sky, salute the Spitfire pilots. No longer greenhorns, this is good flying. (Australian War Memorial)

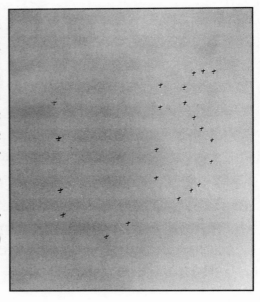

General Brett awarding me the DSC, Darwin, 1942. The general was later sacked by General MacArthur and replaced by General George Kenny.

I meet Generalissimo Chiang Kai Chek, Taiwan, 1952. The new jets were his proud baby. (Official CAF photo)

A pleasant chat with Madame Chiang Kai Chek, Taiwan, 1952. Elegant lady of great grace. (Official CAF photo)

With General "Tiger" Wong, Major Royce Preist, and Colonel Wu, Taiwan, 1952. (Official CAF photo)

the confidence of my troops, I did a slow roll in front of the enemy formation. With my experience of two previous attacks on enemy bombers, I had good clues as to the proper lead requirements for a big bomber. I continued out of my slow roll into a right turn, then leveled out with my nose far out front of the line of big ships.

By this time of the war we had replaced the old iron post and peep ring on the engine cowling with lighted crosshairs superimposed on an angled glass panel mounted directly in front of the pilot's eyes. This was an improvement that permitted sighting with both eyes and avoided the closing of one eye to aim. The point was appreciated, as a combat pilot really needs four eyes instead of just one.

I lined up on a spot about one-third the length of a football field in front of and a few degrees above the line of flight of the lead bomber and pulled the trigger. My lead could not have been more on target if I had done it a dozen times. The stream of bullets from the six guns in my wings poured directly into the leading element of bombers. I had a feeling of elation — we had gotten in on the raiders before the Zeros had gotten to us.

Every fifth bullet in our guns had a tracer that marked its flight. Every other fifth bullet was an API, armor-piercing incendiary, that exploded when its nose struck something. Two other of the five bullets were lead-core, and one was solid-armor-piercing. To my ultimate joy, the lead bomber began smoking as I held the trigger down, ripping into the packed formation.

The technical manual for the .50-caliber machine gun instructs a gunner to fire in short bursts in order to maintain accuracy, but accuracy was not important as I closed in and held the trigger down continuously. The priority at this time was to get off as many rounds as possible, for I was now close and the bombers looked as big as barns. Accuracy was insignificant.

I swept over the formation with good speed and a good feeling on the controls. The enemy pilots had foolishly lowered into the operating range of the P-40 for the first time in my experience. A hard, steep turn at about sixteen thousand feet back to the left in the direction of the bombers blacked me out. I grunted as hard as I could to restore my sight, and when it returned, a dramatic scene unfolded before my eyes. I was just in time to see Lieutenant Miller, my element leader and third man in my flight of four, saw a wing off a Betty bomber, which flipped over into the one next to it. The two enemy bombers stuck together momentarily with propellers and engines flying, but I could observe no longer, as there were two healthy bombers directly in front of me less than seventy yards away, all guns firing.

I had planned to cut back into their midst before the Zeros were upon us and my turn was just right. Being faster than they, I was fast overtaking them. The bombers looked shiny new and I knew I had not seen this airplane in the skies over Java. The turrets in the tail of the planes were firing, and I realized they were 20mm guns because they were firing so slowly, one could have counted the rounds, or rather the puffs of smoke that came from each round. My tracers were going to the right of the gunner, whom I could see plainly. I kicked the left rudder, sawing my tracers across the turret, and the gunner stopped firing.

I realized that the Zeros must be stacking up behind me on my tail, but it was now or never to be able to rip those bombers. I pulled farther to the left, raking the left engine, which started burning, but my speed was overtaking the big ship and I dove beneath it as I sped past.

Now I was approaching the lead ship of this element, and his tail gunner was firing those slow shots at me. With my throttle back and directly in the prop wash of both bombers, I was slowing rapidly. I glided right up to the gunner, and, precisely as before, I yawed the tracers across the turret and he stopped firing. I figured I was a target of the nose gunner of the ship I had just passed, and of a bunch of Zeros too, but I could see no tracers going by, so I kept shooting while switching to the right engine.

About that time a sluice of oil came from the right engine of this last bomber, covering my windshield. I then stalled out, as I had forgotten to add throttle. The P-40 dropped a hundred feet or so in the stall as two burning bombers heeled over above me. I turned away from them as a Zero dove on me. I pretended I did not see him; then, as he closed in, I dove beneath him, making him turn almost straight down. I think that was a fruitless maneuver because it let him get closer to me than he would have if I had dived as soon as I saw him. I jerked up and down, yawed and jinked wildly running for my life, until I figured I had lost him, then pulled up steeply.

I was eager to get back to the bombers, where, no doubt, the fellows were going at them, when another Zero appeared from below. He was climbing toward me, so I turned on him, carefully leveled the crosshairs on his cowling, and fired. From what I learned here, I would have gotten this guy on the next mission, but inexperience denied me the victory. I fired from too far away. The tracers converged, then went on each side of him and also dropped beneath him. I guess he figured he could bag a P-40 without risking a head-on pass, and he jerked up and went above me. I was astonished at this maneuver, for I felt he would stall out in such a steep climb, but he did not. He hung on his propeller as I passed beneath, then cartwheeled down as I pulled up. A little jockeying was taking place, and I soon found I was on the losing end of the bargain, so I pushed over and dove out of the one-sided affair. When I pulled out of the dive, the oil had spread solidly over my canopy and I feared I might overlook some attacker, so I turned for home. Of the 600 rounds of ammunition serving each of the six guns, I doubt if I had more than a handful remaining anyway.

My thrills were not over for the day though. Unknown to me, though much expected, I had many bullet and cannon holes in my plane. Both tires were shot out. I did no victory rolls over the field and I carefully made gentle turns in my approach. As the wheels struck the ground, the tail went up. I jerked back on the stick, but the tail climbed higher. I pulled the stick back to my stomach, but the nose went down and the tail went higher. Then the propeller struck the ground, the engine dug in, and the plane went straight up on its nose and hung there for one hour and twenty minutes — I'm kidding, but it certainly seemed that long. It then fell back down on its wheels, which collapsed, dropping the plane on its belly with a whoof of dust in the middle of the runway. I dashed out of the thing, fearing what might happen next. We found the old bird was riddled with bullets. They used the rest of it for parts.

After the encounter with the very nearly vertically climbing Zero, I realized the danger it represented, that it could approach from beneath you in the blindest spot on the aircraft and shoot you down with your never having seen it. Saburo Sakai tells of doing so repeatedly in one of his books. Thenceforth, it was a dreaded concern on any scramble. I mention this because, along with the other threats, scrambles where no contacts were made were all terror-filled experiences in those early days. The possibility of being caught by surprise at low altitude, from out of the sun, and from below made every mission stressful.

A most gratifying result emerged from this engagement. In Java we were plagued with malfunctioning machine guns. Desperate efforts to correct the unbearable situation finally produced the solution. Delicately fine moving parts demanded an immaculately clean environment. We found we had to remove every gun daily and wash it thoroughly in gasoline to assure its proper functioning. We in the armament shop were immensely relieved. The fact is, I never had a gun misfire throughout the Darwin campaign.

A driver in a jeep picked me up and drove me to headquarters. The squadron doctor was there. He must have had a recent course in combat medicine, for he took me by the hand and led me over to a reclining chair. He told me to calm down and think of some idyllic pastoral scene and forget the day. It may be that I had psychological problems all right; I told him I thought his prescription was a bunch of horseshit, and I got up and went on into the debriefing. I think the doctor didn't like me for some time after that.

It seems we shot down eight bombers and three fighters. Captain Sims was shot down, but landed his disabled P-40 on a grass patch on Melville Island and was unharmed. The enemy ships were Mitsubishi Zeros, and Bettys, the bomber I hadn't seen before. This seems to have been the first smashing victory over the Japanese air forces and the Zero, and over the Japanese armed forces. It demonstrated that the awe was not so awesome — that they could be defeated even by a bunch of gringo greenhorns.

For my action I received the Distinguished Service Cross, the second such medal awarded.[*]

Later intelligence personnel of the 5th Air Force were sent to Darwin to interview me about my close-up observation of the new Japanese "heavy" bomber, the Betty. Our forces were later to see thousands. I was surprised at the amount of detail I was able to give from my subliminal consciousness. The bomber's rounded tail, two side-blisters with small machine guns, a big 20mm tail turret, a top turret, and cigar shape came mostly from my subconscious. My questioners appeared to be skilled in bringing out these impressions that I hadn't realized I had actually experienced.

After the debriefing I was so proud of my trainees I could almost burst. If there had ever been a time in the history of our nation when good performance of raw recruits was required, it was now, and they had come through with glory for which the nation should forever be proud.

Just when the enemy had soundly defeated every arm of every nation that had opposed them; just when they chose to add a technological gem to their proud air force, the Betty; just when the

[*] To the reader not familiar with the rankings of military awards, the DSC is the second most prestigous decoration awarded by the United States Army, immediately following the Medal of

awe of that arm of their military forces was at peak levels throughout the world; just when the morale of all the arms of all the Allied nations was at rock bottom; and two weeks before the Battle of the Coral Sea and six weeks before the Battle of Midway, the absolutely critical battles of the war, where the war would actually turn on their outcome, eight American recruits thrilled the world with a smashing victory. Numerous newspapermen came to interview us, as this was something new on the battlefront. Headlines in Los Angeles, Chicago, and New York carried the story of this victory over the Japanese. H. V. Kaltenborn and other prominent newscasters carried the first cheering news the Allies had seen in months.

For the beleaguered, disorganized Allied nations who had, month after month, suffered the hammer blows of the powerfully armed, skilled, and experienced tripartite aggressors, it was a sustaining breath.

But one successful skirmish in a far-off corner of the globe could not turn the war around. Millions of dedicated servicemen on many battlefronts were to do that. If any action could be said to have furthered the process we began, it would have to be the gallant action of the pilots

---

Honor. The next award for aviators is the Distinguished Flying Cross, the DFC. In all, 555 DFCs were won by pilots in the 1st Fighter Group in WWII. In all the grinding and hazardous work done by these men from North Africa to Sicily to Anzio to Germany to Udive to Ploesti, only three DSCs were awarded.

of the U.S. Navy matching fire with a superior enemy far at sea, in the battles of the Coral Sea and Midway. It was the morale, the courage, and the effectiveness of those men that did it. But one little spark can light a large fire. I don't have to ask what a little spark of encouragement means to a beleaguered force of weary men. I know what it can do, for I was there.

For the most important arm of the most important nation of the Allied warring nations, that spark of encouragement cleared the fog of fear and apprehension and lit a ray of hope and courage. Our little group of P-40 pilots was building scores, and others wanted to do the same. They were actually becoming eager, and I had to warn them that the skilled, superior enemy was still out there. We still had to be extremely cautious.

I can also say that the fighter pilots of all other American air units who heard or read of the Americans shooting down "Japs like clay pigeons" stirred in their flying boots and gained hope and faith that they, too, might become successful pilots and perhaps even aces.

In World War II air supremacy was vital to modern warfare. Hitler abandoned "Sea Lion," the invasion of England, because he did not attain it. The Allies would never have undertaken the invasion of Europe without it. Air supremacy is not won with bombers. It is won with fighters, leading one to say that the fighter arm is the most important arm of modern warfare. For the Zero to continue to make a second-rate force of the

American air forces would have been sinister. It may not have denied us eventual victory, but the delay would have been costly. On 25 April 1942 that delay was shortened, as we probably bagged two of their fighter aces.

It should be explained that a soldier, as a fighter pilot, faces different circumstances from a soldier fighting as one of a squad, company, or battalion of men on a front line. Most of the time, after vigorous action, he finds himself alone and on his own resources. He can decide he wants to avoid the danger and seek safety, or he can assume his obligation to be a good soldier and seek the enemy.

In the interest of brevity, I have not dwelt on the numberless scrambles and missions that resulted in little contact with the enemy. After the Japanese learned of the inability of the P-40 to reach altitudes comparable to the capabilities of their Zeros and later bombers, they flew at high altitudes. As a result, sightings were often made when we never reached their altitude. We had some escort missions with A-24s, but the B-17s and B-24s always wanted to operate at their higher ceilings. There they were much faster than we. So intercepting and ground and sea attack were our greatest failing and we were deficient at the former.

At the reunion of the 49th Fighter Group, Ralph Wandrey, wingman of Richard Bong, America's leading ace, related that the P-38s were always able to climb higher and attack from above against the Zeros. It was what I had dreamed of so often, but was never to do.

After being at Darwin a few weeks our mail got through to us. After the long months since sailing, a little pack of mail could be uplifting to the spirits. Aldine Seeger, the beautiful blond, blue-eyed German-American girl I had dated in San Francisco, had written a number of letters. She told of blackouts along the coast, and of the intensity of the war effort by everyone. She sent a small record that I was able to play on a phonograph belonging to Special Services Section, and on it she told me she loved me. I let Dennis listen to it with me. He said he wished he had a girl who loved him. It made Aldine seem special. On one letter she imprinted her lips in lipstick and said it was a kiss for me. She said she would wait for me. I started thinking more about her.

In the mail Dennis got a model airplane set of an Me-109. He set about constructing it while we were on alert. He was pretty good at it and soon had a sleek little Messerschmitt hanging in the alert shack. While on alert I often busied myself catching the various birds that lived in the nearby woods. We would throw out crumbs from our lunches that we brought from the mess tent. I built a box trap and trailed a string back to the shack, or to the hammock I had made of a GI blanket. Various parrots, finches, magpies, and the like were my "victims," though we always released them.

One day I caught a magpie, and as I was

fondling it, I looked up at the Messerschmitt and an idea hit me. The other fellows helped me rig a string from the nose hub of the 109 to a tight loop around the tail feathers of the magpie. We then turned the bird loose and there went the bird with a Messerschmitt on his tail. The weight of the Messerschmitt pulling down on the tail of the bird put its flight in a high-climb altitude that took him through the tops of the trees just outside the alert shack. There it shucked the 109, the tow string, and a few black and white feathers still attached to the string. The string and feathers lodged in the branches and the Me-109 hung down a few feet, swinging in the breeze.

When Dennis returned to duty he immediately inquired about his model, and of course no one knew the slightest thing about it. He fussed about its disappearance for a time, but the issue finally lay at rest. Then one day he was lying in my hammock, looking skyward, when suddenly he saw the model plane swinging at the end of the string on a branch about eighty feet above the ground. "How in the hell did my Messerschmitt get on that limb up there?" he exclaimed. There were conjectures like "A hawk must have got him and found he wasn't good to eat!" or "Maybe it decided to take off on its own," but Dennis was suspicious for months until someone finally told him the true story when he figured it was safe to do so.

Most of the fellows considered the assignment at Darwin to be a hellhole. But despite the lack of a social life, it was an interesting assignment for me. Ah! Wilderness was everywhere. There was wildlife galore, and hunting and fishing opportunities were great, and there was no dearth of mouths hungry for fresh meat the game would supply. One had to be careful in the woods, however. There were many snakes, and almost all species found there are poisonous.

An odd thing happened to one of our pilots on a practice mission at Darwin one day. Captain Robert Vaught had just taken off, when he discovered a snake coiled on the cockpit floor, ready to strike. The next moment the snake struck, embedding his fangs in Vaught's leg. Too late, he grabbed the snake by the neck, rolled back the canopy, and hurled it over the side.

Most of Australia's snakes are deadly poisonous, and within moments the young officer began feeling faint and realized he must land soon before the debilitating effects could overcome him. He began looking for an emergency landing spot and quickly spotted a ranch house surrounded by a cleared area. He was able to set the plane down without damage but found the house to be abandoned. By now the venom was taking serious effect. His leg was swelling badly and the pain was excruciating. The stricken man lay in his cockpit all day and all night in agony. The next morning his flying buddies set out to look for him and finally located his downed aircraft.

Vaught was without water and he felt that it was mandatory to get to medical assistance. He managed a wobbly takeoff and headed straight for his home field, where he made a crash landing but suffered no injuries. He was hospitalized but recovered and returned to his squadron. His experience added one more entry to the preflight checklist for pilots flying in the Northern Territory: Check for snakes!

After our move from Adelaide River, we went to a strip bulldozed alongside the highway south of Darwin, later named Strauss Field, after our heroic comrade. Taxiways were built that led from the end of the runway into the woods to revetments covered with camouflage netting. As I gained confidence in flying the long-nosed P-40s, I began applying some new skills. When landing, the planes would immediately start kicking up dust with the propeller. This was not so bad on the runway that had a sprinkling of oil, but on the taxi strip and in the revetments, it was thick as pea soup for several minutes until the whirl of the propellers died down. Dust settled on the mechanics, the tools, spare parts, oil and hydraulic fluid containers, the airplane, and its canopy.

Because of the dust I tried something new on landing. I began cutting my switches as soon as my wheels touched down and coasting the length of the runway, by which time the prop would be stilled. With the momentum of the roll, I would kick rudder, turn off onto the taxi strip, coast to my revetment, kick brake into the revetment, stomp brake in the revetment, and spin around and into position facing out of the revetment for exiting. *No* dust was created at all on the runway. An airplane going sixty miles per hour down the runway with its propeller standing still did look unusual, however. Drivers on the road alongside the runway would be bug-eyed. Then to have the aircraft go off the runway, down the taxi strip, and into its small revetment positioned perfectly was certainly eye-catching. My crew chief was so proud that he had a clean airplane, clean tools, and clean parts that he almost became arrogant.

My crew and I won out on another event. As we all flew from a strip, two flights were stationed at each end of the runway. At first it was policy for the ranking pilot to take off first, but my flight repeatedly was out at the end of the runway minutes before the ranking flight leaders at the other end were ready. I complained to Captain Sims that we were just sitting ducks for strafers or bombers, out there waiting for the others to get ready. He then made the rule that whoever was first on the runway could take off. If it were a tie, or close, rank would proceed. After that I don't remember it ever being close. We always took off first. One reason was that I authorized my crew chief to turn my switches on and start inertia before I got there. I then leapt in, continued the start, he buckled my safety belt, then I gave it throttle and was taxiing in only seconds.

I did not take time to strap on the parachute, as a chute is no good lower than three hundred or four hundred feet anyway. In fact, it could be in your way if you crashed on takeoff. So all cockpit checks were made while taxiing and on the takeoff run. I tried to have both mags checked before my wheels lifted off. In the air I would start getting into the parachute after cleaning up the cockpit, and there was always plenty of time up to four hundred feet. I think the ranking flight leaders were too proud to ask what I was doing to always be ahead of them. My number two, three, and four men didn't have to hurry, as the second man had to wait for the dust to settle some before he was able to take off anyway.

Our radar equipment was outdated and functioned poorly. The British had invented the system and we had borrowed it from them. We hurried to catch up in its development and production, but our first sets were untried and flawed resulting in missed interceptions. Surprising to some, perhaps, much of a fighter pilot's work was downright boring because of this.

The sky is a large place, and intercepting another airplane somewhere out there, anywhere from twenty feet to twenty-five thousand feet in an expanse of thousands of square miles that may be cloud-filled, hazy, or obstructed by blinding sun was largely a hit-and-miss proposition. A friend of mine flew his entire tour without seeing an enemy airplane. Colonel Francis Harris flew two tours in North Africa and in Italy and failed to get a good shot at the enemy.

At Darwin, as in Java, on most missions we found no enemy, but he, us. There were occasions when I was leading that I spotted their formations, but did not engage because of disadvantages in altitude, position, or fuel limitations. The last thing I wanted to do was to lead green pilots into a battle that was a loser from the start. I was a strong supporter of the philosophy of playing hard to get, but strike hard when you get a good chance. Once, far at sea, I found myself alone after diving away from a pursuer. I discovered the main enemy formation on the outbound leg of their raid. They were already farther to sea than I, and were twenty thousand feet above me. A long chase would have been necessary and I wasn't sure I hadn't caught a bullet already.

The unknown bullet was always a concern in combat. My dear friend Tom Maloney met the end of his combat career and very nearly the end of his life when, after strafing a locomotive that had blown up beneath him, he developed an oil leak. Like the old story of the horseshoe nail that was lost from the horseshoe that was lost from the hoof that was lost from the leg that was lost from the horse that was lost from the charge in the battle that was lost in the war that was lost, a tiny flaw can cause great loss.

The incident where I had flown so close to the Zero fighter that I had fired upon, and my own exploding shell had struck my own ship, is a good example of what the tiniest bit of damage can grow into.

If the one-quarter-inch-square piece of metal

from the jacket of my own exploding .50-caliber bullet had vibrated free from where it was embedded in the oil cooler, the leak would have brought the plane down at sea, on land, or wherever I happened to be. Just when this might have occurred no one could know, so a pilot had to remain alert after an engagement, for he might be brought down by delayed-action damage like my now-disabled friend Tom Maloney.

On our days off, a friend or two and I would take my little .22 pump rifle and my old hollow steel fishing rod and go out to the tidal flats fifteen or twenty miles to the east of our camp in a jeep and hunt the delicious ducks and geese, or the wild pigs and feral buffalo we found in abundance there. I had scouted the area from the air, noting roads, trails, streams, marshes, and meadows, and had seen big herds of buffalo, thousands of wild ducks and geese and wild pigs. Our larder of canned beef, mutton, Spam, and beef hash became tiresome, and our bag of young buffalo, wild pig, geese and ducks, and fish became a welcome change of menu.

Tides are great in northern Australia, and they come far inland. We used to fish the tidal guts for catfish, which were great eating. Once I put a heavy line in the river, got a bite, and a shark came to the surface with the bait in his mouth. It appeared he was looking for whatever was pulling on the line. He was about ten feet long. After this I quit fishing the river and fished only the smaller tidal guts.

With the .22 rifle I would bag geese, ducks, bustards, a delicious turkeylike bird, young pigs, and cranes. With a Garand from the guard section we would shoot the buffalo and big boars. On one occasion we wounded a buffalo and thought he was down. When we approached, he leapt up and charged us. Two or three fast shots put him down again to stay. We jumped a wild boar out of a brushy clump in the middle of a meadow. We tried to cut him off from another thicket, and he rushed the jeep and put a slash mark on the bumper. We sure jerked our feet up into the jeep when he came charging.

In the wet season, marshes covered the flats. In the dry season they dried into smooth meadows where we occasionally came upon a wild dingo. We would give chase and, with the windshield lowered and battened on the jeep, it was a wild ride with .45 pistols blazing and rifles banging away. By ridding the game herds of dingoes, we felt that we were compensating nature for what we were taking for ourselves.

Our success became so well-known that Major Wurtsmith called from headquarters and asked me to take him hunting. He brought skeet guns and training ammunition, and we had a ball shooting the wild geese and ducks that were so numerous. The geese had odd habits. The first one I ever saw was sitting on a limb about forty feet up in a eucalyptus tree. He wound up in an evening meal as a victim of the little .22.

There were hazards in the wilderness, especially leeches, the world's fastest swimming creatures. Step into a clear pool, and zap, a leech would shoot across the pool and onto your leg like a bullet. Snakes also were abundant. Once while crossing a meadow, one, about fourteen feet long, was gliding along. I jumped down from the jeep to look at him and maybe prod him, when he turned toward me and kept coming. I soon slowed, then stopped, then turned back toward the jeep. The snake kept coming as we sped away. I still don't know what he had in mind.

One day little Les Johnsen, my old friend from the Java escape, came over from his unit, the 9th Fighter Squadron, a few miles up the road. We decided to drive back to his unit. The road in between had been recently reworked, and a furrow of loose gravel was pushed to the center of the road. Les weighed about 145 pounds. He was driving an army command car, a heavy, stiff-geared personnel carrier. We passed another vehicle, and up ahead a big truck was approaching. Les pulled back to the right lane in front of the truck, but the left front wheel tracked down the furrow of heavy gravel, directly into the path of the big truck. I saw him struggling with the heavy wheel, so I reached over and yanked hard and we swerved out of the way of the truck. Les told the story to my brother years later when they met, by chance, in Norway.

Bombs from night bombers were one of the threats. They seemed to be working at it full-time. Our attack in the Solomons may have diverted them from their intentions at Darwin, for after Guadalcanal things seemed to subside at Darwin. Our quarters there were five-man tents. One would have perished without a mosquito net. Nights were hot, usually with little wind. We had an out-of-tune piano, and Lt. James Alford was a good pianist. He was appreciated. I think the piano was loot from the nearby vacated town. I trust we returned it to its proper owner when we left. Meals were poor until I would go hunting or fishing.

Lieutenant Clarence "Johnny" Johnson of the 8th Squadron, from Fort Worth, Texas, was a superb pilot. His father had owned an airplane when Johnny was a child, so he had soloed at about twelve years of age. He had many hours of time when he entered cadet training. One day, on a mission, he came out of a big wheeling battle and lost his bearings. In the Northern Territory in those days there was one north-south road out of Darwin, but no others. Johnny missed the road, a virtual beacon for lost pilots, and flew west two hundred miles until he ran out of gas. He bent the propeller when landing. Lieutenant Richard Dennis and I and a couple of mechanics flew in an Aussie Hudson to the site and landed in a large meadow near the P-40, where Johnny had landed on a nearby beach. We took him a replacement propeller.

We had learned where he went down via radio signal from an old Spanish missionary who served the Lord and a band of wild Aborigines in the area. While there, we were treated to a peek back in time to the Stone Age. The Aborigines had just come in from a four-hundred-mile trek from a wilderness area, according to the missionary. Most of the women had no buttocks, especially those suckling babies. Their butts were flat and wrinkled.

Those Aborigines had built homes of eucalyptus tree bark they tore from the trees, bent in half, and lapped in a circle. By bending the slabs toward the center of the circle, they fashioned huts four feet high for shade and shelter. By bending one slab in the middle they had a door; home sweet home in a few hours!

An interesting side study occurred. To beat the heat, Dennis and I were bare-chested and only in our shorts. A couple of teenage girls with budding breasts displayed an interest in us by pointing, giggling, and making suggestive sexual motions. I said to Dennis, "There is your chance for a girlfriend, Den." He declined with a whack at my head.

The mechanics and Johnny got the prop back on the P-40, and Johnny took off from the beach and beat us back to base.

Johnny and I met in mock combat one day, and there ensued a whirling, swirling battle that went from twelve thousand feet down to the treetops. We were meeting, passing, then turning hard back at each other head-on, so that neither was able to get on the other's tail. It was my first mission in a P-40E, and I was afraid of the turns, fearing I would snap and spin in. We broke off near the ground with a draw. I congratulated Johnny on his pilotage, and he was proud. I was glad it turned out that way, as flying was Johnny's life, and to have him lose might have made him doubt his ability. A few days later Johnny got his chance at a Zero, and in a courageous fight lost, with serious wounds as a consequence. When we landed, I went over to his plane, which was next to my own revetment. He just sat in the cockpit. I jumped up on the wing and saw the blood coming from his head and neck. I yelled for the ambulance. He did a great job in getting the airplane back on the ground. Johnny returned to the States when I did, was given command of a P-39 squadron, but lost his life in a P-39 that tumbled in flight and crashed to earth.

It seems that tragedy was the prevailing theme in combat, but occasionally funny things occurred. One time, some of the fellows got together and pooled their funds to purchase whiskey. They entrusted the money to a fellow pilot who was going south for a few days' R&R. The courier returned thoroughly inebriated, sans whiskey. That day a native had come into camp with a huge python he had killed. The inebriate was so drunk, he flopped on his cot in deep slumber. The whiskeyless victims decided to help wake him up in the morning. This was done by wrapping the python around his body from feet to head with the snake's head on the slumberer's chest looking directly into his face. The observers said that permanently broke the fellow from drinking.

Another time later in the war, some navy pilots flying F4Fs, whose carrier had been sunk, came in to land on one of the 49th's fields, which was fitted with perforated steel planking on the runway. One of them lowered his tail hook and rolled up a few yards of the runway on landing.

One day I found myself alone after a big hassle with a flight of Zeros, when I spotted one well below me. He had probably made the mistake of following a P-40 in a dive. I probably had three thousand feet of altitude on him as I dove, so by the time I came in range I was at a speed of around 425 mph.

Again my inexperience made me almost lose the contest. He pulled around in a steep left turn. I had never fired at a plane in a hard vertical turn. I was surprised at the amount of lead required in a steep turn. At first I could have led him 100 yards; the wise thing here is to overlead, then he has to fly through your fire at least once, even if he pulls ahead of you in the turn. I hadn't, so I then tried to catch up to him, but it was too late and I was soon behind in the turn. But, it being a high-speed turn, I pulled tighter and tighter, and was gaining, but I was on the verge of blackout so I grunted as hard as I could to help fight it. The tracers appeared to be going in a half circle under my wings. I held the trigger down and pulled tighter until he was passing out of sight under my wings. To my great relief, there was a big explosion, my plane lurched upward, and fire and debris flew in all directions. When I straightened up and looked down, there was a ragged frame, assorted junk, and one piece of a wing that fluttered like a maple seed toward the surface of the sea. I circled and cleared the sky around me, then watched the wing strike the water and slowly sink into the depths, the round red sun on the wing disappearing into the deepening blue of the sea. Then out to the side I saw an open parachute. I thought, ha! I'll go over and thumb my nose at him, so I flew by and found that he was not in the parachute. We had heard these pilots did not wear the chutes buckled while over enemy territory. It was true. The straps were flapping in the breeze. I guess some of the pieces of debris I saw were my opponent.[*]

Now I had a problem. There was no one in sight, in the air, or on the sea, who might confirm my victory. But wait. I had an idea. Why not fly through the parachute and take some of the rags home with me? That would be confirmation for sure. In the meantime the chute was floating inexorably toward the surface of the sea. I backed off to make a run on the chute, but got to thinking what might happen if the metal buckles or heavy straps or parachute cords got tangled around my propeller, or banged into my radiator,

[*] After the war I learned from reading Japanese ace pilot Soburo Sakai's book *Samurai* that many of their fighter pilots disdained wearing parachutes while flying against the Americans.

or the webbing over my canopy, then I would shoot *myself* down. Nor did I know how the trapped air in the chute would affect an aircraft going two hundred miles an hour. So I gave it up, and I don't know yet what might have happened, but I did lose confirmation for the kill. I was miles at sea, with no air/sea rescue, and no radio bleepers. Over fifty years later I was watching a television show on experimental flight operations when a drag chute accidentally came open and jerked the tail off the aircraft. It appears that I chose the right course, as I *am* here to write about it.

On our day off Randy Keator and I took a jeep and two Garand rifles and went out on dusty dirt roads beyond a cattle station called Humpty Doo. Randy had escaped the Philippines and we talked of the war's outlook, and of how long it might take to recover the thousands of miles of oceans and islands that had been taken by brutal force. We spoke of our dear POW friends who would be ground under the heel of the enemy's boot for interminable years.

As we moved along, we came upon a wild pig asleep in its wallow. It was Randy's first trip with me, so I let him shoot the big pig. Farther on we came upon a herd of buffalo, and I shot a young bull of about 450 pounds, just right for choice, tender meat. We next saw a dry streambed that had a large, shallow slough at one place, so I noted it down for a return trip. I wanted to bring a net and sweep the waters for stranded fish that might be there. I bagged some wild doves, almost as big as a chicken; good eating. I also wing-tipped a large black parrot that we caught and examined. I was a little careless with handling it, and it grabbed me by the thumb and bit it absolutely flat at the nail. My sore thumb was only about one-quarter-inch thick for several minutes until I rubbed circulation and life back into it.

Farther on we came to a grove of bamboo grass and drove into it. There, alone, stood a solitary buffalo bull. The animal was gigantic, and looked twice as large as the average, with sweeping horns some six or seven feet wide. Those horns must have been the world's record, and I would have loved to have had the head for a trophy, but during those times we had no plans for the morrow. We just admired the magnificent beast and drove away. He had had such powerful domain over his past, I suppose, that he did not run. He just stood his ground as if to challenge anything we tried to do. We returned to camp with three pigs, a buffalo, and several of the large doves and geese. The mess sergeant happily took over.

For the next few days at the alert shack we worked fashioning a fishing seine out of camouflage netting. We tied bamboo joints at the top and scrap metal and old airplane parts for weights on the bottom. When I next had time off, I took a truck and twelve or fifteen enlisted men and drove out back to the dry streambed and the shallow slough.

The slough was about sixty yards long and fifteen yards wide. We waded into the water and pulled the seine the length of the pond. At the end we had felt nothing large in the net. There was an obstructing tree where we couldn't sweep out the end with it. I waded into the small encircled area of pond, and all of a sudden eight or ten huge fish flew into the air in a big uproar that scared the hell out of us. Most of the fellows dropped the seine and ran. I yelled for someone to pick it up, and we corralled several twenty- to thirty-pound freshwater fish and myriad varieties of smaller fishes. We took them back to camp and had a big fish fry.

About this time it appeared that the enemy was making plans to invade. They started sending bombers over every night to circle our bases and keep us awake by dropping a bomb every few minutes. The practice was annoying, to say the least. The bomb bay doors had a funny sound when they were opened, and we would wait until we heard the sound, then we'd jump out of our cots and dash for the slit trench in back of the tent. One night I must have been careless and went back to sleep. I heard a whistle and dove for the trench, landing on a body. I said, "Oh, I'm sorry, I didn't know you were there." He said, "Ah, that's okay, I'm lying on somebody myself."

Bill Herbert, Richard Dennis, and I went out in the jeep one day, hunting on the flats. Bill wanted to drive. He goofed around and ran into a tidal gut and stuck the jeep. We had to walk out. At first we built a fire and cooked a bustard, then ate some of him. But after dark set in, the mosquitoes moved out from the swamps and started the bloodletting. We all pulled up a large mass of grass and crawled beneath it, but as soon as the mosquitoes could climb down through the stems, they were all biting us again. We saw we couldn't spend a night out there and not become 100 percent anemic, so we started walking out. But which direction? Fortunately it was a clear night and we had the Southern Cross to navigate by.

I had flown over the area and had seen a vehicle track to the north perhaps some five miles. We took off in the dark with a sliver of a moon to navigate by. I figured if we went due west, we should hit the vehicle tracks. We crawled through thickets, waded a swamp about three hundred yards wide that fortunately didn't go over our armpits, and just when we were growing discouraged, we came upon the tracks. Then we had to decide which way to follow the tracks. We chose to head north, which meant toward the coast. At about 2:00 A.M., after a few miles we came to the same Humpty Doo we had visited before. Here, there was a cattle station ranch cabin, where an Australian and two Aborigines were sleeping.

They invited us in, and we eagerly entered, as the mosquitoes were after us quickly whenever we stopped walking fast. The cabin had mosquito netting for a screen door, for which we were thankful. We flopped on the floor, as we were near exhaustion. The Australian then telephoned our unit, a jeep was sent for us, and we were back in our own tents about dawn.

Somehow, in our relations with the Aussies, our squadron wound up with a Tiger Moth. This was a 1930s edition of a training biplane with fabric covering and a tiny engine. Richard Dennis and I would fly out, land on the meadows, hunt or fish, and fly back in the evening. One evening we were coming back and Dennis was flying. He flew down over the runway, attracting the attention of the pilots and crew. I stepped out on the wing and was holding on to the spars while Dennis was looking out the other side of the cockpit. I tapped him on the shoulder, and when he looked around he nearly leapt out of his seat. He started yelling, "Get back in there! Get back in there!" Back on the ground he insisted I was crazy. I was a little surprised, as Dennis was a rather wild kid himself.

As mentioned, the bombers were coming over more at night in May and June. The searchlight batteries would catch them in their lights. I went to Captain Sims and asked him to let me go up and try to get them at night. He was bucking for promotion and didn't want to risk anything going bad: denied.

The bombing continued, and seeing them up there in the lights was getting to me. I took it up with my crew chief, and he agreed to take a jeep to the end of the strip and keep the lights on until I was airborne. I figured I could get one of those big sitting targets for sure and then the CO would be happy about it. It didn't turn out that way. Unfortunately, up until then, the early warning unit on the coast had informed us of approaching bombers as soon as they detected them, about thirty to forty-five minutes before they reached landfall. On this night they decided to thwart the enemy by waiting to sound the alarm and let the troops sleep thirty or forty minutes longer, and awaken them only a few minutes prior to arrival. I decided to engage them anyway, but when I took off, the bombers were already overhead and in the spotlights. A couple of minutes later they were out of them, so I had no time to climb to fifteen thousand feet for an intercept.

Now I was really up in the air. I had no chance to be a hero and bag that bogie, and I found that the jeep light my crew chief turned on when I buzzed the strip was too weak to see the strip by. I had to ask for help from the Australians at Bachelor Field, the former civilian airport and now Aussie bomber base, to turn on their runway lights for me to land by. With the enemy overhead, I understood their hesitancy. So I circled for an hour or so, and after the bogies had left landfall, I landed. The squadron sent a jeep over for me with an irate squadron CO in it. Even the group CO came up the next day and did his share of chewing.

At a reunion of the 49th Fighter Group at Reno, Nevada, in 1996, a number of our members were riding to the Reno airfield to watch the air races. On the charter bus was veteran Robert Baden. He turned in his seat and said, "Jim, one of those memories that remains with a person throughout life was that black night when we enlisted men parked the jeep at the end of the strip and lit the oil rags along the sides. The throb of the Allison in-line engine against the background of the whine of the Jap radials is something I'll never forget. With such makeshift facilities, we were scared to death you would never make it back down." Their fears were justified, for they did not know I had as an ace in the hole the well-equipped Australian bomber base, Bachelor Field, to land at.

Things seemed to let up a little, as I guess the enemy had shifted its plans about Guadalcanal and New Guinea. We had raids, but I had found no favorable opportunities until around the first of August. We had a standing procedure that a flight of four would take off and stand by over the field as the mission pilots returned to protect them from attack while landing. My flight had the protecting assignment on this day, and as soon as all the others were down, I set course fast for Melville Island with two others and started a wide circle looking below. I had been thinking about what I would do if I were the enemy, and I would probably let down where it was much warmer, pull off my oxygen mask to rest my face, and relax for the trip home. They would, of course, fly over land as long as they could, preferring that to flying over the hazardous sea. I was now free to do what I had resolved to since 7 December 1941 — hunt Japanese.

Whatever the case, when I looked down, there were three Zeros in V formation several thousand feet below, right over the island. Today our flight was only three, Lts. Earl Kingsley, Larry Eisenberg, and me. I called my flight and said there were three Zeros below and ordered them to close up. Kingsley closed quickly. Lieutenant Eisenberg at that moment called back and said his engine was running rough. I looked back just as his broad silhouette flashed against the sky as he turned tail for home. This left Lieutenant Kingsley and me to deal with the three Zeros on our own.[*]

I felt a touch of hesitance with Eisenberg's departure, leaving only two of us against three of the vaunted Zeros, but I figured with any luck we could take out at least one and run like hell if we lost out in the maneuvering.

With Eisenberg's departure I was faced with a hard decision. Wingmen are justifiably critical of flight leaders who lead them into fatal situations. P-40s in one-on-one situations against the vaunted Zero was considered dangerous enough, two against three could be disastrous. But time did not permit for pondering; I just thought, we'll

[*] Kingsley later said, "We should have shot Eisenberg down along with the Japs."

have to suffer the consequences if it goes bad.

I flipped the P-40 over on its back and pulled through in a twisting turn to align myself with the direction of their flight. I did little throttle adjustment, as I wanted to keep as much speed as possible if I needed to escape.

Down, down, straight down we went with the building whine of the engine, the popping sounds of the canopy at high speed, and the roar of the wind building toward 500 miles per hour. I adjusted rudder trim as yaw increased so I could have a neutral aiming platform and pulled out of my dive directly behind them several hundred yards back.

I believe the Japanese pilots, at this time of the war, were suffering from a strong amount of pride. They tell in their writings of their disdain for wearing parachutes, perhaps refusing to admit that they just might be shot down by an Allied pilot. I suspect they deigned to keep a furtive scan of the skies, which might imply fear or a need for caution. This attitude played right into our hands, for a fighter pilot who isn't looking around is one who is easy to kill.

Whatever the cause, the three Zero pilots directly in front of me were not looking around as I stalked them. Closer and closer I came with my heart beating like a tom-tom in my chest. Not yet, I told myself, don't spook the biggest game you will ever have for a target.

I could see clearly the bright red rising-sun insignia on the wings and tail. Not yet, I warned myself again. Take dead aim and make very sure I at least take one of these guys out of the picture. That will leave only one each to contend with.

At 100 yards I put the crosshairs on the canopy of the right-hand plane in the formation and pulled the trigger. Six .50-caliber machine guns roared without a stutter, and the canopy of the fighter seemed to melt. I held the trigger down until I saw that the plane was shattered. Then I hurried to swing my guns onto the lead fighter only a few feet to the left of the stricken Zero. With the trigger full down I swept over the lead ship, missing his tail assembly by only inches as I hauled back on the stick and shot straight up. I rolled over and hung there and observed the scene below.

The lead ship was in a gentle turn to the right, smoking, and Lieutenant Kingsley was on his tail, firing. The other Zero was flying straight ahead with light smoke coming from his exhaust indicating he was at full throttle. I nosed down and came back down on his tail, and he made a steep turn to the left. I closed to within a few feet with six .50-calibers roaring. Then I was in the midst of a big red ball of flame with pieces of things flying through the air. Kingsley finished the other one, and this made it a clean sweep. My little trap had caught the trespassers.

An example of the one-sided scoring in the air war at that time is shown in Saburo Sakai's (Japanese Ace) recording of his unit's operation at Lae, New Guinea, in April 1942.

5 April 1942: Four Zeros escorted seven bombers to Moresby, shot down two enemy fighters with loss of one Zero.

6 April 1942: Four Zeros engaged seven enemy fighters over southern New Guinea, shot down five, no losses.

7 April 1942: Two Zeros intercepted three enemy bombers, shot down two, no losses.

10 April 1942: Six Zeros escorted seven bombers over Moresby, shot down two enemy bombers. PM: Three Zeros intercepted several enemy bombers, shot down one bomber, no losses.

11 April 1942: Eight Zeros intercepted four P-39s and shot down all four. No losses.

17 April 1942: Thirteen Zeros on escort, lost two bombers.

19 April 1942: Nine Zeros intercepted six enemy bombers, shot down one bomber. No losses.

21 April 1942: Fifteen Zeros on sweep over Moresby, shot down two bombers, six P-40s. No losses.

24 April 1942: Fifteen Zeros on sweep southern New Guinea, contacted seven P-40s, shot down six. No losses.

29 April 1942: Two Zeros intercepted three B-17s, shot down one B-17. No losses.

After we landed and debriefed, my crew chief came to me and said, "Lieutenant, did you know you nearly shot yourself down today?" I said,

"How do you mean, Sergeant?" He said, "Did you have blue ammunition today?" I said, "Yes." He said, "When I inspected the plane after you landed, I found this embedded in the coolant radiator. When I dug it out, it began to leak. How close did you come to the plane you shot down?" He pulled from his pocket the nosepiece of a .50-caliber API* bullet. I said, "Feet, maybe inches. I feared I had pulled out too late once. I scared myself pretty good." What had happened was that my explosive bullet burst when it struck the lead Zero and one of its fragments flew into the radiator at the nose of my plane as I passed over.

I received the Silver Star for the elimination of that little band of Zeros. Lieutenant Kingsley received the Distinguished Flying Cross for his part.

I'm sure the air crews back at the enemy unit wondered what on earth happened to their three buddies, as they waited for their return, for there was no one left to tell the tale.

* Armor-piercing incendiary.

VII

Could the Tide Be Turning?

Australia and New Zealand had been screaming for England to send them some air defense ever since Japan started its rampage through the Southwest Pacific. Both countries had loyally supplied their youth for the defense of England and the Empire; now they expected a return favor when they, too, were threatened.

Although England needed every plane for her own defense, there was no way she could ignore the plaintive cries of her faithful daughters of the Empire. She sent her best; a complete wing of fifty-six brand-new, Spitfire VC fighters and the best of the experienced Anzac (Australia and New Zealand Army Corps) pilots commanded by Wing Com. C. R. Caldwell, an ace pilot with twenty-two victories. By January 1943 the number of planes had reached 100.

With the arrival of the Spitfires, our fighter group was to be withdrawn from the Darwin area and moved to New Guinea, where the Japanese appeared to be placing more emphasis.

Before our move to New Guinea, the Spitfire personnel asked us to talk with them about tactics, enemy activity, enemy aircraft, and pilots. I was one who joined the discussions. When I got my chance to talk, I offered my opinion of the circumstances, the outlook, and the dangers. I told Caldwell that I was familiar with the Battle of Britain, where I understood many of them had fought; that I was aware that the Spitfire was a beautifully maneuverable aircraft that had easily outmaneuvered the German planes; and that I was sure they felt it would do the same for the Zero fighter. I cautioned them to find out first if the Spitfire could "cut it" with the Zero before assuming it could, because a Zero was light as a feather and could turn on a dime. I wanted them to consider the possibility that the Japanese pilots and planes might be superior to the Germans they had encountered.

The meeting continued for two or three hours, but just as it ended I told the assembled group pilots, many of whom were aces, that I would like to say once again that they must check first on who could outmaneuver whom. "Yes, yes, thank you." Sadly, in their first big encounter after we left they attacked a large Japanese formation and lost fourteen Spitfires and several pilots. It was a fiasco prompting an investigation by higher Australian command. General Kenney, theater air commander, threatened to place them with the Americans to teach them how to fight the enemy.[*] It is understandable, however, that

[*] General George Kenney, in his book *General Kenney Reports*, states: "I sent Bostock [Air Vice Marshall, Royal Australian Air Force Chief of Air Operations] to Darwin to talk to the kids and to tell them if they didn't stop dog-fighting I'd send them to New Guinea to serve with the Americans and learn how to fight the Japs properly . . . they had to learn the hard way." New York: Duell, Sloan, and Pearce, 1949, p. 240

they would do what came naturally to them.

The Fifth Air Force made some arrangements with Australian education institutions to set up a course on the problems of high altitude operations, and I was one chosen to attend. I was pleased at this, because my older brother, Jackson, a physician with the army, had been sent to Australia, and I wanted a chance to see and visit with him. I boarded a C-47 and landed at Melbourne, where my brother had a hospital company, and where the course I was to attend was located.

My brother and I met, and after a good visit I asked, since he was a bachelor, if he knew any girls there yet. He said he had met an Australian lady, and he was sure she had a friend.

I should pause here and explain that I had never been enthusiastic about my brother's choice of female friends, a fact I should have remembered. While working his way through ten years of medical school, he like me, had never been able to date and entertain many girls. He had always taken up with some woman who had her own money but was definitely no late model. This used to irritate my mother no end. He evidently was in a rut on that and didn't have confidence in himself to chance a date with a cute girl, although he wasn't bad-looking.

We met the ladies at his friend's apartment, and, as is often the case when a girl chooses a date for you, I was not overjoyed with the selection. In fact, it was so disappointing that I started thinking how on earth I could escape from the trap and made good use of the limited time afforded me by the course. Time was of the essence.

The women were nice, friendly ladies, and I had to protect their feelings, but I still wanted to leave them. I didn't yet know which one was to be mine. I feared each choice equally. I had it! My brother was a doctor and my brilliant idea should let us both escape, leaving no international bitterness, and still have the evening for "dear" hunting.

I was sitting on a couch, and suddenly I bent over with a terrible cramp in my torso. My brother quickly came over to attend to me, asking where the pain was. I whispered that it was in my heart, that it was short of love, and the prospects of corrective treatment were sterile. Then, just loud enough for him to hear, I said, "Let's get out of here!" He told the ladies that he'd better take me to his dispensary, and we left.

Outside, I said to him, "Jackson, we don't have to settle for these institutional types. We want some cuties. We aren't looking for the professors, we are looking for the students!" I didn't want to hurt his feelings, but time did not permit dallying. I said, "Let's go to this huge skating rink downtown and skate in the opposite direction. Then, when we find the prettiest girls on the ice, let's invite them for dinner." He said, somewhat indignantly, that he would throw a party for the forty nurses in his hospital company, and I could make my choices. I certainly didn't fight that idea, but I said, "Let's make the most of tonight."

So we went to the rink, where about two hundred people, mostly girls, were skating. I asked Jack to pick out one he liked. I found a rosy-lipped little beauty about eighteen and introduced myself. Then I enlisted her help to introduce my brother to the girl he selected, and soon all was copasetic. We invited them to dine with us, and we had a happy evening. I hoped that this experience would help bring him out of his rut. I told Jack not to go back to the older lady, but ask this little chick out again.

At the party for the American nurses, several good-looking young ladies attracted my attention. All there were previously aware of my earlier war efforts — the Australian papers were full of the 5 August victory — and Jackson blew it up more.

A full-breasted little Italian gal caught my eye, and she seemed interested in war stories. She danced well, was one of the prettier ladies there, and was real fun to be with. She reminded one of the phrase "So round, so firm, so fully packed." About five feet four inches tall, full lips, brown eyes, with a mischievous, coquettish look. Every man, I'm sure, wanted to be her patient. I sure was hoping we would get a hospital company sent to Darwin.

The next night I called the Australian girl I had met at the skating rink and we went to a picture show. When the Pathé News or Aussie News came on, the interviews following the Darwin air victory were rerun. She looked at me, then back at the screen, and asked, "Isn't that you?" I agreed, and tried to act modest. The following day classes ended, and my brother and I had our pictures taken. I then packed my bags. Peace had flown. I returned to Darwin.

At the alert shack, a hammock I had constructed sparked a confrontation. Miller was a big lad from Philadelphia. He was proud and well-educated (a masters degree, I think). He came from the well-known big city while I was from the country. He had a dominating character and I am certain he felt superior to me in every way. He was slightly larger, but not particularly well muscled. On my day off he would lie in my hammock, which was fine. One day, after a day off, I climbed into my hammock. Miller was on duty too. After a while he came over and said it was his turn to have the hammock. I asked whom the hammock belonged to. He then tried to push me out, and roll me out; he tried lifting my feet out, then my arms.

Now, this breach of conduct was enough to provoke me to take him on in a fist fight, but officers are not supposed to fight. He expressed surprise that he couldn't throw me out of my hammock. I told him I could beat him at anything he chose. He scoffed at that. I said that since we couldn't fist fight, we could see who was the better man by a series of physical tests.

Among other challenges, we had a footrace, we broad-jumped, and standing-jumped, did pushups, muscle-ups, and wrist-wrestled, not one test of which he won. I said, "Now, aren't you glad we didn't fight, or you would have gotten the hell beaten out of you?"

The contest was exhausting, which was sad to reflect upon, for I'm sure our bodies were short of oxygen. At that instant we had a scramble. We took off and climbed hard. At about 21,000 feet, Miller dropped back. I said, "Close it up, Miller." No reply. I repeated the order. Then I feared anoxemia.* "Miller, Miller, Miller!" I shouted into the mike.

In spite of the fact that this was a combat mission, and I was under the command of Fighter Control, Fifth Air Force, I long felt I should have turned back and tried to whack his wing with mine to get his attention. We found Miller's body in the cockpit of his mangled plane near the field.

It is surprising how callous men can get toward death. Perhaps it was fitting. But after Miller's death Dennis and I drove out in the wilderness. We had played with him; we had fought with him; we had fought beside him; we had eaten with, bunked with, and been with him constantly sixteen hours a day for many months. And I was glad I hadn't gotten mad, lost my temper, and

* Anoxemia: An abnormal codition due to deficient aeration of the blood, usually at high altitudes; also called balloon sickness or mountain sickness.

tried to beat him up over the hammock affair. Right after Miller's death I was promoted to captain. That his name was on the promotion list to First Lieutenant made his death no easier.

With the Spitfires coming in, we decided to give them a little show. We did a little practicing, then flew over their headquarters at Bachelor Field in the pattern of a giant "US." It was pretty good. Then we went down and beat up the place. I did a loop off the deck, which in that era was of note and caused comments. It is simply a loop begun at the level of the runway and finished at the level of the runway, and obviously must not be short on the bottom. Dennis wanted to do it with me, but I was afraid to let him. With today's fighters it is not worthy of mention, but the Spitfire pilots were saying, "Did you see that P-40 do a loop off the deck?"

With our replacement by the Spitfires, we soon left Darwin. We flew across tropical Australia, and landed at the east coast city of Townsville, Australia, south of New Guinea. We reported in to the office of the base commander, a beer-bellied old colonel. He assigned us revetments for our planes and quarters for us until the airfield in Port Moresby was ready to receive us.

In the colonel's office there was a pretty girl who I introduced myself to when the colonel stepped out. She was friendly, and we were chatting when the colonel walked back in. He immediately called her over to his desk for something, and it was obvious that he coveted the girl himself. I had already obtained her phone number, however, so I told her where he could hear that I would call her in the evening. He told us pilots to wait outside the office.

Helen Hansen was a loving girl who wore the cutest and most tasteful dresses, skirts, and blouses — so feminine. One felt an immediate urge to kiss her. It must have been hard for the old colonel, working beside her. Her auburn hair with little curls at the temples gave her green eyes, clear north-European complexion, and long, black lashes a really devastating charm. I couldn't believe she was not fully booked. Later on she did tell me that an officer I had met had pursued her in spite of rebuffs, and appeared at the girl's house one night and came in with his pants off. I told her I knew him, and I'd beat the hell out of him if he did it again.

She lived in a house in the suburbs of Townsville with three other girls. I picked her up in a cab that night and we went to a show, and had malted milks afterward. I dated her every night we were in Townsville, and made it a point to drop by the colonel's office and tell her I would see her at a certain time. The puffy old buzzard looked like he wanted to have me arrested every time, as I tried to make my greeting to her more intimate because of his possessive attitude.

One day we took a short boat ride over to Magnetic Island, where we spent a day on an idyllic beach with the delicious fragrance of wildflowers filling the air. We swam in crystal-clear water and sunned on the clean, white sand, and I admired her physical assets. We followed a footpath that ascended a steep hill that overlooked the little bay. From there we could see three brown-mottled sharks about eight to ten feet long swimming within a few feet of the shoreline. Earlier I had swum out to the shark net that closed off the bay, and when I got there I found the net was broken by rust. After that we stayed close to shore. That afternoon we caught the boat back to Townsville, and that night we went to a steak fry with her friends, who were a mix of Australians and Americans, and had a wonderful time. We all seemed to like one another a lot.

Again my thoughts ran to the stupidity of war. It must be that man sat down and tried to think up the stupidest thing he could possibly do in life, and decided on war.

But time was running out for this brief period of peace. Soon we were to fly over the coral reefs to the embattled island of New Guinea. I said good-bye to Helen and promised to see her again if I lived.

While at Townsville we had heard rumors that a rotation system was being considered for pilots who had been exposed to the most violence. It sounded like I would be high on the list considering my midair collision just before Pearl Harbor, the landing accident at Amberly Field, Brisbane, and the various combat sorties.

This threw me into a quandary. Just now I was starting to believe I had enough experience in combat to feel confidence in keeping myself from getting killed. I was eager to lower the boom on those back-stabbing, sneaking, brutal snakes in the night that murdered my countrymen by pretending to deal in peace while they raised a bloody knife to stab us with.

Well, I would have made them pay, and I did a few of them. I wanted to use my skills to make more of them pay; and with an airplane like the P-38 that didn't have to fight the enemy from underneath, I think I could have racked them up by the dozen. I had hopes of getting into a P-38.

When it was announced that I was on the list for combat relief, I went to my squadron commander and said I felt that I should stay with my comrades and continue to fight. My squadron commander was not a man of steel. He had a wife and kids in the States. He said, "Aw, if you stay over, they'll want the rest of us to when it is our time. No." I should have gone over his head, but I was not knowledgeable about those things, so I wound up in Europe flying tail-end Charlie, following some less-skilled leader and suffering his less-skilled decisions. I might have been group commander by then in the 49th. But that is dreaming.

I went on to New Guinea, but presently orders came through returning me to the States. I returned to Townsville briefly. I told Helen Hansen of the developments. The pretty thing was both sad and glad for me. There was a tear in her eye as she said, "Good-bye, Yank." There was also one in my heart.

From Townsville I flew to Amberly Field, Brisbane, and put up in the BOQ — the bachelor officer's quarters. I found an old friend, Lt. Paul May, who was quartered there. We had come over on the *Polk* together. May had been assigned test pilot at Amberly to check the planes being assembled there. He was later killed when someone rigged the ailerons backward. This made the plane turn left if you controlled to the right, and vice versa. Doubtless he rolled over just after leaving the ground on takeoff.

May and I went to his room in the BOQ and he was telling me about a bizarre situation on the American part of the base there. Some major, a nonflying officer, had gone on a drunken spree and had threatened to shoot the base commander, had kicked an Australian boy who worked in the officer's club, had urinated in the glasses at the bar, and was still scaring the base commander to death with threats. He added that the man roomed just across the hall. After being exposed to the serious business of fighting a deadly enemy and doing the best you can with little, it galled me to hear of such malicious conduct.

At the moment May was telling me all this, a noise and loud swearing was heard in the hall. The door next to ours was slammed open and I heard a man say he was going to get a gun and "kill him." Well, the last thing I wanted to do, after going through the dangers of aerial combat, was to get killed by some drunken jerk slinging a gun around. I jumped up, opened our door, and asked the man what he was doing. He asked me what business it was of mine. I said he shouldn't be threatening to kill people. He said, "Go to hell, get out of here!" As he bent over a footlocker, I took him by the shoulder, hoping to reason with him, but he jerked away. When he started cursing me, I struck him squarely on the chin. He dropped momentarily but recovered and drew back to strike. I slammed him three or four strong blows to the face, paused a moment, and said, "You are going to the brig." I told May to call the MPs.

The major started to curse me again, and I slammed him two more blows. Now his arms were hanging, and I grabbed one and jerked it high behind his back. He cried out almost humorously, "Where is the brig? Where is the brig?"

I held the dummy's arm behind his back until the MPs arrived and then I released it and him, to them. I told them to put him in the brig and keep him there until ordered to release him, by order of Capt. James B. Morehead.

The next morning, figuring I might be detained by the incident, I hurried down to operations, climbed on board a B-24, and left Australia and any involvement far behind.

Our first stop was New Caledonia with its vivid red soil. Next we landed in the Fiji Islands and spent the night. I looked up my old friend, Maj. Henry Viccellio, commander of a P-39 outfit there. In the unit was my longtime friend Rex Barber, the pilot who shot down Yamamoto.

I spent the night with Henry and we talked about old times at Hamilton Field, the war, and the fun we had hunting and fishing. The next time I saw Henry was at the Pentagon, and it was Lieutenant General Viccellio then.

After a pleasant visit with "Vic," the big ship took off for a tiny dot in the middle of the Pacific Ocean. The navigator had the ticklish job of finding Howland Island, more than two thousand miles north of the Fijis. Through the Plexiglas nose of the B-24, interesting ocean scenes were visible. At one time we flew dozens if not scores of miles over one great school of fish that looked as if they were two to three feet long. They must have numbered in the billions. Sharks, whales, porpoises, sea birds, and fish provided us entertainment.

The course was true, and we landed on a small bit of sand that protruded only a few feet above the ocean. It had one palm tree at the end. A short while before, Capt. Eddie Rickenbacker was en route to the Southwest Pacific theater when the navigator lost his bearings, and they were forced to land in the open ocean. Some of the crew perished, the rest being rescued after long exposure at sea. Thoughts of the incident were in mind on those long flights over water, and with only a dot in the ocean to find. After refueling, the next leg of the flight sought tiny Johnson Island, another two-thousand-mile distance. Again the navigator was on the money, and we set down to refuel for the next leg.

I felt sorry for the personnel assigned to these lonely stations. They should have been screened for their preferred sports, and should have been selected from those who, like myself, felt that anyone not fishing is just frittering away his life.

After Johnson Island came Hawaii. At the end of this leg the blunt form of Diamond Head shoved its mass above the horizon, and we landed at Hickam Field. We all went into Honolulu to a nightclub for dancing and mixing with civilians. The next day we set out on the last fourteen hours of our twelve-thousand-mile journey without serious incident, and landed at familiar surroundings at Hamilton Field, California.

I felt satisfaction and regret; I felt sadness and joy at the completion of my tour in the Southwest Pacific theater. I felt I had been a good soldier, but had qualms about leaving my fledglings to the ravages of war without me, especially when I later learned my faithful wingman, Dennis, had been lost in New Guinea.

However, I thought I could be of value to the green fighter pilots I would be training in the States by saving them hard lessons learned the hard way in a hard war.

I must confess, after having seen one of the new P-38s perform there at Townsville, I visualized becoming a leading ace in the theater. One of the young pilots just coming into the theater when I was leaving downed forty of the enemy, and General Kenney said he was a poor shot. I was already experienced and a good shot, and had dreamed so of having a good plane to go after the bastards with. That pilot, by the way, was named Richard Bong.

VIII

A New Menu

I was placed on thirty days leave after returning from the Southwest Pacific theater. I returned home the local hero as a result of earning two Distinguished Service Crosses, the Silver Star, two Distinguished Flying Crosses, the personal commendation of General Marshall, and the attention of the national networks and newspapers. What was more interesting was that I seemed to be a hero among the female population. This made for a more interesting vacation, and I had a grand time renewing old acquaintances and making new ones.

At the end of my leave I reported to the headquarters command on the West Coast, and I was offered command of a fighter squadron. When I asked what kind, I was told a P-39 squadron was available.

Since I had flown P-39s in Australia, my attitude toward being assigned either a P-40 or a P-39 was poor. When we were at Hamilton Field before the war, we flew P-36s; these were really honeys to fly, so I was looking for improvement. We had been told of a fighter being produced by North American Aircraft Company that was close to one hundred miles per hour faster than either the P-40 or the P-39. We heard that the army had turned down purchase of that marvelous plane, and so the British had contracted to take all the company's production.

I'll tell you that if you are being pursued by an enemy plane that is just a little faster than the plane you are fleeing in, your thoughts turn to the rejection by your country of a plane that one hundred miles per hour faster. You may think you'd like to have that decision maker in your gun sights.

The first time I flew the P-39, I thought it was coming apart as I taxied out. I feared its last landing may have been a doozy, and its crankshaft was now out of round. When a pilot first flies a particular type of airplane, he has no way of knowing its characteristics. Against my better judgment I went ahead and took off. It nearly shook my goggles off before I got airborne. When I got back and asked someone about my grave misgivings, he said it was normal.

I already had my fill of flying the P-40, so instead of taking the advancement, I asked about P-38s, and was told an operations post, only, was open. I said, "I'll take it." The P-38 with two engines and two high-altitude superchargers, both longevity policies on a pilot's life, proved too attractive.

During my leave I renewed my romance with Aldine Seeger, the pretty girl I had met in San Francisco when I was stationed at Hamilton Field, and sometime later we were married. It was a poor match. One came from harshly realistic, austere beginnings, the other from a sophisticated, advanced life of few wants, few requirements. Temporary duty and long separations in foreign lands, also add little to the environment for marriage.

I was assigned to the 333d Fighter Group, a replacement training unit located at Van Nuys, California, and was soon advanced to commander of the squadron. The unit served the dual purposes of training replacement pilots and doing antisubmarine patrol on the West Coast, flying out of Van Nuys and later at Olympia, Washington.

Duty hours were long and the pressure was constant. A big political, Hollywood-appointment-type bird colonel was in charge of the area training and defense program. He was bucking for a promotion and pushed the units constantly to attain more flying hours and turn out more trainees regardless of quality and thoroughness of training.

I was striving to give the young pilots training in the skills vital to a combat pilot. I had found a big, vacant area nearby what was a seasonal flood control reservoir that gave winter floods backup space and was not used during the dry season. We sent attendants out to it with cloth panels for targets, and to keep anyone from going into the area.

The training was going great, as our practice range was only a few minutes distant from the field, but the colonel got word of it and put a stop to it. What would happen to his prospects for promotion if some accident should occur? I was disappointed that he refused to stick his neck out a little for those who were soon going to risk their lives for their country.

I felt very defensive of my comrades who were fighting for us overseas. On one occasion a trainee went AWOL and shacked up in a hotel with some wench, and missed several days' training. When we located him and returned him to base, I was so furious I told him if his punishment were left up to me, I would cut off his head.

After Maj. Arvid Olson was transferred and I was advanced to squadron commander, I had the chore of moving the squadron, first to Olympia, Washington, then to Ellensberg, Washington, and then back to Ontario, California. We maintained the West Coast alert, trained hundreds of replacement combat pilots, and made the important moves without serious difficulty. I was promoted to major.

After a year's stateside assignment, in February 1944 I was sent to the European theater. Another officer and I teamed up together for companionship. At Casablanca we boarded a B-26 and landed at Naples, where we saw wrecked airplanes and bomb damage everywhere. When we debarked into a cold, horizontal rain, my friend said, "I will be glad when we get inside, so I can tell whether I'm going to stop shaking or not."

I then reported to the headquarters of the 1st Fighter Group at Foggia, Italy. We were housed in five-man tents, heated by the small, round,

18-inch, cast-iron, oil-burning stoves. Those tents were cold in February. One doesn't normally think of Italy as being on the same latitude as Philadelphia, but it is. The summers are sunny and warm like California, but the winters are damp, rainy, and cold on the boot of Italy.

I was assigned as commander of the 71st Fighter Squadron, but the former commander was still in place. He had a local girlfriend, a nurse, he had fallen for. Although he had finished his required missions, he did not wish to be rotated at the time. This made for an awkward situation for me since the group commander had little command ability and stayed drunk much of the time. He let this situation drag on for weeks with the two commanders in place, using dovetailing the transition as an excuse. As a result I was scheduled to fly tail-end Charlie, also known as Purple Heart Corner by both commanders and pilots, for sixteen missions, probably with the old commander hoping that I would not return, leaving him in command, thus delaying his rotation and possibly gaining another promotion for himself.

When I first reported in, I made the mistake of wearing my combat ribbons, and I was not well accepted. The pilots' attitude seemed to be "Who does this guy think he is, a war hero come to show us how to fight a war?" I should have been able to read people better than that, but petty jealousies seem to magnify in combat units.

This attitude became apparent after I engaged

two Me-109s that were attacking one of the squadron flights. I pursued them, which was a no-no in theater policy, and brought back good strike film, which was ignored by command review. I was further rebuked and relegated to tail-end-Charlie missions ad infinitum. At this point there enters into the battlefield action an age-old problem, that is, poor theater tactics and poor policy orders from headquarters. A stupid policy prevailed at the time. Things weren't going well, but at least I was getting in my missions in the gorgeous fighter plane I had prayed for in the Pacific. Moreover, I was proficient in it and I was especially confident. Oh, if I had only had one in the SWP.

On my arrival in the theater I was vexed at some of the policies, one that involved me particularly. Orders were that the fighters were never to leave the bomber formations they were there to protect. The theater was short fighters, as the Eighth Air Force in England had priority allocation. In the MTO we weren't allowed to go after enemy fighters unless they were attacking.

At a glance this policy appears to be sound. But it was made by a man who did not wear warrior moccasins and did not tread the skyways. What those orders said was that I was to turn away from the enemy now directly in front of my guns and rejoin my unit. I had maneuvered to the tails of the enemy and fired many rounds into the rear plane. It stalled suddenly in flight and I dodged up and over it in pursuit of the other. So by the time I passed over the rear enemy plane, I was aware that I should be rejoining my unit. After a good burst at the fleeing enemy, I pulled up and headed in the direction of Ploesti, with no punishment administered to the remaining fighter.

When in war, nothing is as good as a dead enemy. What the orders should have read was "Leave the bombers only when in hot pursuit." Then there is a good chance of making the quarry a dead enemy. That way, you don't have to worry about him later that day, or the next. That policy gave much comfort to the enemy, giving him confidence that he was safe. All he had to do was to turn away from engagement and hunt for another weak sport. I should have stayed in the SWP! Sadly those orders stood throughout my tour.

After pulling up, a battery of antiaircraft weapons opened up on me, and I got a chance to appreciate what the bomber boys went through on their missions. While twisting and turning to avoid the hostile fire, my mind was ever on the thought that each moment was possibly my last on earth; one hit and the lights could go out.

By the time I had emerged from the cone of fire, I had lost my unit and I returned to base alone. Again I made a mistake by not going to the group commander and explaining the entire episode, but I said nothing. This let my partner commander do so first. By that time it was built into a major crime, and the group commander had to do something about it. At the squadron debriefing, my bed-mate commander publicly denounced the dastardly deed, to the satisfaction of the gathered troops, who still wanted to see the big shot from the SWP and all his DSCs taken down a notch. I was verbally reprimanded by the CO.

Something should be said about the difference in a soldier's attitude and morale when one's own army is on the offensive in a somewhat balanced situation, in contrast to one where defeat comes at every turn, and invasion and capture threaten. With the latter, a soldier's feelings are much like one condemned to die. A fatalism comes over him, and he starts feeling he is to be the next one on the list. He feels no need for any consideration or preparation for this life; thoughts for living are only on a daily basis. The reverse is true where the fighting is equal, or the soldier is well trained. Then he feels it is the other fellow who is going to be killed, that it will not be he. This optimism is also bolstered by good training. If he feels he is well trained, then confidence rises.

Eric Anderson, DSC, an infantry officer who fought from the invasion of Italy to the end of the war, felt he was the finest-trained soldier in the U.S. Army, and though he was in countless battles, he said he never felt any great amount of fear.

When I began my missions in Europe, I felt little fear, whereas, in the SWP, untrained, outnumbered, outclassed in skill and machines, most of the missions were terror.

Jesse Bullock, DSC, infantryman wounded five times in about as many invasions in the Pacific, said of his first invasion in the Aleutians that he was green and poorly trained. There, he was sent out on patrol. He crawled over the tundra, hugging the ground like a lizard. Ahead was a large rock standing several feet above the ground. He crawled up to it and stood up behind it to take a good look at the enemy area. As he stuck his head around the rock, a hairy, unkempt Oriental face looked around the rock at the same level, at the same time. Jesse said the enemy soldier threw his gun six feet into the air and ran like a rabbit. I asked Jesse, "How far did he get, Jesse, before you got him?" Jesse replied that the two were in about the same shape, and so he got away. I said, "You mean, Jesse, that you and the enemy were only a few feet apart?" Jesse said, "A few feet? Hell, I could have kissed him!"

During two years of flying I realized that I would likely be coming up against more well-skilled enemy pilots, and I spent long hours developing my own skills. I found that negative Gs were hard to coordinate. That meant that trying to lead a plane while pulling negative Gs was difficult, so if you are hotly pursued, it makes a good escape maneuver. Push over into negative Gs and jink wildly.

I also found that if you have the advantage, and can dive on your opponent, always convert your speed into altitude by hauling straight up after your dive to a near stall. A second advantage can occur here; turn onto your back so you can survey the battle scene below, given there is no enemy above you. At near-stall speed you can turn your plane on a dime. Push full rudder and your ship will turn 180 degrees in a hundred yards and quickly take the heading you wish. While you hang there, looking straight down, you can wait for the enemy to go in whatever direction he chooses, and when he does, slam full rudder or elevator without snapping. You quickly get to the heading to follow on his tail. At higher speeds the plane will snap on you, and you are out of control for a time. There are volumes to be learned about the tricks to aerial combat, but these are just a couple of lifesavers.

When asked about the fighting ability of the P-38, I thought it was as maneuverable as any I flew. The reason the P-51 racked up many more kills than the P-38 in Europe was that a '38 could not dive, and the German fighters could easily dive away. Compressibility was the problem, and when in a dive, the P-38 went out of control, so it was avoided at all costs. Bailing out was also a hazard with the continuous horizontal stabilizer directly behind the cockpit. It could be done but had to be done right. The extra engine was a beloved gem when flying far at sea or far behind enemy lines. All the other deficiencies became minor in view of those considerations. When I had the opportunity, I sought mock conflict with

P-51s, P-47s, and P-40s, and I never lost a dog-fight with any of them, even though they could all dive away from the P-38.

Other pilots who flew P-51s felt the P-51 was superior. C. E. "Bud" Anderson, author of *To Fly and Fight: Memoirs of a Triple Ace*, had many mock dogfights with P-38s. He says: "I always felt that I was on the winning side flying the P-51." I have several hundred hours in a P-51, and I would choose to fly a P-38 in a dogfight between the two, any day.

Combat meant different things to different people. Some pilots loved to fly so much, I think that they even enjoyed combat. My old friend Gen. Clayton Isaacson had several combat tours; I think mainly because of his love of flying. As a general officer, on his leave time he would fly crop dusters for the fun of flying. Some pilots came to dislike flying; one once said he "would never set foot in another of the goddamn things if he didn't have to." For me, the first few years were thrilling, and new planes like jets were ex-citing; later it just became a job. That is one reason I took early retirement.

As for the misery quotient, in Europe the early-riser missions were the worst. Being awakened for a long mission in a freezing-cold tent, shiv-ering and groping in search of your flight clothes with thoughts of much antiaircraft fire and ban-dits trying to explode you and burn you to death are not of what vacations are made. When scenes are shown today on TV of the agony of the men of the German Sixth Army before Stalingrad, when the Russians captured those poor devils, my memory is jerked back to those early winter-morning missions in Europe. It wasn't that cold, but I know of few things more miserable than awaking at 0400 hours in a black tent in freezing cold and heading out in a snarling airplane, perhaps to meet your maker.

The group commander, Col. Robert Richard, after I had approached him to make a decision with the command problem in the 71st Squadron, advanced me to the position of group operations officer. This was a far more pleasant arrangement, and there I was able to influence policy and tactics. Colonel Richard evidently was beginning to like me, even asking me to live in his chalk-rock house with him and the adjutant.

In an area between Bari and Rome, there is a large underground formation of chalk rock. It is easily cut and worked into construction blocks. It seems that the southern half of Italy is constructed of chalk blocks. There the rock mines are so extensive they are called the catacombs. Many of the air units bought blocks and constructed even large buildings for various purposes. One bomb group built a congregation hall and different units used it for social purposes. In winter the rock structures were warm, and in summer were cool.

The colonel liked to play poker, and almost every night there were poker games. I had played some poker while in the Pacific. There, I had asked my brother to buy for me a book on the game. I had studied it carefully and applied some of the teachings. In Italy I found my opponents to be unschooled and undisciplined, and winning was not difficult if one stuck with basic principles. Of course, I professed to know very little about the game, which was no stretch of the truth. They just knew less. Important examples of those principles were, one, play conservatively, and two, bluff only to build the pot. Have the cards when you bet heavily. With some tact I was cleaning up on the staff, including the CO.

Famed pilot Chuck Yeager once said, when on the subject of recorded aces, something to the effect that some recorded as aces were really not aces, and some nonrecorded were aces. So true. Recording victories is far from being an exact science. Part of that chore became mine after I went from the squadron to ops.

A good example of that was when, on a fighter sweep up the Po valley in Italy once, my flight was attacked by the Yellow Nose boys. This was a famous aggressive German unit of Focke-Wulf 190s that did a lot of damage to our air effort in the MTO.

We broke into a counterattack and we flashed by one another at close range. One came by me within a few feet, then dove straight down toward the earth. My flight leader thought that I had plugged him, and when we landed and were being debriefed, he said, "I saw you get that Focke-Wulf, Jim." I had to say, "No, Stan, I didn't get him. I never even got my sights on him." An opportunist might well have agreed and chalked up a victory to himself, as he had confirmation right there. In the SWP theater there were two pilots, a flight leader and a wing man, who, when separated from others in an action, repeatedly returned with "victories" for each; each confirmed by the other. Other pilots in the same unit began to wonder about their outstanding success. There are cheats in every game.

There was a general policy that the wingman was never to leave his element leader. This is a good policy, as it helps maintain an integral fighting unit, but there are exceptions to this rule that sometimes prove wise. On a mission over Budapest, our flight came up against some Me-109s. They were at about 35,000 feet, where maneuverability is decreased. The friendly flight leader must have been inexperienced at high altitude, for he was losing the turning contest, and the flight of 109s was closing in on our P-38s. Being tail-end Charlie, I was the first in line for execution. Orders or no orders, sometimes one has to act. I jerked combat flaps — 20-degree flaps to decrease turning radius — left the flight, cut across the circle, and closed in on the enemy. When I got close, all the 109s dove away, and I returned to the flight, still wondering if the flight leader would have just sat there in that dumb, shallow turn and gotten us all killed. Back on the ground I said to him, "Man, when you see you are losing out on what you are doing, you have to do something else. Combat flaps, steepen your turn, or something!" As I have said, combat can mesmerize; this may have been an example.

On just about any mission far into enemy territory something would occur to pick up the pace of living. On a mission to bomb the Brenner Pass between Italy and Austria, I was flying an old dog of a plane. Someone must have landed real hard in it. It slopped around in formation and guzzled gas. I was busy as a cat the whole time. Over the target, somehow, the flight leader crossed in front of the bombers and came right over the target just as the antiaircraft fire arrived at our altitude. It was the first time I had come close enough to get bounced around, and I heard several bursts. The question always is, will the next one be it? One bounced me in the air several feet, and my first impression was, yes, this is it! Back on the ground, with some of the boys out counting holes, the squadron leader caught hell. For one small point, I wouldn't have cared if the old dog I was in had been shot down. On the way back, my gas gauges started showing low readings. Halfway back on that mission one tank was dropping toward empty, the other showing ten gallons. I felt like kicking the damned thing. Brenner Pass was known to be loaded with many big ack-ack guns, so the mission was flown at well above 30,000 feet. Halfway back I thought of leaving formation, but the Yellow Nose boys hung out in these parts, and they were a handful enough when you had lots of friends and fuel.

Back over Foggia the left main tank bounced on empty. I had milked all my other tanks dry, my props were clocking around 1700 rpms, mixture was back to just above a cough, and I was picking up the microphone to call the field for emergency, when one or two of the "holed" boys were calling for the same. So I simply had to sweat it out. Now the left main showed zero, the right main showed five gallons. To shorten the story, I landed without incident or accident, but I was so disgusted with the whole mission that I didn't even check to see if it was a faulty gas gauge, a leak, or what, but my comments in the Form I, the flight record, were voluminous.

After moving up to group operations officer, my responsibilities included laying out the missions on the map, the routes, timing rendezvous, briefing the missions, and dozens of chores that fell to no one else. It was most satisfying work for someone eager to pursue the enemy. The commander started giving me more responsibility for tactics, helping to lighten the burden of working under fault-ridden policies and decisions. I felt I was able to save many lives because of my former experience and knowledge. An example of one of those important situations was when we were scheduled to strafe an enemy airfield near the coast where the Germans had moved in some dive-bombers with the capability of hitting nearby troopships. The CO had planned to take the unit in at treetop level to reduce the chances of casualties. This tactic does reduce the casualty rate, but it is also much less effective than coming in at altitude, where there is plenty of time to find your target and line up your sights on it.

I argued that the mission was too important to do half a job — that we should try to eliminate every plane on the field. Colonel Richard said he didn't want to get his boys killed going in where ack-ack had such a clear shot at them. I acknowledged that this was true, but one bomb on an Allied troopship could kill many more men than our whole group comprised. I said, the mothers of the boys who occupied that ship were as dear to them as the mothers of the boys who flew our planes, so it simply boiled down to figures; did we want more casualties, or fewer. The colonel finally let me have my way, but the mission became a sweat because I had my neck out. For that reason I led the mission myself.

On approaching the target field, I could see there were no planes on it; there were no planes to attack, so no attack was made. The luck was mine, for if we had gone in at treetop level, the enemy guns would have had a crack at us. As it was, we avoided it completely and avoided casualties.

One of the next missions I flew was the big bomber raid on Monte Cassino, where we were trying to pulverize the place in order to help our troops take the formidable fortress. The memory is still fresh in my mind of the scene of the concentrated bombing of the hilltop and the monastery, the boiling smoke and dust, the turning of the long bomber train as it swung for home. Another time our unit joined in the air effort against the desperate Anzio beachhead. Many brisk fighter skirmishes occurred over Anzio.

The 1st Fighter Group was embarrassed before the world about this time, when one of the pilots whom I earlier considered a flaphead shot down a German Red Cross hospital plane. I felt like ripping into the pilot, yet it is one of life's situations where little can be done. After it was all over, he would probably have appreciated a beating with a cane.

After the tactical bombing of Anzio and Monte Cassino, the mission again was Ploesti and its rich targets, consisting of nineteen square miles of oil refineries and production facilities. After the war these raids were determined to be the most productive of all Allied bombing efforts. With our repeated raids the Germans were finding it hard to repair and return the wells and refineries to production, and German tanks and personnel carriers were running out of gas on the front lines.

Funny things do happen in combat, but only seldom. One of these rare events occurred high over Ploesti one day when the American formations had climbed as high as they could to avoid the German antiaircraft artillery. The P-38s were at about 35,000 feet. At this altitude, temperatures range about thirty to forty degrees below zero. Some planes were colder than others, and this day I had a cold one. About this time I had to urinate. In the cockpit of a P-38 a relief tube was provided, a funnel-type affair that was a son of a gun to hit under most favorable conditions. Under the conditions at the time, it was almost impossible. About the time I had liberated the diminutive, shivering, shriveled blue organ from its lair in the heavy clothing and started a stream, fast action began on the combat scene. My flight slammed into a steep turn, followed by heavy G forces. By the time the enemy or the Allies escaped, and I was about to level out and check on the damage after the rude shutdown, I found a more diminutive, more shriveled, bluer organ, frozen in a sheet of ice, demanding great care in applying restoration measures. I will spare you the story of the time I had dysentery.

Back in Foggia, things were going well personally for me. Though the pressure had been on me earlier, flying mission after mission as tail-end Charlie over Ploesti, the most heavily defended target over Europe, I complained not a word. In fact, after I gained a position of greater authority, that is, operations officer, where I could assign myself any flight position I wished, including the lead position, I scheduled myself to fly tail end. That was my opportunity to show the 71st Squadron I didn't notice the obvious dig and "punishment" I had received while flying there. Actually, I felt such a release flying over Europe compared to the strain of the early days flying against the Japanese in the Pacific that I was totally confident in any flight position. This was for two or three reasons. By then I had really learned how to fly, I had an airplane that was better than any German fighter plane, and I felt I could handle all but a few of the top German pilots. I did meet one one day, though, that I realized was superior, certainly in knowledge, but that meeting involved only one brief encounter, perhaps fortunately.

A large flight of Messerschmitts attacked our four-ship flights of P-38s over western Romania en route to Ploesti. I turned into them, making it a head-on pass. I carefully leveled my wings as they approached, worked the gun sight into position with just a little elevation, ready to beat him to the trigger. Then I worked the sight down as required elevation receded, so I was beautifully set for him to come into range. At a certain distance he pulled away at just enough angle to go by me unscathed. He knew what that exact distance was! I did not. He knew if he pulled away farther out, I could have jerked my nose into his path; if he had pulled away any later, I may have already killed him. He knew that distance well. I never really learned it. My experiences were too few to have learned that fine point, but that old pilot had had many more. He went on in to make a pass at the bombers I was supposed to be protecting, and I was caught off base.

On 6 June 1944, D-Day, our mission again was Ploesti. I was leading one of the group squadrons with fifteen other P-38s and climbing to rendezvous with a group of B-24s over Yugoslavia. Up ahead, on the same course and the same altitude, two tiny specks appeared. As the distance closed, it was clear that they were single-engine aircraft. I added throttle and moved out ahead of the squadron a few yards, followed by fifteen ships in close formation. We closed the distance rapidly and I took careful aim and fired at the first Me-109. His canopy blew apart, and the rear Me-109 became a sheet of flame. The other enemy pilot started to turn, then flicked into a dive. The enemy pilots had never seen the sixteen planes and presented a stationary target. The sixteen P-38s never broke formation and continued on their way to rendezvous with the B-24s on their way Ploesti.

The victory was not a particularly proud one, as there was no fight to it. On the other hand, when it was learned that this very day was D-Day on the beaches of Normandy, it was gratifying to feel I had done my bit for the cause.

An unhappy episode developed with the recording of this kill. An author once interviewed me with the view toward writing of my experiences. He asked how many victories I had totaled, and I replied eight. Later he called me back and claimed I had misrepresented my victories, that he had checked the records and they showed only seven. I was embarrassed and wrote for the records myself. Sure enough, only seven were recorded. I protested to no avail. I was disgusted.

It certainly did appear that I had laid claim to a victory I did not possess; I felt my reputation was damaged, and it reduced the feeling of contribution on an important day of the war. I wrote the Air Force Historical Records office and asked that a search be made of the issue; result: claim denied.

In 1991, while attending the American Fighter Aces reunion in Arizona, I met Dr. Frank Olynyk, the official recorder of the AFAA,* in the hallway of the hotel. We spoke, and Frank remarked, "I came across one of your victories the other day, Jim." Frank had been reviewing 1st Fighter Group records and had seen it there. I asked if he would send me a copy. I sent the record to the Air Force Historical Review Board, and the victory was again awarded. What had occurred was that the headquarters of the Fifteenth Air Force in Italy had lost all records covering the dates from 3–8 June 1944, but the 71st Squadron still had a duplicate copy. The loss is easy to understand when day laborers who don't speak English are employed to move hundreds of boxes and thousands of pounds of gear in wartime conditions.

Although I was confident of my ability in this beautiful war machine, there were daily reminders of the deadly nature of the job. Twice, before moving out of my five-man tent, all of my companions were lost, and I was alone. Four more

* American Fighter Aces Association.

Mediterranean Theater of Operations

pilots replaced them, but once again I was alone with no one to talk to.

The attrition rate over Ploesti and some of the strafing missions ran high. One of the costlier missions of the 1st Fighter Group occurred on 10 June 1944. The diary of the 71st Squadron is quoted on this mission verbatim:

This is a day we will never forget. Wing [higher headquarters] dreamed up another nightmare and we had to buckle up to sort of endure it. The deal was to send 36 planes from 82nd Group on a dive-bombing raid to Ploesti with 39 ships from the 1st Group as top cover. The 71st put fourteen planes in the air. Sending two fighter groups all the way to Ploesti, alone, attempting to dive-bomb the oil installations with P-38s and a concentration of flak and ground fire un-equaled anyplace else in Europe was a per-fectly outlandish proposition. It proved to be an extremely costly and tragic affair.

The 82d went first, flying on the deck with the bomb loads, hoping by staying low to avoid radar or any spotting by ground ob-servers, while the 1st was supposed to supply protection and cover getting them to the tar-get. Shepherd was leading our squadron whose position was covering the rear of the entire formation. A couple of hours out, get-ting close to the target, with radio silence, the formation somewhat spread out, everybody craning and looking and no one appeared to see the Luftwaffe up in the sun.

Somehow word had been relayed of the formation's direction and the Germans put over 100 airplanes up in the sky awaiting the arrival of our flights of 38s. They came screaming down with the advantage of height and speed, landing smack in the middle of the 71st Squadron, hoping to the pick the rear end of this attacking group and create instant chaos in the process.

On the first break (hard-turning maneuver), Baker got lost and probably got himself shot down. Hisey's wingman came back early of course [probably Turner], and so he was flying Shep's wing. Then three of them jumped these two, shooting up one of Hisey's engines and he called for help. Then he saw three of them coming down on him and told the rest to let go, that he had had it. Hatch got five 190s and one damaged, one probably. Hoenshell got two transports and one F. V. Hoenshell is still missing. No one seems to know what happened except that he might have been that ship on single engine with six 109s on his ass. Fergy and Bridges covered the 82nd into the target and strafed on the way back, landing at Vis [an island in the Adriatic used for emergencies] for gas. Jackson got hit and exploded in mid-air. Potter got shot down. They heard Willie Bro Black screaming as he went in. Janci got it and

246

Smith is missing. All in all, nine men were lost. From our account, we shot down at least 12 German aircraft. The pilots who returned, exhausted, strained, gaunt, and very angry, are dying to get revenge.*

I did not fly this mission. With summer weather coming on, longer missions were planned and flown. In a position to choose my own missions, I chose the longest and the toughest. On one to Hungary we came upon some Me-110 fighters attacking a squadron of B-24s.

I selected one as he dove away on seeing the American fighters. Again the faulty policy of not permitting "in hot pursuit" cost the Allies a victory. I was on the 110's tail and getting hits when I remembered my other incident where the CO had reprimanded me for following the enemy, and I broke away to return to the bombers, with only a "possible."

The war was going fast and furiously. Bomber groups were being added to Gen. Ira Eaker's strategic bombing forces. One of the proudest days of my life was when all the flying units in the theater were held on the ground for a period of two or three days, then assembled for an all-out raid against the oil targets at Ploesti, Romania. On 23 June 1944 all our squadrons, plus spares, were scheduled to protect a B-24 group occupying a link near the center of the great

---

* Two-inch-diameter areas of hair on one returning pilot's head turned snow white that night.

sky-train. I scheduled myself to lead the group. As I circled the lead squadron in wide climbing turns, in order to give the following units opportunity to quickly join up, there were American bomber (some 761 aircraft) and fighter planes as far as the eye could see. It sent chills down the spine to see thousands of American airmen together, ascending into the sky in tightly organized units, advancing on the brutal enemy in defense of freedom and democracy.

The great mass of airplanes snaked across the sky for perhaps 100 miles, and just to see such a sight with units already well out over the Adriatic Sea, yet some still taking off from the many airfields, made me feel proud. I would have enjoyed bagging an enemy that day, but my only chance came when a German fighter swung in on my charges but was shot down by the bombers themselves just when I was about to line him up in my sights. It was a clear day over southern Europe for that mission, and much damage was reported. Six hundred and seven of those bombers reached the target, delivering 1,526 tons of bombs. Twenty big brothers did not return. Back on the ground, the tired crews had a feeling of fulfillment and satisfaction at having participated in dealing a heavy blow to the enemy.

On a fairly short mission into Yugoslavia I discovered my coolant flaps were not functioning. This meant I was probably losing hydraulic fluid. I should have returned to base immediately, but I was leading the squadron and hated to mess up the lead. Probably a more important reason was that I did not want to mar my record of never having flaked out on a mission.

Some pilots have been known to do so for more than one reason, some suspect. One lieutenant at Foggia had been scheduled on twenty-one missions and had completed less than half of these. Command alertness here has to be questioned. So I continued the flight by pumping the coolant flaps open by hand pump every few minutes when the coolant temperature would start to rise.

When I returned to home base, however, I tried to pump the wheels down, but no go. In order to reduce my guilt, I called on the radio to the group engineering officer and asked him to dig out the technical orders and read to me the exact procedures for lowering the landing gear when out of hydraulic pressure. Captain Elfridge Austad did so, and I followed the instructions, but still no wheels. In a further attempt I circled the field and shut down both engines. Figuring to minimize damage to the engines, I feathered both propellers and set up my traffic pattern. On my base leg I cleaned up the cockpit and finished feathering the props. On the final approach I wasn't satisfied with the positions of the dead propellers, concerned that a single vertical blade (three-bladed propeller) would dig into the soil worse than two-angled blades when they hit the ground. I got involved toggling and overshot the field. Now I had to crash-land. I chose a nearby wheat field and settled in on my belly, pranging both propellers and most of the airplane. It was a sorry performance.

About this time the group was designated to get some of the new P-38 10-L0 models. They had arrived in England and had to be flown to Italy. Major Francis "Bucky" Harris, fourteen other pilots, and I were ordered to England to ferry the new planes. Bucky and I caught a B-17 flying up to London. On the bus into London we struck up a conversation with two American nurses. We had much in common with the girls and made dates with them for the evening. My date was really cute; Bucky's wasn't so hot. We took the girls to dinner at the London American Military Officer's Mess. We officers were placed on R&R status by group headquarters. This gave us lodging at a fine hotel in downtown London, chits for the military officer's mess, and other benefits.

We had a fine meal, drinks, dancing, and lovely feminine companionship that we were starved for. After six months of army cots and dirt floors, Spam and bully beef, it was simply one of the greatest evenings of our lives. Vive the world's nurses! Unfortunately the girls were en route to some station and had only two days in London.

We still had another seven or eight days leave remaining. At that time the Allies were on the move in France; Paris had been taken. In the officers mess we two majors struck up a friendship with two B-17 pilots who were also on R&R. One of the bomber pilots said, "Why don't we fly over to Paris?" In one voice we all said, "Amen." That night, two weeks after liberation, we were in Paris.

In a Parisian nightclub, Bucky and I met two young girls. Mine was a pretty brunette, Bucky's wasn't so hot again. The femininity of the Parisian girl is unmatched in the world, or so it seems to me (it may just be the hype and surroundings), but this slender brunette with dark eyes and sheer garments, which she had probably inherited from her aunt and broke out after liberation, was stunning. Both girls were good dancers. It was a gorgeous evening. The girls could speak a few words of English, and the boys were struggling to dredge up some of their college French. The girls' adorable accents and everyone's attempts and bloopers with different languages were a constant source of amusement. There is an old saying, "You don't have to know the language!" It was a most pleasant interlude of socializing with our Allies and seeing the lights of Paris. The next day we rejoined our new friends, the pilots of the B-17, who flew their big bird and us back to England, so Bucky and I had to be content with one gorgeous night in Paris.

Arriving back in London, Bucky and I returned to our triple-A hotel. After catching up on our sleep, we returned to the diggings around the officers' mess. We had tried a meal in a London restaurant and were shocked at the British table fare. Ersatz food sure enough! The sausages were half ground alfalfa. There was a limit of one on the eggs, and chicory was the coffee. We certainly never realized what sacrifices those sturdy British people were undergoing.

From London we pilots were ordered to report to a large depot in Birmingham. While waiting for transportation to arrive, the baleful wail of the famous London air raid sirens split the air. Just then the put-put-put sound of a V-1 rocket reached the streets as one of Hitler's terror weapons streaked overhead. There was a moment's silence, then a loud explosion, then the sounds of ambulance sirens.

On arriving at Birmingham, I took care of some paperwork, and then we were taken to an air base nearby called Mount Farms, where we found our new 10-L0 model P-38s with a three-hundred-gallon auxiliary fuel tank under each wing. During my briefing I cautioned the pilots on fuel management and to take extra care to avoid dropping their external fuel tanks. All aircraft were started successfully all checked in on the R/T, and I took the taxi strip.

Coming up was one of those humiliating times of life; I bumped the tank-eject button and laid two three hundred-gallon fuel tanks right on the taxi strip. All had to wait for the leader to taxi back and have new tanks replaced. Finally, back on the runway, the squadron roared off to traverse the south of England down an airfield near Land's End at the southwestern tip of England, called St. Mawgans. All landed safely and we were put up in a nice hostel near the field. The weather was stormy and we were warned to stay on the ground until it improved.

There was camaraderie in the comfortable British facilities provided by congenial allies. But I was feeling a little sad about life in general. I walked down to the shore and stood on the rocks some fifty or sixty feet above the roaring sea. At times the churning surf would slam against the seawall and shoot up the precipice, and I would have to dodge back to avoid a good wetting with saltwater. The lonely sea reflected my mood. The circling, surging currents of the ocean and the ripping gusts of wind seemed to depict what I could see as a confused world of love and hate, of tenderness and violence, of peace and of terrible war. And I knew I had to reenter the terrible part.

Next morning dawned clear and bright. I rebriefed my pilots; they all got their steeds started and lined up for takeoff. Over the field they joined up like pros, and I set course directly across France with a potent force of new, deadly American-brand fighting machines. Over the English seacoast we rose; next came the English Channel with thoughts of its turbulent history over the centuries. Then came the neat, lush meadows and farms of Normandy with signs of the multiple effects of the war. Farther on we crossed the Rhône River, and ahead loomed the imposing fortress of the Alps of southern France and northern Italy. Off to the left lay the Brenner Pass and memories of being caught there in the heavy antiaircraft artillery barrage. After we crossed the Alps, we dropped down into the upper reaches of the Po River and the hangout of the Yellow Nose boys with their FW-190s. Come-on-up was the emotion at this point of the voyage. But we saw no Focke-Wulfs and the long boot of Italy had to pass beneath before our ferry mission was complete. Soon it was, and we were circling our own field with a satisfied feeling that all our new war babies were safely at home in their nests.

Thinking back on that small segment of the American military forces, the power it represented is amazing. We were all combat-experienced pilots. With the new wing-tip tanks and two three-hundred-gallon belly tanks, we could hit a target one thousand miles away with sixty-four .50-caliber machine guns, which alone could cut an airport to pieces, or each carry two one-thousand-pound bombs that could sink a large ship or decimate a column of troops and light equipment. We had every confidence we could handle any like number of enemy planes on earth, and since we were flying more than one thousand miles over enemy territory, we would have welcomed any such challenge. Of course, we were armed to the teeth with gun switches at the ready.

Those sixteen P-38H 10-LOs, fresh out of their crates, represented millions of dollars in American assets and thousands of hours of toil and support of our fellow citizens. They deserved our careful custody, for they would deliver one of America's heaviest punches, and I had intended to deliver them safe and sound to their destination.

One of the roughest targets in southern Europe was the munitions factory and Messerschmitt plant at Wiener Neustadt, Austria. At the briefing on a mission there, the intelligence officer warned of some six hundred fighters being stationed around the target. As a result, I took the group to a 36,000 foot altitude in order to counter the overwhelming number of fighters. It turned out to be a mistake that I regretted long after. Fighters attacked my charges five or six thousand feet below and shot several down before I could intercept. I was too far away to be effective. Although we did get a couple of the enemy, damage had been done. The recent Ploesti fiasco probably influenced my caution. As an afterward to that mission, I was introduced to a veteran in Petaluma, California, in 1989 at a social function. We talked and learned we had both been in the Fifteenth Air Force in Italy. The man was a bomber pilot, and said that he had been shot down in July 1944 over Wiener Neustadt, Austria. I felt like apologizing to the man, as he said he was shot down in a B-24. We were escorting B-24s that day.

On one of the missions to Ploesti it looked like the long trail of good fortune for me was about to end. The objective was to strafe an active airfield that served as a hive of fighter activity for the defense of the Ploesti complex of oil fields and refineries. I led the 71st Squadron at low level, skimming the power lines, farmhouses, treetops, and mountain passes in an attempt to avoid detection — it was an exercise in futility in my opinion.

This type of mission is one of the most nerve-racking of all. Although Intelligence plots a route to avoid all antiaircraft weaponry, sometimes they miss, and sometimes the enemy moves their location, and you stumble across them, like a foot soldier advancing across a hidden mine field. Also, the pilots have no altitude advantage; it is total disadvantage if enemy fighters catch you coming in. Third, there is danger that results in almost certain death if something goes wrong mechanically, for example, engine or control problems or structurally, that is, plane damage from colliding or striking trees or lines, with no chance to bail out or find a place to force-land. Added to this is the stress of flying formation in air that is almost always rough and bumpy, that jerks you up, down, and sideways while your wingtips are only a few feet away from your companions'. If it is a hot day, cockpit heat can be intense (I would rather fly an ordinary combat mission than fly a peacetime training mission of great duration at low levels), so this mission was tough long before it got tougher.

So far the squadron had flown through five hundred miles of enemy territory without major interference, but that was only so far. My navigation was true and up comes the enemy base, right on target.

When the German lines were shrinking in the east with the Russian advance, in the west with the Allied advance, and in the south with the invasion of southern France, this caused a concentration of German guns. They had been building guns as fast as they could for their expanding fronts and increasing number of targets. Now they were pulling them back into their installations such as airfields, oil refineries, and so on. Even early in the war the Ploesti oil fields had been laced with every type of small, medium, and large antiaircraft gun known to the Germans. Now, in some places, there was hardly room for their placement; some areas looked like cabbage patches from the air.

On this mission we were trying to reduce the air defenses over Ploesti by strafing aircraft and supply sheds on a heavily defended airfield that was not suitable to a low approach, so I pulled up to a couple of thousand feet, then pushed over for a diving attack. As I led the sixteen planes from about two thousand feet, the ground and sky lit up with fire, smoke, and myriad streams of tracers. Someone on my right blew up; someone on my left was hit. I found a good target and gave it the full four .50-caliber and 20mm fire. Suddenly my left engine belched smoke and oil drenched the engine nacelle. I held the trigger down until I swept low over the target, and then chopped the throttle and feathered and cut the switches to try to avoid the expected fire. With full throttle on one engine, the plane yawed dangerously, but by cranking trim I could tell she was straightening up some, and I was slowly acquiring a balance between power and trim and she was becoming a flying machine again. With a careful turn I got her headed back toward Italy instead of Russia.

The six hundred miles home was to be alone, and more thrills were yet to come. Somewhere in eastern Yugoslavia, just skimming the trees, I came across a column of German tanks with their crews lolling on top of their machines. When I opened up with my remaining ammunition, there was a wild scramble. I figured I didn't do much damage except what they had done to themselves in scuffed knees and elbows, and the blow to their dignity. I made it back to Italy and got the faithful machine on the ground in one piece, where she was put back in order to fly another day.

By a flip of the coin, the group and I missed out on a mission that I much wanted. Arrangements had been made through diplomatic and military channels for a number of bomber and fighter units to raid targets in Hungary and Romania, then continue into Russia and land, stay overnight, then refuel and rearm, and return to base for a second raid on the enemy. One P-38 fighter unit was to go. It came down between the 1st FG and 82d FG. The 82d FG won the toss. We talked with some of the 82d FG pilots after the mission, and they said it was most interesting, that things were harsh and stiff in the Russian military. An incident brings this out. Two B-4 bags (personal baggage) were stolen from one of the B-17's flight crew. They reported the theft to the Russian base commander, and to their shock he had the two sentries assigned to guard the American planes shot right there. They decided they would not report any more discrepancies.

Flying in the European theater was different from the Pacific. It was interesting to fight a different enemy, and it was a relief to be able to fight on equal or better terms. But my true love was to avenge the dastardly deeds of the world's most bestial nation, Japan; to kill the troops of a nation that employed terror, torture, and unspeakable cruelty and who had executed my own personal friends in ceremonial acts of murder. My dream had been to fly a P-38 where I had flown the P-39s and P-40s, as had my pilot replacements like Bong, McGuire, and MacDonald, who had less experience than I at the time of arrival of the P-38s in the theater.

Since I fought the Japanese, the Germans, the Italians, the Koreans, and the Chinese, people ask about the differences. There were differences. Basically, I think for a broad answer, the east thinks one way, the west another. In the Far East I was cautious about what to expect, like having a greenhorn in a poker game. In the west it was as if we all were old poker hands. The Japanese taught their pilots that once they latched on to an enemy, their attention did not deviate until the enemy was destroyed. It happens that this was a good policy for bomber and torpedo pilots, but a trap for fighter pilots. During training they made their pilots sit in a barrel for hours and look out the open end in order to impress upon them to concentrate on the target. I considered this dumb, and it helped greenhorn American kids blow them out of the sky when they were concentrating elsewhere with no thought who might be on their tails.

I used to teach my students *never* to maintain concentration on the target for any length of time before checking their tails. It was true; some victories were lost by not concentrating on the target, but we were not willing to exchange an American life for an enemy's. It wasn't easy to slip up on a German pilot. I thought most pilots I had observed cleared their tails (the deadly spot for getting shot down) far too seldom. I learned to fly close formation while looking all over the sky at the same time. This may be due to the experience of flying in Java where the Japanese roamed the skies constantly in search of the dwindling Americans. I kept my neck going 180 degrees to the right and left constantly. It is a pain in the neck (pardon the pun)to have to do it, but it cannot be neglected; it is only your life at stake! Half the fighter-pilot casualties would be alive today had they known of their enemy's approach from the rear. Nearly all pilots that I have observed would fly several moments without clearing their tails, including the Americans, but not the ones I trained.

A friend once told me of being separated from his unit over France. He headed back toward England and saw four P-51s above, all heading home. He added throttle and closed in to fly formation with the other four. After a rather hairy round of combat he was calming down and enjoying the comfort of the company of the four other friendlies, when he came to the realization that the friendlies weren't friendly. They were Me-109s! They never saw him, and needless to say, he eased back on the throttle. I asked him how many of them he got, and he replied that he just kept easing back on the throttle.

America built 99,742 fighter planes during WW II. She lost 25,000 planes over Europe alone. Those 25,000 lost produced 99,000 casualties. If we had been better prepared, we would not have lost half that number. That lack of preparedness was felt in so many ways.

IX

His Life in My Hands

An active career in the military service often makes it harder to live with oneself. When you become a leader of men, especially in combat, your moves, actions, decisions, and policies cost lives or save them. As an element leader (two ships), a squadron, group, or wing leader (one or two hundred ships), your responsibility is there, and you must do your best for your fellow soldiers. Many men whom I have commanded would be with their families today if I had done a better job.

A strafing mission on airfields in northern Italy is another of those instances where conscience dwells with memory. I was flying wingman to the leader of a four-man flight (I often flew missions as wingman though I had the option of the lead). When the squadron came upon the field, my leader was flying some fifty feet above the trees and structures. Since we were over the target, I broke radio silence and called, "Door Knob Two, lower your altitude, you are too high and make an easy target." The pilot may have had an aversion to flying low, and he remained at about the same altitude.

After shooting up the place, including some airplanes, we sped on away from the airfield, but Door Knob Two still flew high above the others.

Presently a fire appeared at the leading edge of his right wing. It was a small fire, and at first I hoped it might go out, but as we climbed away from the target, I, only a few feet away, could see that it was increasing. At first we sweated gaining enough altitude for the pilot to bail out. Pulling away from the target near the city of Verona, the fire increased and was soon spouting flame like a geyser. Now we were over Venice, climbing hard to avoid small-arms fire, and the flame grew larger. I was holding my breath, feeling that the bird was either going to blow up or the wing come off. I kept expecting the pilot to bail out, for the fire had burned fiercely for a period of six or eight minutes. It finally dawned on me that he was probably mesmerized. I picked up the mike to call and tell him to bail out. At the instant I pressed the button, the right wing broke off and the plane went into a spin. I yelled, "Bail out, bail out!"

An airplane that loses a wing starts spinning and is hard to get out of. A short distance above the surface of the sea a parachute showed. Bernie had been able to free himself, and there was hope he would live. The plane struck the water just off the shoreline, and we all searched diligently for a bobbing head and a spreading white chute. Then, sadly, came the message: a spreading blossom of scarlet red against an ocean of blue. Another mother of the world would grieve tonight. War had taken her son.

At the poker table one night, Colonel Richard

was having his drinks and grew boastful. He was saying how the older classes of pilots went through much more thorough training, adding that they could fly rings around the present-day trainees. To counter, I made the remark that some of our boys were pretty good pilots. The colonel took umbrage at the remark and said that he could take me any day. He said he would have Engineering set out two ships so he could prove it the following morning.

Now, Colonel Richard was not a big person characterwise. I hated to grapple with my CO when I knew I could not gain by showing him up, but I couldn't just chicken out, the match was on.

In the pilot replacement training squadron that I commanded for a year in 1943, I scheduled many plane-to-plane simulated combat missions as I tried to reduce buck fever in my trainees on their first encounters in combat. As a result, I did a lot of it myself and really learned how to fly fighter plane versus fighter plane; in fact, I originated a move or two for myself.

When the colonel and I took off for the joust, we agreed to meet at twelve thousand feet at the same level, going in opposite directions, passing, and then the contest was on. When we met I wanted to be going as fast as possible. It did not appear that he was. As we passed, I pulled back hard on the stick and zoomed straight up as far as that P-38 would go. Colonel Richard did a left turn, then started a climb, seeing I was above him. At this point I was probably a thousand feet above and had rolled over on my back, watching which way he was going to go. I was just above stall speed and hanging there until he cranked in more turn, heading for my tail. I slammed full rudder. This cannot be done at higher speeds or your plane will snap, and you lose control temporarily. My plane swapped ends to the right, and I was now going in his direction. I dropped behind him and cut off his hard turn to the right, and I came out right on his tail. He did a number of maneuvers in many directions, loops, split Ss, steep turns, and others, to absolutely no avail. I felt bad riding him so mercilessly.

I soon ceased my pursuit and then made matters worse. I told him to get on my tail and see if he could stay there. His performance was so pitiful that I think I would have washed him out of flying school. Maybe I didn't blame him so much for choosing short missions when he flew with the group, a fact he was accused of. Richard couldn't even stay on my tail and I didn't do many wild aerobatics. Of course, he was forty-two, out of shape, puffy, and not spirited. I was twenty-six and in good shape. It was not a fair match, but I didn't issue the challenge. After leaving the colonel's tail again, I flew out to the side, then back, and joined formation on his wing. Back at base, he said he would have cleaned my plow fifteen years ago.

A day or two later Richard was still chafing over our flight. He had had a few drinks and was saying that I might have outmaneuvered him, but he, Richard, could throw me in a wrestling match. It seemed he had done some wrestling in college. Oh, me, I thought, spare me. This is not the course one wants to take with his commanding officer. But, again, I was caught up in the circumstances. So there was a wrestling match.

Richard was a husky man, but whiskey and cigarettes took a toll. He could probably have outwrestled me in his youth, but I refused to fake the match and threw him to the ground. Again Richard was embarrassed. It had been rumored I was in for a promotion, but it was now off. It had been a trap I was unable to escape. A few weeks later the adjutant told me that the colonel had put me in for promotion twice in the last month but had jerked them back both times. I had no idea why!

In midsummer the long missions continued. One day the Fifteenth Air Force put on what must have been the longest mission of the war for fighters before the B-29s came along. The media has spoken about the Yamamoto mission being *the longest* of missions; it was a long, hard, low-level (all ground-hugging flights are hard) mission, but not much longer than half the mission to Krakow, Poland. When I stretched the mission cord across the map that morning in the briefing room, the simultaneous gasp was heard on the flight line two hundred yards away — seven hundred miles! The spiders on their webs in the corners of the old, white chalk Italian farmhouse we used for group operations fled for the safety of the cracks in the plaster. We thought Ploesti was a tailbone killer, but this would be more than one hundred miles farther. To fight through to Krakow over hundreds of German airfields, and thousands of home-based fighters, and thousands of antiaircraft guns would be a formidable mission. It was our way of saying, "Okay. You asked for this. Now come up and fight."

The weather was clear, and the great skein of bombers climbed high. Like flocks of mixing waterfowl, the following flights of bombers and fighters etched the skyline as far as the human eye could see. The lead crews would be bucking the first slashing attacks of the defenders of *DER VATERLAND*. Like on those deep American bomber raids on Germany out of England, the blood would soon be flowing.

The bombers climbed as high as they could. They were in rarefied air and on oxygen hour after hour, and the gunners and fighters of the home team gave as good as they were getting. It was an open challenge to anyone who "thinks he can stop us; let him try; we're giving you all day to do it."

And it was all day. In early morning the battles began in earnest. They extended over hundreds of miles. Had it been an air show, and the route been straightened out, half the population of the United States could have watched, as it would have stretched that far.

As for me, I did little fighting. After turning off the target, my turbo-supercharger warning light went on. I banged on the instrument panel, but the light persisted. I was flying tail-end Charlie and had to throttle back or risk the danger of killing myself. A turbo-supercharger is a gadget something like a water pump that pumps added air into the air intake of the engine. Like a water pump, metal cups spin at high speed, and if abnormal conditions exist, these parts can fly apart like shrapnel and can be as deadly as bullets. This meant I would not be able to keep up in formation. I had to drop back and soon found myself alone with seven hundred miles of enemy territory between me and home. A short time off the target a flight of five Me-109s passed right beneath me. I'm sure they figured I was wounded, but they were looking for bigger game and I couldn't do anything about it. Those buzzards still had on their belly tanks! On impulse, I almost swung down on them, but decided not to do so considering the shape I was in. One additional concern was that I didn't want to lose my precious altitude; it gave me some security from the fighters and big guns. I could have dropped down and joined a formation of bombers for protection, but that seemed kind of degrading. They were slow as the seven-year itch, and actually, I rather enjoyed being on top of the world, tooling along at thirty-seven thousand feet, watching a world busy at war. Over on the right two bombers were trying to fly formation.

One had two propellers feathered, the other an engine smoking slightly, and obviously having trouble. Up ahead about eleven o'clock there was a sudden flash, and pieces of a B-24 flipped in crazy circles, and a parachute blossomed among them, all headed for Poland. I wondered if the man were alive, or had his chute been blown open in the explosion. Behind at the eight o'clock position a string of Focke-Wulfs were making passes on a group of B-17s.

At one point, a strange volley of shells exploded above me, and what looked like white sheets of cloth came out of them and started spiraling toward earth. I wondered if the Nazis had invented some terror weapon to mimic half-opened parachutes falling to earth. I later reported this to G-2 as something "unusual or a first reporting."

Farther along on the return leg, a single Me-109 passed quartering beneath me, very close. He still had his belly tank on, and this was too much for me. I flipped the P-38 on its side to begin a dive, but the little bastard dropped his tank and did a split S, so I preserved my altitude. Another six hundred miles of smoking bombers, of observed executions of fellow fliers in crippled birds, and the continental mass of Europe passed beneath. Then the Adriatic came into view with the Alps to the west. The Alps looked diminished and unusually unimposing because of my altitude. Over the Adriatic I started my letdown. For one thing, my oxygen gauge was reading close to zero. Hurrying down, I could see straggling single bombers making desperate attempts to reach the island of Vis, the only airfield north of the battle line, still well south of the valley of the Po.

Before it was over, another wrenching event occurred: A wounded B-24, with two props feathered and one engine smoking, was trying to reach a tiny vineyard on the coast. It looked like he was too low to make it, but, what a pilot! He put her down in the first thirty feet of available soil. Grape stakes went flying, but she didn't catch on fire and stopped rolling at the end of the vineyard. Grateful airmen emerged from the battered bird, doubtless to kiss the ground they walked on. Maybe they kissed the pilot, too. A magnificent job of flying!

The scenario of war reeled on. Ploesti was proving a double-tough nut to crack. Early in the war Germany realized the vital importance of the Romanian oil fields to her war effort. Consequently, she placed one of her brightest, most patriotic officers in charge of its protection. He was an aging veteran of WW I, Gen. Alfred Gerstenberg, a soldier of vast combat experience who understood the problems of logistics, supply, and air defense. As a German who had lost one war, he was determined she would not lose another. Immediately upon his assignment he set to work like a beaver installing Europe's most formidable defenses. He and his troops worked night and day in a rush order to guard the gigantic oil complex of Ploesti that comprised

Europe's most productive petroleum assets. They were composed of thousands of oil wells, vast tank farms, acres and acres of huge refineries, and soon after the general's arrival, far-flung fields of antiaircraft defenses. Intelligence was reporting one thousand antiaircraft guns as early as 1943. More aircraft were shot down over Ploesti than any target in the world. The extended approaches, the outer circles, the inner circles, and the critical, intricate heart of the target received Germany's finest defensive weapons and its highest priority. The beaver's dam was taking shape. The wily old fox even hit upon the idea of building a false set of refineries, tank farms, and oil wells that gave a fifty-fifty chance that air raiders would strike at the decoy instead of the precious real thing. If he could throw up so much gunfire and such a swarm of fighters and set fire to thousands of smoke pots to blanket the target, he might create enough confusion to get his enemy to waste bombs and bombers on the papier-mâché fake refineries.

Sadly, for America, like the Desert Fox, this soldier belonged to the enemy ranks. And *his* enemy did just that: We did waste our bombs on his decoys.

On one of America's first raids on Ploesti, 178 B-24 bombers, on 1 August 1943 were assembled in North Africa. They flew low level, only a few hundred feet high, in a daring and risky attempt to knock out oil production. Fifty-four of those bombers were lost in a blood-smeared fiasco, much of which struck the decoy instead of the refineries, and the damage to the real target was quickly repaired. Casualties on that raid totaled 532 killed, wounded, or captured.[*] Figures such as these caused America's air arm to suffer more casualties than either the army or navy in WW II, and Ploesti contributed her thousands. A total of 59,800 American airmen attacked Ploesti during the war; 2,432 were lost. It was the third most heavily defended target in Europe.[**]

Along with guns of every caliber, Ploesti got high priority on fighter planes. Eric Hartmann, Germany's leading fighter ace, shot down seven American P-51 fighters in one day there. As a result of the intricate defenses, Ploesti proved to be one of the toughest and most important targets of the war. More lives were lost, more bomb tonnage expended, and more aircraft lost there than on any other target, yet it dealt Hitler his hardest blow. As soon as damage was produced, the Germans would be back with thousands of troops and slave laborers repairing the breaks. They fought like tigers, they worked like beavers, and the carnage of war marched on.

On one mission, a swirling mass of fighting was going in all directions. The squadron was all split up, and I found myself alone. I spotted an Me-109 below me that had set up an approach

[*] Dere and Foot, *The Oxford Companion to World War II*, Oxford University Press, 1995, p. 890.
[**] Figures quoted from *Air Force Spoken Here*, Adler and Adler, Bethesda, Md., 1986, p. 386.

on a B-17 already in trouble. At this point there were two choices a fighter pilot could make. One, he could turn, fly back to the rear of the enemy, then turn and approach from the rear and below the level of flight, which is the fighter's blind spot, or he could dive on him in full view and drive him off. In this case there was no time to execute a maneuver to the enemy's rear, for the risk was too great that the 109 would get to the B-17. I dove on the Messerschmitt, which did a split S and dove straight down. I tried to follow, as I was closing the distance, but I felt my ship start a nibbling at the controls. This was that critical warning a P-38 gives as it is about to enter that death trap, compressibility. I eased the twin-tailed craft upward and thus lost a possible victory for the Allies. Later, the Lockheed Company designed dive brakes to correct this problem.

Many pilots lost their lives to the phenomenon of compressibility. It seems that when an object reaches a velocity of about 740 miles per hour in the air at sea level, it creates a shock wave. This is at the speed of sound, and for a long time was a mystery that killed many airmen and baffled scientists who struggled with the barrier it posed. It was this threat that was solved by the brave and daring feat of flying done by Charles Yeager in the X-1 that broke the "sound barrier."

Today, of course, our faster planes, even fast transports, exceed the speed of sound. The problem was whipped by adjusting the design of the craft for penetrating the barrier — facts that were not known when the P-38 was designed.

In both theaters of war, more pilots were lost from accidents and weather than to combat, by a ratio of more than 2:1. On one mission, performed by the 1st Fighter Group as a fighter sweep and challenge to Germany's elite Focke-Wulf units in the Udine area of northern Italy, my squadron was returning in threatening weather.

A strong front had built in behind the flight, and as the leader approached the boiling air mass, he misjudged its height, and the entire flight of thirteen remaining planes was caught in the turbulent, surging front. I was flight leader of the left rear flight of four. This meant there were two planes on my left, one on my right, four directly in front, and eight more on my right and right front. Updrafts and downdrafts threw the planes around like leaves. Unfortunately, the formation was in a steep bank as it entered the clouds. Midair collisions were a grave threat, and may have, in fact, occurred.

There is a serious problem that can rear its ugly head in the pilotage of aircraft. An airplane can be flown by visual reference to the ground, the horizon, and other surroundings. It also can be flown by reference to blind-flying instruments such as airspeed indicator, gyroscopic instruments, and others in the craft. This can be done in solid cloud cover or in the black of night. But when flying visually, and suddenly one has to go on instruments, the transition can be hazardous.

One of the more serious problems at that time is vertigo, the sensation of whirling about sickeningly. Coordinating the indication of the various instruments that tell you if you are diving, climbing, turning, on your back, or what, and doing it instantly in order to save your life, is stress in the extreme.

It was fortunate that I had had a previous helpful seasoning with this taxing experience. In 1943, while stationed in Washington State, I took off on a flight to attain my monthly night-flying requirement of four hours. All towns and homes in the area were on blackout alert. There was no moon and the sky was overcast. The runway was dimly lit. After the plane passed the end of the runway lights and was airborne, there was nothing to be seen. Total pitch blackness, no horizon, nothing was present for visual flying. I quickly forced myself to focus on the instruments, and from the favorable beginnings of straight and near-level flight I was able to avoid striking the ground, trees, or structures, kept from stalling at low level, and successfully converted to instrument flying for the rest of the flight. Any sort of struggle or bobble with loss of altitude would have meant sure death by my crashing into the big timber country of the state of Washington that night back in 1943.

Now, finding myself in dense clouds with no visual reference, and with my instruments spinning erratically, I had the same feeling of desperation. All other planes were lost from sight and were, of course, involved in their own struggle to right themselves and save their own lives. Some pilots spun down out of control but were able to recover before they hit the ground. Some came out from the edge of the clouds upside down, while others were in odd positions that they recovered from. One bailed out to become a prisoner of war and three crashed to their death. I came out on one edge of the cloud mass without major gymnastics, set course, and landed at home. There the waiting and sweating began. Some of the planes landed with stress damage; for four the waiting went on.

Some chores of the senior staff officer seemed worse than the stress of combat itself. Once, during the invasion of southern France, when the group was operating off a dirt strip bulldozed out of rough, hilly brush country, a rush order was issued to the unit late in the day. I took off with one squadron immediately to answer the call of a ground controller to intercept some Junkers 88 bombers that were bombing our troops and equipment along the front lines. On reaching the area, the controller vectored the squadron to a sector at very low altitude. By now it was late dusk. Too many instances of mistaken identification occurred during the war with disastrous results, where our own troops and guns fired on friendly aircraft. So I circled the action at a safe distance, hoping to catch the Germans coming off the target, but refused to take my men in low where trigger-happy gunners, often untrained in aircraft recognition, were spoiling to catch an "airplane" in their sights. In all likelihood the enemy would have been there and gone, and the P-38s would have become the targets when they appeared on the scene.

On returning to the narrow little strip the bulldozers had cut in the thick brush, I got down all right as leader, although it was a pitch-black night and the runway lighting kit had gaps in it. Unfortunately, the number three man had landing gear trouble and cracked up in the middle of the runway. Now we had real trouble. No other fields were available nearer than Sardinia or the Italian mainland, and there was not enough fuel to get to either place. There were twelve planes circling in the dark trying to land on a narrow strip blocked by a downed aircraft. In such a case, an operations officer can go off his rocker.

A mad scramble was made to find the bulldozer and its operator and get the pancaked P-38 shoved off the runway. Before this was accomplished, pilots were bailing out, landing in the small trees and brush in the surrounding hills. Astonishingly, no pilots were killed, but seven P-38s were lost because their fuel ran out before the runway was cleared.

The next few days were spent pulling P-38s out of the hills into a boneyard near the strip. Parts are always a problem in any overseas operation, causing defective planes to sit on the ground out of the fight. A good maintenance officer is always looking for a source of extra parts, and those cracked aircraft represented a gold mine of engine and airframe parts he could horde for months to come.

Missions came thick and fast in late July 1944 during and after the invasion of southern France. There were troops to support, bridges to be blown, counterforces to interdict, counter air to dispose of. On the second day I was leading a flight of eight P-38s on a mission to bomb a road bridge over a canyon. I was searching with my map on my lap, when Capt. Tom Maloney, leader of the second flight of four planes, called out an attack by seven Me-109s that were diving on us. I turned to meet them head-on, then cranked back hard to the right, putting the friendlies onto the tail of the bandits. Some of these continued the dive, while others turned to fight, finding quickly that they were now the targets. I straightened for a moment for the flight to release bombs, then followed one of the Germans; Tom followed another. My target appeared to be smoking and the pilot bailed out. I turned to pursue another, which dove for the chasmlike walls of the Argens River near the Grand Canyon du Verdon, a dramatically rugged area of southern France. My P-38 was overtaking the Messerschmitt as we descended into a great canyon with walls towering on both sides. Just behind the first plane, two more Me-109s flashed by just in front of me, both in easy range, but the luck was too good to be true, for a fourth fighter appeared three hundred yards to the right of the flight of three. The fourth enemy fighter then pulled to my right to fall in behind me, making me a target. The two nearest bandits seemed unaware of my presence, and continued straight ahead, a perfect target of two. I hoped I could shoot down the two enemy dead ahead before the one to the rear was able to shoot me down. I was centering my circle and dot sight on one of the planes ahead, when I decided to double-check my enemy to the rear. In the rear-view mirror I saw the pilot begin firing. Damn! With three fine targets off my nose, I was forced to abandon my pursuit. I jerked back on the wheel — the P-38 has a wheel for control instead of a stick — and my plane shot straight up alongside the massive canyon walls into a loop. I would try to outmaneuver this one bandit and get one at least. As I topped the loop, I could see a fifth plane, a P-38, behind the 109, and, it, too, was firing. In an instant the enemy was on fire, and as I continued the downside of my loop, and pulled out between the canyon walls, the German plane crashed against the stone walls in a fiery end.

Memories such as those of the smoking parts of the plane, engine, propeller blades, wheels, wingtips, perhaps arms and legs, emerging from the fiery splash, and bounding down the walls of the canyon, will fade only when life does. One carries them to his grave. On the mission Tom was credited with two, Lt. Robert Longworth, one, and Maj. Jim Morehead, zero!

In this brief combat action, reactions came into play that can be explained. During the war the British conducted a study on the fighter pilot in combat. The study found that on the first few missions the average pilot was worth little or nothing. The trauma and the paralyzing fear of being placed in the line of fire of machine guns tends to mesmerize the pilot. Eric Hartmann, Germany's leading fighter ace, flew ninety missions before he had his first victory. On his first mission he broke away from his leader, got lost from his flight, and returned to base alone.

The excessive surge of adrenaline, caused by the confrontation of the human body to the oppressive presence of danger or other unexpected or surprise encounters is difficult to control. On occasions where pilots were present during violent combat engagements, there were gaps in their memory, and they would ask their comrades what took place at the time.

In the Pacific, early in the air war, where death was likely in the one-sided Allied battles with the Japanese, in the Java and Sumatra campaigns, mental blackouts were common.[*] A wingman once asked me which of us had made the initial attack in one particular engagement. On another occasion, a pilot estimated there were fifty enemy aircraft opposing us, when it was closer to five.

In a vigorous dogfight I completely misidenti-

---

[*] *Bloody Shambles*, Vol. II, chapters 2 to 5.

fied a German fighter one time, believing it to be an American P-51. With this mental/visual deception being a fact of life, perhaps judgment should be eased in cases where friends are sometimes fired upon in the belief they are foes.

Our next mission was to bomb and strafe the marshaling yards at Lyon, France. We worked over a roundhouse full of locomotives, and then a truck convoy on the way back. It was a most satisfying mission, as I got to rake a whole roundhouse full of locomotives all gathered in a bunch; less satisfying, though, since most were not fired up, and no explosions occurred. I bet they had a lot of repair work, though, tracing and fixing all those bullet holes. On the way home we caught a truck convoy on the road where I strafed along the ditch banks where the drivers and troops usually ran. They figured one soldier casualty counts for many vehicles in damage value, so I always tried to bag a few casualties by strafing ditches, although I guess the men on the ground felt like that was playing dirty pool.

These missions were dangerous, and we often lost men, but they were satisfying at the same time. You could see exactly what you were accomplishing, whereas, on bombing raids, we seldom saw much of the results.

On Corsica I got a chance to enjoy one of my favorite sports, wing shooting. Major Francis "Bucky" Harris, commander of the "Hat in the Ring" squadron, and Colonel Richard, group commander, checked out twelve-gauge skeet guns and we walked out into the hills of the Corsican countryside to hunt the famous red-legged partridge of Europe that lived in the vast, brushy habitat there. Having been hunted for centuries, the bird is difficult quarry. We bagged a few of the big partridges that weigh about a pound and a half each. They flush with tremendous speed, and cut rapidly one way or another, or dive behind a tree or obstruction, thus making a sporting target. They have beautiful white meat and large breasts and plump legs. We took them to camp, cleaned them in water from a small trout stream that ran beside the bivouac area, and later I fried them in butter borrowed from the mess. Most of the birds were young birds just maturing and they were delicious. They fried up brown with a condensed milk and flour batter. Colonel Richard and Bucky said it was the best meal they had had since arriving in Europe.

It was a blistering hot day and we returned to camp about noon. As we approached the stream I placed my billfold on the ground with my gun and walked into the stream with all my clothes on. I walked on in until I was completely under, to the surprise of Bucky and Colonel Richard. Then I splashed some water on them and they ran.

On the hunt we came across two grave sites with wooden crosses at their heads. On the top of each vertical cross arm was a Nazi helmet. They were evidence of the campaign on Corsica that freed the island, providing the base for our flying operations. I wondered just how many American boys' lives were required to put the two Germans in their graves. My thoughts ran to the scourge of the human race: war itself. Now two German mothers, who had suffered the pain of childbirth, who had suckled those babies at their breasts, had changed a thousand diapers for each, had taught them to talk, to run and play, grieved. They had provided their food and clothing, training and schooling, had loved them. They would remember a thousand intimate incidents normal to parenthood; they would forever remember.

My own mother, when speaking about the loss of one of her sons, once said:

> The loss of one's child is the worst loss of all. Fathers, mothers, sisters, brothers, friends; the loss of none is more wrenching than the loss of a child, for a thousand intimate, endearing memories, from babyhood to boyhood, to maturity, lingers on in the mind.

Runway lighting was a persistent problem on the narrow dirt strip on Corsica, so Colonel Richard ordered more equipment. A B-17 loaded with several thousand yards of runway lighting cord came in to land at the strip and discharge the material. Bucky and I were watching the big plane as it descended on the final approach leg.

Suddenly the tail dropped, the nose lurched upward, and the big ship stalled and crashed. In seconds it was a burning inferno. No firefighting equipment was available at the strip, and soon all that was left was a pile of ashes and nine, gleaming, ivorylike rounded objects the size of footballs, shining through the ashes; human skulls. Of the nine crewmen and passengers, there were no survivors.

Weight and balance specifications had not become widespread regulations as yet, and the young lads who crewed the big bomber were not aware of the great danger of loading the airplane tail-heavy. They had loaded thousands of feet of lighting wire in the rear of the ship, making it tail-heavy. As they slowed the plane on the final approach, the tail dropped, the plane stalled from about fifty feet, and crashed, and all were burned to death. Speaking of war mothers, here were nine more to grieve.

On one mission out of Corsica, the commanding officer was the leader. It was a seek-and-destroy mission at low level, where targets of opportunity, such as locomotives, truck convoys supporting the enemy front lines, and the like, were sought to strafe and disrupt. We were flying in a long valley in southeastern France and the northwestern corner of Italy, surrounded by the snow-covered Alps that loomed far above. I was leading the right front four of the box formation, while Colonel Richard led the left front four-ship flight as well as the squadron. I saw a German staff car speeding down a deserted highway, reported it to the colonel, and asked and received permission to drop down and strafe it. I descended in a wide circle and approached the front of the vehicle from straight down the road ahead. In the P-38 fighter, with two engines with counter-rotating propellers, there is little or no yaw. Yaw is the ever-changing effect of the torque of the engine on the craft as the plane changes speeds. In the P-38, this phenomenon is eliminated. It was late afternoon, the air was calm, and the area was shaded by the towering mountains. I placed the sight receptacle on the car's windshield and fired. When 20mm cannon shells and fire from four .50-caliber machine guns strike glass, it just seems to melt. The windshield evaporated and the car jerked to the right and plunged into the right-hand bar ditch; it lay smoking with no sign of life emerging from the wreck. Shady, no wind conditions make for good air-to-ground gunnery, and I don't think a single bullet missed the vehicle out of a burst of sixty or eighty. I hoped that a couple of big-shot Nazi generals were aboard the car.

I hesitate to tell the rest of the story, but Colonel Richard, feeling eager after my pass on the staff car, was anxious to find a target. Farther along we came across a horse pulling a cart. Richard said he was going to go down and get it. It was one of those times when I wished I had spoken up, but I didn't, and I have regretted it ever since. Richard peeled down on the target, fired, and left a crumpled horse cart and a struggling, wounded horse. I looked no farther, as there was nothing to be gained, but the earlier feeling of satisfaction of service and accomplishment was lost.

Strafing and dive-bombing missions were the steady menu at this stage of the invasion. Our troops were throwing back the Nazis and the front line was moving toward Germany. It is interesting why America was able to enter the war well behind and prevail over advanced military experts. Reading Audie Murphy's moving book *To Hell and Back* will tell you something about why the Americans won the war. It wasn't won with luck, or because God watches over the naive and the Americans; it certainly wasn't superior arms, as the Germans seemed ever ahead of us on arms.

World War II in Europe was won by young men from a toughened generation who possessed the mettle to face the hell of a struggle with a superior enemy, just as the early struggle in the Pacific was won, where the advantages were with the enemy to an even greater degree. To preserve her freedom, America had to lean on the bloody backs of those young men to whom she should forever be grateful. Her failures, which she should resolve never to repeat, thrust those young men into the maw of the grinding machinery of war, unprepared. Like that unforgettable unit leader, Lt. Comdr. Wade McClusky, at the battle of Midway, while still searching hundreds of miles out in an empty sea, running beyond his fuel supply, who bore on in the face of cries of desperation from his wingmen. He found the enemy and did his heroic work. It is a peculiarity of human nature that a man like a McClusky or a Foss has never been honored as much by his country as one who played ball for 3,031 consecutive days; repeat *played*. Many fail to recognize the significance of that grit, its effect on the war, and the lives it saved.

On a mission to dive-bomb a bridge somewhere north of Marseille, I located the span that had no apparent flak defenses. I yawed my rudders back and forth, which is the standard signal for going into string formation, peeled into a dive on the bridge, and missed. On the way back I was busy wording excuses such as: I didn't know just how low I could go before being hit by my own shrapnel from the bomb, or that awful draft out of the canyon bounced me off target, or I felt I should leave a target for "you guys to aim at." None of them sold. One pilot did wipe out the bridge.

The invasion of southern France on 15 August 1944 was highly successful, and soon the Allied armies were striking deep into the country. The need was pressing for fighter escort for the strategic targets that were being attacked by the Fifteenth Air Force deeper and deeper into enemy territory. The group returned to Foggia.

Flying a P-38 in the war was a most interesting assignment, for its versatility gave it a wide range of missions and targets. For example, the record of the 71st Fighter Squadron, 1st Fighter Group, January to June 1944, p. 190 reads:

The range of the P-38 and the nature of the war spread the squadron fighter activity over an amazing range of territory. Between the stinking squalls of winter, and the elusive sun, our pilots went to Wiener Neustadt, Ragensberg, Klagenfurt, Steyr, Yugoslavia, among other places. In March, still playing cat and mouse with the sun, trips went to Florence, Toulon, Monte Cassino, Vienna, Venice, Klagenfurt, Yugoslavia, Verona, Steyr, Verona, Sofia.

Again:

They all came back like a bunch of kids today. A fighter sweep and though they missed the target and goofed up the mission, it was a raving success. The object was to hit some airdromes near Venice and get the 109s as they were coming off the ground, only they missed the right airdrome and hit another, shooting the hell out of it and strafing a train, a seaplane base, a road and, in general, anything that came into sight or anything that moved or looked shootable. And everyone got back. That sure builds the morale, a couple of deals like that and they sure seem to have a great time on a show like that.

Again:

The target was Ploesti today and it seems to have gone off okay with none of our pilots getting hurt. They were jumped by 109s, but successfully drove them off.

One of the first missions scheduled after the tactical workout of Corsica was escorting the heavies to one of Germany's most defended cities, Munich, site of Adolf Hitler's infamous "Putsch."

On penetration, I took the group high so as to hold a position of advantage over the hundreds of defending fighters en route. Very high and climbing, cracking cold and anxious, I checked my oxygen gauge. At the instant I looked down at it, it was racing backward and coming up on zero. I quickly called Red Dog leader (squadron commander of 27th Squadron) and asked him to take over the lead. I then peeled out of formation and headed down for breathable atmosphere, for at a thirty-five-thousand-foot altitude, the human body expires in about one minute.

The group policy was, when deep in enemy territory, two pilots were to return; one was to escort the other back to friendly skies. I vehemently disagreed with that order, because there were always wounded bombers aplenty with ten-man crews to escort and help, and they needed protection a lot more than a sick or wounded fighter plane carrying only one American soldier.

So I fudged on the policy, as we had not reached the target yet, and I returned alone. It takes a lot of time, money, planning, and effort to put a military aircraft over a target. Since I was there, I felt it was useless to return to base without accomplishing anything, so I dropped down on an industrial-looking town and strafed some important-looking buildings, continuing down the main street, firing bursts to terrorize the place, and to let the people know they had a war on their hands.

I thought it was a shame to haul all that ammunition home, so I rampaged across the countryside, shooting everything that seemed to have military significance. It was fun letting the German homeland know that it was a fight they were in, but I kept a sharp eye out for interceptors, who I knew would have loved to gang up on me. After a time, the blue of the Adriatic Sea came into view, but not before my gas gauges started showing low readings.

At the regular briefings I conducted daily, I explained the availability of the small island of Vis, in the upper Adriatic, off the coast of Yugoslavia. Now, after roaming southern Germany, Austria, and northern Italy at low level, I decided to use its availability to land and refuel. This would give my briefings a more personal touch too. So I set the P-38 down on the red dirt strip, then taxied along behind a jeep and into a gassing revetment. As the crew finished gassing, a siren sounded. As I looked up, I saw a string of bombers, almost to the horizon, limping into emergency landings on the island. I had never before been exposed to such carnage. I was soon to be sorry I had chosen this plan. Burning airplanes, crashing airplanes, skidding airplanes, cartwheeling airplanes, were short of the runway, long off the runway, all over the runway. Ambulances were dashing here and there. Bulldozers were busy pushing airplanes off the runway. Fire trucks were spraying, blood was running out of rolling aircraft, and inside some of those planes it looked like a butchering pen. Medics removing dead and dying men somehow kept their cool and made order out of it all. They deserved medals. I walked to my plane and climbed in, hoping to catch the first lull in a maelstrom of wounded birds, fluttering in to bring their sad cargo to earth, some for their last flight.

Waiting at the end of the landing strip, I feared one of the disabled bombers would crash into my plane while I waited for the green light. But I got away with a half tank of gas, which was ample for a return to Foggia, where, after some three hours past any possibility of return, I had been given up for lost. Vis had no time to be sending out routing messages noting my being delayed at their station.

Colonel Richard was a strange man. I always tried to understand him and please him where principle was not sacrificed, and he apparently had grown fond of me. Our poker games had been pleasant and I shouldered the bulk of the burden of command, leaving him free to enjoy his cups. Now, with me apparently gone, Richard was upset. It was dusk at the landing field and everything was shut down for the day. Richard was actually grieving for his roommate. So when engines were heard overhead, he rushed out to see who it might be. With the command jeep and driver not at his quarters at the time, Richard had half run to the airstrip. I parked the ship on the line, filled out the Form I (flight log), set the control locks, and was climbing down from the cockpit of the P-38, when Richard rushed up. He had been drinking, but he grabbed me in a big hug that surprised me. I was forced to revise some of my opinions of the colonel's motives when he had earlier argued about "his boys'" lives on the missions. His emotional concerns were assuredly genuine, but they have no place in war. I caused my best friend's death when I ran through him with my propeller in the landing accident at Brisbane, Australia, but I had to live with it. Richard had tears in his eyes as I explained the long delay in my return as we walked back to quarters. No one in the group had landed at Vis before, and the possibility that I had done so had not occurred to anyone.

I had a friend and former flying school classmate stationed in Italy flying B-17s at a nearby bomber base. We got together for a visit and the friend, James G. Ellis, broached the subject of trading airplanes with each other. His proposition was to exchange two old, non–combat-service-able planes, a B-17 that 1st Fighter Group could fly for parts, supplies, and luxuries, and an old P-38 that the bomber boys could tool around in to see what a fighter was like. I spoke with Colonel Richard, and the deal was struck.

Later, after a staff meeting, Richard asked me if I would like to fly over to Egypt. We could pick up some morale-boosting goodies there and spend a few days' R&R. Bucky Harris was also invited, and the three of us fired up the old war bird and flew to Cairo. Ellis had checked me out in the B-17 when he delivered it, and Richard had had some time in one somewhere earlier in his career.

On arrival in Cairo, we took in the famous sights, such as the pyramids and the Sphinx. We took a taxi to the end of the road. There, a native had a few camels and horses that he hired out to tourists to ride around the structures. Bucky and Richard hired horses, and I a camel. As we rode to the pyramids, the grizzled old camel saw a small bush that he wished to graze on, and turned aside to go to it. I said, "Come on, Clyde, I want to go with them to see the pyramids." I could imagine Clyde saying, "No, I'm sick of seeing pyramids, and am just about fed up with foreign tourists. Not one of you knows how a camel feels about this beast-of-burden business, and besides, I'm hungry. This bum who is supposed to be our master feeds poorly." I said, "Come on, Clyde, we're getting behind." But to Clyde, who was accustomed to pleasing tourist clients by pleasing himself, my opinion was unacceptable. He turned back toward the bush. Soon a regular dust devil developed there in the Sahara Desert with me figuring to teach this tourist-spoiled critter a few manners by a real live rootin'-tootin'-shootin' Oklahoma cowboy, who knew how livestock should behave. At the same time, Clyde figured to teach his one thousand and first tourist how livestock had their way in the Old World. His techniques I had not counted on. He turned his head and neck around 180 degrees, opened his great maw, showing two-inch-long canine teeth, and with a great roar attempted to pull his mount from his back. I jerked the opposite rein with all my might, and kicked the angry animal in the mouth with my heavy GI shoes, as I realized there was real danger in this huge animal. If the beast had dislodged me from his back, he might have pawed and bitten me to death. Clyde finally gave in to the new master and dutifully headed for the pyramids as ordered with a kick in the sides to boot. In the meantime, I was giving thanks to the Lord that I won the battle.

We three lodged at the famous Shepheard's Hotel. I remember the beautiful masonry in the structure. That afternoon I went out on the street for some shopping. On the street a hawker approached me, offering to sell me "feelthie peectures." I declined. Farther along the man approached again, "Feelthie peectures for ten piastres." Again I declined. Further on, "Feelthie peectures five piastres." Again I declined. Further on it was two piastres. I finally decided it would be easiest to buy the "peectures" and be done with the pest. I gave him the two piastres, stuck the envelope of pictures in my pocket, and returned to the hotel. In the hotel room I opened the envelope to look at the man's filthy pictures. It made a memorable story for me, as the envelope contained blank pieces of stiff paper. I just sat down on the bed and laughed at being duped.

That night we went to a nightclub and watched a belly dancer. Later we met two girls who were on vacation, one a French girl about thirty-five years old, who accompanied Colonel Richard. She was neat and stylish and seemed quite bright and proud. The other, a girl of about twenty, was from Madrid. Both girls were comely and we were having an uproarious time with the languages. With Richard's girl being French, we had three languages going. I speak some Spanish, and so was able to tell how I approved of her beauty, her dark Spanish eyes, her lovely olive skin, her elegant figure, and her clever repartee. Both girls were pleasant to be with, and we danced and partied and were together for the three days. Then, too soon, the demands of war interceded. Again we crossed the desert sands of the vast Sahara and the blue Mediterranean, finally settling onto the grass field at Foggia on the boot of Italy.

"Back at the ranch" the missions had been going well, and Colonel Richard finally promoted me to lieutenant colonel and had given me a party. But unfortunately my dear friend and combat companion, Tom Maloney, had been shot down, and was missing. Tom was one of the most popular pilots in the group. He was a kind, soft-spoken southerner who always took on the toughest missions. He was a superb flier, a good shot, and was one of the leading aces of the group.

Later we learned what happened. On a strafing mission Tom had come upon a train loaded with German trucks. As he strafed the trucks on open flat cars, one blew up, and he had to fly through the debris that knocked out the oil lines on both engines. He was able to nurse his ship out over the Mediterranean Sea, where he ditched it in the sea south of the Rhône River. He was able to swim ashore, but as he ascended the beach, a land mine exploded in his face. His flying career was over.

Tom crawled the remaining length of the beach. His shattered legs became infected while lying in a marsh, able only to crawl. His legs became infested with maggots, a fact that may have saved his life. He was later discovered, starving and helpless, by our own soldiers. Tom's life was saved, but he would pay the price of war, that of a crippled, ever-suffering veteran who had offered his life for his country.

One of my last missions was escorting a lone B-17 that was set up to test a guided bomb. I watched as the bomb curved and changed course in its downward flight. When Iraq took such a drubbing in their "mother of all drubbings" in the Desert Storm war, I felt a little pride in the efficiency of the guided bomb, feeling I had had a tiny part in its development. I just may have helped launch the first one in combat.

One of the more disappointing, least effective missions I remember was led by a brigadier general on a bad weather day to northern Italy. A few groups of B-17s tried the primary target but could not get through. They tried a distant secondary target and still couldn't get through. Finally, to the disgust of all, they flew out over the Adriatic Sea and toggled the load.

As many airfields, as many ports, as many factories as there were in range of that bomber force, to have that leader dust those bombs had to be repulsive to all present. And everyone's neck had been exposed to danger, as with other missions, yet they did not receive credit for the mission.

The missions slowed in late 1944 as the winds of winter approached and my fifty missions were nearing completion. On my last mission over southern France, a big dogfight ensued at the head of the group over the target. Focke-Wulfs were wrapping it up with P-38s of the group. Leading the 27th Squadron following on, I arrived just as the Focke-Wulfs dove away, but I was able to confirm one kill for one of the pilots of the 71st Squadron.

Finally orders came in November 1944, confirming that I had completed my second tour of duty as a fighter pilot. I checked the new operations officer in on the job, signed off all my files and responsibilities, said good-bye to all, and caught a C-47 to Casablanca to wait for a flight on a four-engine C-54 to the States via the Azores.

My tour in Europe ended much the same way it had ended in the Pacific, in violence. Often, at isolated stations, especially overseas in the combat zone, military discipline lags, and soldiers tend to forget their military training and relative status. That evening I went to the officers' mess hall for dinner. I sat down at a dining table, waiting to be served. There were three other officers at the table, and I greeted them. My greeting was ignored, which is quite rude among officers. They were loud with raucous conversation, also rude, but I had no obligations or special interest in this small station other than to complete my flight arrangements home. That, too, was doubtless the same status as 90 percent of the hundreds of officers who passed through that way station to and from the active theater. I made no comment and simply turned away from them. Their conversation continued with apparent pointed remarks such as "Big shots coming through," and the like. Then the waiter came with coffee and I asked the more talkative of the first and second lieutenants to please pass the sugar.

The officer said, "You want some sugar? I have

some sugar and I'll decide when you can have some." I said, "You better take stock of who you are and what you are saying, Lieutenant. What is your name and assignment?"

At that point I took a pen from my pocket and began searching my clothes for a piece of paper. The officer said, "Oh, you are going to be chickenshit about it, are you?" I said, "Lieutenant, you have just made this a personal matter. Let's you and me go outside." I got up, the lieutenant got up, and we walked to the rear of the mess hall and out the back door.

Outside, I turned on him and struck him in the face. He obviously knew nothing of fistfighting. His arms just seemed to be in the way as I struck him repeatedly. Suddenly he started yelling "Stop this, stop this" in a very official-sounding way. Amazing! I said, "As soon as I teach you a lesson, young man."

At that point he reached into the pocket of his raincoat for something, and I fled instantly around the corner of the lighted mess hall. As I turned the corner, I looked back and saw him extract a whiskey bottle from his pocket. Relief! as I feared he might have been a Military Police officer run amok with a gun, and that he might have shot me. Now I knew, so I stopped and started back.

Beside the mess building there were bordering rocks about hand size. I reached down and grabbed two. I yelled to him to put the bottle down and fight fair. He drew the bottle back menacingly and I let fly a rock. It struck the flap of his raincoat. He continued to hold the bottle high. I switched hands with the other rock and wham! I struck him in the middle of the thigh. He went down holding his thigh, and I left the premises hoping the fool had sense enough to keep the incident out of military circles, for a big flap over it would sink him, and hold me over for a court-martial or some such thing. Apparently he kept quiet, as nothing ever came of it, and I returned to the United States the following morning on a C-54 by way of the Azores.

X

The End of All Wars,
Says Who?

After returning from Europe in November 1944, I was assigned to a staff job in a P-38 replacement training unit at Santa Rosa, California. I checked young pilots out in the twin-engine fighters, gave lectures on combat, and did accident investigations in the job of air inspector. Then a few months later I was transferred to Chico Army Air Force Base, California, as inspector general there.

I have spoken of the grave responsibilities one acquires as he advances into positions of authority in active military flying units. While at Chico, I was assigned air inspector. A group of B-29s was transferred onto the base. One day, as I watched a B-29 enter the traffic pattern for a landing to the south, I noticed how large his pattern was compared to that of the smaller fighter planes. His pattern took him close to the foothills on his downwind leg. I thought at the time that perhaps I should change the pattern approach to a right-hand pattern that would take the planes out over the valley instead. However, none of the pilots flying the planes, or officers of the unit, had made any comments about it, so I did nothing. About three days later weather moved in, and a B-29 on the downwind leg of the pattern crashed into the hills. Only one man miraculously survived. It is one of those terrible memories; if only I had acted!

In August 1945 the base had been assigned a squadron of the new American jet fighters, the Bell P-59. The base commander was transferred, leaving me in his stead. I was anticipating checkout in the revolutionary new fighter when the war ended, but the P-59 unit was transferred to Nevada and I stayed on as base commander.

Was it World War I or World War II that was supposed to be the war to end all wars, or was it both? Little matter, the world went right on repeating history, for as soon as, or even before, the war was over the democracies and the communist world were back in a state of mistrust and suspicion of each other. In fact, another war began immediately, the Cold War.

The Cold War had considerable significance on my life. I had intended to leave the service after the war and become a merchant. I had saved my money and had several thousand dollars in the bank. I dreamed of opening a sporting goods store in some good game country like eastern Washington. For me it would have been a labor of love, as I was a dyed-in-the-wool outdoorsman.

I asked for a discharge, and in late 1945 I was released and took my family (wife and son, Jimmy) home for a visit to Oklahoma. While there, a friend asked if I would like to work for the state, accrediting GI Bill trainees. At the same time, the air force was expanding its permanent forces, and offered permanent commissions. I applied and got the job of accrediting GI Bill training programs.

This was an interesting job wherein I set up job programs in American agriculture and industry for the retraining of ex-GIs. It gave me an opportunity to observe industry over a wide spectrum, and I learned a lot about America and how it works. It made me a political conservative and a believer in the American entrepreneurial philosophy. With favorable prospects of the Air Corps becoming a new entity, openings for regular officer ranks were being offered. I applied and was accepted.

In July 1946 I reentered the Air Corps with a permanent commission and a temporary rank of lieutenant colonel. I was then sent to squadron officers school. After finishing the school I was assigned to the delightful duty of air instructor to the National Guard air units of North Dakota, South Dakota, and Minnesota.

The air units of the three states were equipped with P-51s, and with B-26s for administrative uses. I was well fitted for the job and the flying activities, as the P-51 was much like the old P-40, and the B-26 was an easy transition from the P-38, both being twin-engines. I found the B-26 barrel-rolled about as easily as the P-38.

One day while flying the attorney general of Minnesota to a conference, I did a barrel roll before he knew what was happening. After he calmed down, he wanted to do another.

Famous marine fighter ace, with over three times the number of aerial victories as mine, Joe Foss, was commander of the P-51 squadron at Sioux Falls, South Dakota. Someone said to me shortly after my arrival, "So you've come to instruct Joe Foss how to fly!" I said, "Well, in this case I have come to listen."

Actually, I found Lieutenant Colonel, later to become General, or Governor, Joe Foss, whichever term you prefer, to be the humblest of men, and the soundest. We spent two different assignments together and used to enjoy one of our favorite sports together, hunting. Our paths have crossed on many occasions, and we have been friends for almost fifty years. Our youthful lives had much in common, both having been farm boys, struggling under similar circumstances.

From the Minnesota assignment I was transferred to a newly inducted Guard group at Madison, Wisconsin, where they had a squadron of F-80 Shooting Stars. There I checked out in the F-80, and found it a nimble fighter plane. I liked it. Later I was sent through the jet tactical training course at Nellis Air Force Base, Las Vegas, Nevada, flying F-80s and F-86s.

While flying an F-80 on a mission at Nellis, I had a flame-out at sixteen thousand feet over the gunnery range, forty miles from base. I called *mayday* (an emergency warning) to Nellis tower and headed back to base. I tried a couple of air starts, but no luck. I kept getting lower and lower while trying to get as close to human activity as possible — vast stretches of Nevada are totally unoccupied. I wanted to be as close to ambulances and human beings as possible if I were injured bailing out. But, to my astonishment, I was getting close to the base. At about ten miles out I was down to about four thousand feet and realized I would have to bail out soon or try to land it.

There is a lot of open desert around Nellis, but it's pretty rocky too. A forced landing could easily result in fire and a crunched cockpit. You hated to smash a million-dollar machine. Being experienced at bailing, I wasn't afraid to do so, but I admit to a great amount of indecision at that point.

As I started to pull up and step out on the wing I looked at the base again. It seemed to me I was lower than the normal traffic pattern, and I had no power, yet I was getting darn close to the field. I had to decide, or soon I would be too low to bail out. I decided to stay with it. I was giving my location steadily over the radio, then the tower said they had me in sight. I reduced speed to around glide speed, about 150 miles per hour as I recall, and I could see it was going to be close. The field was all clear and I could see the ambulance and fire trucks at the side of the runway.

Instead of being below me as normal in the traffic pattern, the field seemed to be more level with me. I didn't dare lower flaps or gear. I planned a belly landing. At 90 degrees off the end of the runway on my turn, I dropped my nose way down to avoid stall and glanced at the air-speed indicator. It read 170, faster than I expected. I grabbed the landing gear lever and dropped my wheels on the final approach, got a green light, pulled back on the stick, and sat the little silver bullet down on the broad expanse of concrete.

I rolled two-thirds down the runway as the emergency vehicles sped along behind me. I braked at the first exit, turned off, and rolled to a silent stop as the fire truck sped up. There was no whine of the jet engine, no flickering instruments indicating multiple functions on the instrument panel, just silence in the cockpit. But I was down on the ground with an un-dinged million-dollar baby and a pilot in one piece. I was thankful. In his book: *Yeager: An Autobiography*,[*] Gen. Charles Yeager states: "Nine out of ten pilots will be killed if they attempt a dead-stick landing in a flamed-out jet."

At Nellis I was no favorite with the instructors. On the gunnery range I persistently bettered their scores, and they did this sort of thing every day. On the dive-bomb range I did not miss a single bull's-eye, and the short, pudgy instructor was so small about it, he didn't even congratulate me on the score, which was rare for a student and even an instructor; nor did he do so on the forced

[*] Charles Yeager, and Leo Janos, *Yeager: An Autobiography*, New York: Bantam Books, 1986, p. 186.

landing. Maybe it was because he should have told me I was not supposed to make forced landings in jets.

The ground gunnery work was all done in the F-86. It was a little Cadillac and a sweetheart to fly. I felt like it was me, just me flying up there, and she was our first supersonic. This was a relief after flying all my career in planes that shuddered, went out of control, and came apart if you dove in them too fast. Dive this little baby as fast as you wished, so long as you are over your sonic boom range or the open ocean, as sonic booms are not welcome to the local populace.

In February 1953, after finishing the course at Nellis, I was sent to South Korea as a replacement pilot for losses or rotations in the fighter interceptor units fighting the Chinese and North Korean Communists there.

I remember the first of the flight to Hawaii's Hickam Field in the old C-54. I was in the middle tier of seats, and fourteen hours of breathing nicotine from smoke you could cut with a knife from a hundred smoking passengers left me ready to go AWOL. And there was about forty hours more of the same to come.

At Wake Island it looked like nature was just barely able to make it an island, as it seemed that only a few feet of white sand protruded above the surface of the sea. Scars were still evident from the previous war, ended less than a decade before.

When we landed at the end of the last leg of

the long aerial journey, I was placed among people who, in my previous experience, had been total beasts. They had stabbed with bayonets when they took our soldiers prisoner, my dear companions who had worked to keep me flying. They had strafed my wing mates, helpless in their parachutes. They had starved and beaten to death others they had captured. They had done the most unimaginably horrible deeds that one human can do to another, all of which were still fresh in my mind.

They all seemed to be pleasant enough, which only reminded me of Mr. Nomura back in December 1941, smiling and dealing peace in Washington while he knew full well Pearl Harbor was being attacked. I had best get over to Korea.

I left Tachikawa late one evening and landed at Pusan one early morning in February 1953. Four other officers, all majors, and I were driven from the airport to the railway station to catch a train to Taegu. In February it is bitterly cold in Korea. I remember a thick glaze of ice on the cobblestones. I remember a little legless Korean boy coming out of the darkness of the small railway station on a sort of broad skateboard, upon which he sat. He was begging. I had a silver half dollar in my pocket. I never felt better for giving money to a beggar. I was disappointed he did not recognize what it was, and almost reluctantly placed it in his pocket. But I knew it would be of value to him anywhere.

It was a cold, sleepless, bumpy hundred-mile

ride to Taegu, where the Fifth Air Force headquarters was located in the mountains of southern Korea. We found quarters, caught a little sleep, and reported to the adjutant the next morning.

The adjutant greeted us, accepted our orders, studied them momentarily, and then said he might have bad news for us. He said there was a shortage of pilots in the dive-bomber units, and there was a surplus of F-86 pilots in the fighter-interceptor units. He said there was no certainty of it, but the general had instructed him to say it was just possible we all might have to be assigned to dive-bomber units. Of course, we protested. "What, how on earth could this be?" The adjutant replied that if anyone did not like the idea, the general had said that he could see him. We were instructed to return the following day for our assignments.

When we left the office, I said to the other four that I thought this was a poor policy and something should be done about it. They agreed, and I asked them if they would go with me to see the general about it, as we had been invited to do.

Oh, that was something else. Finally they said they would if I would do all the talking. Agreed, I returned to the adjutant's office and told him that we would like to see the general about our proposed assignments. He said, "What?" I repeated the statement. He said, "Are you serious?" I said, "Didn't you say if we did not like the prospects, we could see the general?" He said,

"Well, yes, I suppose I can arrange it." I said, "I thought you said it was set that we could see the general." He said, "Yeah, but I didn't know — well, come back tomorrow morning and I'll let you know." He was so surprised that someone would actually say something to the commander about the problem that he was nonplussed.

That night at the officers' club I met an old trainee of mine who had been in my squadron. We had a great visit and he filled me in on the doings of the theater. I mentioned to him what the adjutant had told us, and he said he knew all about the problem. He said the general had ordered him to make a staff study of the situation and he had just completed it.

I asked how it was possible that replacements trained for months in one skill, in one class of equipment, would have to be placed in a totally different category of work. He said it was quite simple, that it was entirely the general's fault. Several months earlier the F-86 units were short of pilots, so the general (Richard M. Carmichael) had made a quick fix of the shortage by offering transport pilots, bomber pilots, reconnaissance pilots, or whatever, the opportunity to fly the F-86 if they would sign up for another tour. Promptly the F-86 units were filled, while the dive-bomber units continued heavy attrition with no increase in replacements.

I asked why he hadn't stopped the program, and he said he had just done so. I thanked my old friend, Evvie, for the information, and the following morning reported back to the adjutant. He said that we could see the general at 1500 hours.

We five field-grade officers reported to the general's office. His aide, a master sergeant, asked us to be seated, and he would advise us when the general was free. Some twenty or thirty minutes later the general came to the door and we saluted and entered. He invited us to sit.

The general's desk was situated in the corner of the room. Five chairs were placed in a semicircle around the desk.

He began by saying fighter pilots were among the best of pilots, that they could fly anything, and he knew because he had been a fighter pilot once. He went on to explain that there was a problem in the Korean theater, unfortunately, with having more interceptor pilots than dive-bomber pilots, and when such a problem was encountered, he did what duty compelled him to do, that is, he made the difficult decision to correct it. Then he asked, "Just what would you gentlemen do if faced with the same situation?"

No one answered, for the other officers had said that I was going to have to do all the talking. I didn't answer because it was a leading question, and he hadn't asked it directly of me. We just all sat there. This apparently flustered the general somewhat, and he added, "Well, what would you do about it?" Still, we all just sat there.

Now, he was getting red around his collar. The officers in front of him were being almost insubordinate. He decided he would force the situation. He was embarrassed to have to look down to find the name of one of us on the list in front of him. Time weighed like a heavy cloud hanging over us. You could almost hear our pulses, but his approach was so obvious and displeasing that I refused to say anything until forced to.

He looked at the list with a quick sweep of his eyes. He saw the top name on the list, the ranking officer, Morehead.

A silver oak leaf and a gold oak leaf are difficult to distinguish at the eye level, and we were all sitting at the same eye level. The four majors were beginning to look at me expectantly. Then the general said, "Okay, Morehead, I said, what would you do about this situation?"

Unfortunately for him, he looked at the wrong man when he asked the question, and the major was about to say that he was not Morehead, when I had to speak. I said, "Well," — long pause — and the general's face was red, and he was embarrassed and angry, and he quickly turned to me. I said, "General, I wouldn't care to say anything unless I had the freedom to say what I thought and a few minutes to say it in."

With evident relief the frustrated man threw his arms in the air and said, "Go ahead, go ahead!" I said, "Sir, I believe every officer sitting here would go to Heartbreak Ridge (a famous battleground on the Korean front at the time) and man a machine gun if it became necessary. But these men are specialists, having been highly trained at the cost of tens of thousands of dollars of our taxpayers' money. They are in the pipeline of estimated replacement requirements, and to arrive at that assignment and find the pipeline clogged with untrained pilots is certainly a disappointment." And remembering Nathan's words to the guilty David, "Thou art the one," I said, "And I happen to know it is all your fault."

General Carmichael was a highly decorated man. His combat career had been long, hard, and faithful. He was one of those pilots in the B-17s caught coming in to land at Pearl Harbor on "infamy" day. He had led the first B-29 attack on Japan, was shot down over Japan, and was held prisoner. His decorations were equal to my own, for he wore a Distinguished Service Cross, a Silver Star, Distinguished Flying Crosses, and administrative medals galore. He was a West Pointer and a disciplinarian. He jumped to his feet and stormed, "Just a minute!"

I said, "Oh, I thought you said I had the freedom to say what I thought." With his face and neck beet red, he swallowed hard about three times and sat down. I said, "Sir, I realize it is too late to do anything about this right now, but I think it is a deplorable situation, and I hope to God you will do something about it."

His body was almost limp as he said, "Well, I'm doing the best I know how."

It was obvious to all of us that it was time to end the discussion, and we all rose as one. He stood, we saluted him, said "Good day, general," turned in an about-face, and left.

That evening I saw Evvie, my old friend at the club. He came over to me and said, "What in the hell happened in the general's office today?"

It is an interesting fact about the memory; in dramatic situations, as so often in combat, one can remember the minute details forever. I remember the conversation in the general's office that day almost word for word, as with many other quotes I have made in this book.

I did not wish to boast about the straight words we had given the general that day. I said, "Oh, I don't know, why?" Evvie said, "The hell you don't." I said, "What do you mean?" He said, "Oh, yeah! Meyers, the adjutant, said Master Sergeant Hatch said after you guys left the general came out and said, 'Worst ass-chewing I've had in years!' Now, what happened?"

I told him briefly, but made him swear not to spread it. I didn't want talk about how we told off the general; I was interested in getting the poor situation corrected. Needless to say, we all were sent to dive-bomber units, and the possibility was lost that I might become the only fighter pilot to bag an enemy plane in each of our last theaters of war.

I was assigned to the 464th dive-bomber group at Kunsan, on the west coast of Korea, flying F-84s, known as Thunderjets, where I began my tour. I checked out in the new jet and started learning the airplane's characteristics.

My first mission was to bomb some railroad tracks. I missed, and I thought of the waste. I could have dropped it on either rail of the track if I had been in the plane I was trained in, the F-86.

Our missions ranged from the front line to the Yalu. Korea was a hard-bitten scene with bitter-cold temperatures, and we were required to wear plastic dry suits beneath our heavy clothing. They were miserable to get on, as they fit close to the body, and a claustrophobic person would have had trouble with them. Their purpose was to give you extra time for rescue if you bailed out into the sea. The temperature of the shallow Yellow Sea was frigid, as was the Sea of Japan, and a few minutes were all a pilot could last before becoming paralyzed from the cold water. We did have a helicopter stationed on our airfield for rescue if we went down at sea or in the rugged terrain.

Vivid memories remain of the Korean tour. There was the great frozen expanse of the Chosin reservoir and the rugged, tortuous terrain our men had to fight in. Looking down from a mission, you knew there was agony going on in the ground war below. Once I was dive-bombing a reported supply dump on a hillside. From several thousand feet up, it all looked like just another grassy hillside to me, and I thought intelligence had come up with poor information again. But, according to instructions, I dropped my egg at the confluence of an eroded draw and a tree line.

As I got closer in my dive, it did look a little lumpy there. As I started to pull out, whoof! went half the hillside in a massive sheet of flame, and I got a lift on my pullout.

In most assignments, fighter pilots are authorized so many rounds of shotgun shells per month with which to practice leading the target. Skeet was the normal practice, but I often used mine on the real thing. In Korea there were many ducks and geese. The helicopter rescue boys next door had their own little house and housekeeping arrangement. We would prepare any ducks or geese I bagged there and feast while others ate C rations.

In the bitter cold I would go out in the rice fields and hide in an old slit trench or behind some creek bank and wait for waterfowl to come in.

I mention memories; there is one I shall never forget. One very cold evening I was walking up a hill, stair-stepped with tiny rice paddies. In the dusk I could see a thatched hut with a curl of smoke rising from the roof, then the acrid smell of a grass (the standard fuel of the rural people) fire reached my nostrils. To bring climax to the scene, the cry of a baby came to my ears through the gusts of a bitter wind. What a narrow thread the happiness of that little family hung on; how uncertain their future seemed to be with one half of a nation striving to kill off the other half.

Another time I was walking up a frozen streambed. As I rounded a bend, I came upon a young Korean mother kneeling on the ice in which she

316

had chopped a hole. On either side of her was a small pile of clothes. She was washing them in the frigid water. Her hands were red as fire from the cold. It made me think of what America considers the poverty-stricken.

One day General Carmichael came to the base, and I was there when he walked into the headquarters. He was friendly and talked with me about my assignment. He seemed to have no malice for me, and I certainly had none for him. Everyone makes mistakes, and he was correcting the one that affected me. I'm sure I did not exude enthusiasm about dive-bombing (cannon fodder, as we used to say).

Before my tour was up, the Chinese, whom we were fighting, opened another front with a threat to Taiwan, by an attack on the Quemoy Islands in the Formosa Strait.

Our headquarters was notified that a field-grade officer was needed to head a contingent of instructors and advisers to be sent to Formosa (Taiwan) to bolster and train the Nationalist Chinese Air Forces there and upgrade them to jets. I applied for the job and was notified immediately that I had been selected. I have the feeling that the good general remembered the incident in his office and was trying to make up for the past. He showed he was a man of character. Since the F-84 and the F-86 were the type of fighters we were sending to the Nationalist Chinese, my experience in both of them made my selection logical.

I was placed in command of a team of instructors and American maintenance personnel with T-33 jets, two-seater training planes.

I had never instructed in dual-seater planes. I had checked pilots out only via piggyback, or wingside, but to go from propellers to jets, it's best to give them dual-seater time. So I was in for new experiences.

During WW II we hosted a large number of Chinese pilots at training fields in the States. Horror stories were rampant about the things the Chinese students would do. I suspect American students would have done as many dumb things if they had been in another land and were not able to speak the language. Aside from a few exceptions, however, our team had outstanding success. One occurred to my own student and me. It highlighted my own ignorance as well as a backward reaction by the Chinese student.

I was letting my student land the T-33 himself for the first time. I was observing. As we came over the end of the runway at about a fifty-foot altitude, the student became nervous and slammed forward on the stick, which, in his mind, would push the plane onto the ground, the opposite of the prescribed procedure. One pulls back on the stick gently as the plane settles.

His action started a dive into the ground, nose first. My hand should have been on the stick following his moves, as it was thereafter. Anyhow, I grabbed the stick and jerked back hard. The nose came up just as we struck the ground, fortunately on all three wheels at once. It is the hardest I ever landed in a plane, and it knocked the breath out of me. I pushed the throttle forward and kept the plane flying for a go-around while I got my breath back. I had the structural engineers go over the plane thoroughly before I would let it fly again.

One of the T-33s was in the hangar for an extensive check. We roped it off and placed a full-time guard on it to keep the curious Chinese workmen from climbing on it and possibly tripping the rocket seat ejector. One morning, to our dismay, we arrived at the field to find that the guard had gone, literally, through the roof. He had climbed in, fiddled with the cockpit mechanisms, and had been ejected. He did not live to tell the tale.

By living in China, one learns more in depth of the Chinese culture and the degree of the differences between Chinese and Western culture. For example, a man used to walk down the street in front of our hostel each night, playing a fife. One night I saw him in the car lights, and he carried a blind man's cane. I asked Wong, my houseboy, why he walked the street each night. Wong said he was a masseur. I said, "Oh, how nice, how nice to have a blind man do masseur work, work he could do with his hands." Wong said, "Yes, very good masseur." He added, "His father masseur, grandfather masseur, great-grandfather masseur." I then said, "How could that happen, his father and grandfather all blind?" Wong said, "Put eyes out with hot iron when baby."

As late as 1954, we saw Chinese women with tiny feet, feet that had been bound since childhood. Normally they were from rich families, and did no work, as some could not walk. I asked a British missionary who had grown up in China how it was done. He explained their feet were wrapped tightly with strong bindings. He said as children they cried all the time from the pain.

General Chiang Kai-shek had been eager to update his air forces because the Red Chinese were receiving the Soviet Union's MiG fighters. So our program was a special project of his and Madame Chiang Kai-shek's. They would visit our unit frequently for the latest update. Dinners and evening entertainment were regular treats. I remember one dinner of twenty-one courses.

The waters around Taiwan were clear and the underwater scenery was spectacular. The Chinese had a Stearman PT-13 trainer that I had access to. Captain Simon Schmidt, a ground support officer, and I would take the plane to the nearby Pescadores islands. There was a little airfield right by the ocean's edge.

We would fly over with our face masks and underwater gear we had made from oxygen bottles — (we claim to have invented the first scuba). On the beach we would hire a native to take us out around the coral to dive and explore. One day I was down about forty feet when I came upon a dark cave. I cautiously approached it, half expecting a long arm of giant squid or octopus to ensnare me, when sure enough it did. I didn't see it, but it had me around the neck. I sprang off the bottom with a mighty leap, porpoised near the boat, and scrambled toward it. Then I saw Smitty writhing on the surface beside the boat, convulsed with laughter and trying to get his breath. Then I realized the source of my torment. My faithful partner, my friend, my pal, had been watching me through his face mask from above, and recognized my apprehension as I approached the cave. He had swum down and grabbed me by the neck, then returned to the boat. I said, "Smitty, you dirty dog. I'll get you for this!"

We speared fish, caught crabs, and probed among the ocean's secrets in the unmatched world of beauty beneath the waves. I'm sure the native boatman long wondered why my sportsman pal was so overcome with laughter, and just why I had rushed to the surface and went high in the air like a leaping dolphin that day off the Pescadores. But old Smitty paid dearly for his practical joke.

The native returned us to the beach, and we stowed our gear and mounted the biwinged open-cockpit bird for the return flight to Taiwan. About halfway back an ocean liner steamed along far beneath us. It was a perfect setup for my plan. If the engine of the plane were to die, we would have a source of rescue.

I eased back on the mixture control (fuel shut-off valve) until the engine missed. I acted very concerned. I looked back at Smitty with the most frightened look I could muster. I pushed it forward again. A few moments later I eased it back again. Pop! sput! sputter! then silence. I yelled, "Bail out, Smitty!"

I watched his face in the rearview mirror. He turned white and yelled back, "Now?"

I yelled, "Jump, Smitty!"

He kept yelling, "Now? Now?" He undid his safety belt, rose up in his seat, and at that moment I pushed forward on the control and yelled, "Wait!"

A moment later I started the sequence all over again and milked his emotions a couple more times until I felt properly avenged. Back on the ground I mused seriously as to what may have gone wrong with that engine. I topped it with the remark, "These damned Chinese mechanics!" It was some time before I revealed to Smitty how dearly he had paid for his deep-water prank. Even then he tried to kill me.

The Chinese Nationalists on Taiwan were now preparing for their last stand. I was impressed with their work. We converted more than fifty pilots from props to jets in a few months, and had a formidable fighting force of F-84s and F-86s to meet Mao Tse-Tung's MiG-15s.

I had to be careful how I complained about opposition that I received from my Chinese coworkers. I never learned, but a couple of Chinese commanders who gave me trouble with my policies just seemed to disappear. Chiang Kai-shek watched our operation almost daily, and I am sure he knew of any complaints I had, for I always seemed to get anything and everything I asked for. Just exactly what "corrective action" he took in the matter, I was not sure.

My team wound up our operation on Taiwan with much good luck and excellent results. In fact, among all the Air Force MDAP (Military Defense Assistance Program) teams worldwide, we held the lowest accident rate at the time.

My commanding officer, Col. Edward Rector, one of the world's great officers, pilots, and gentlemen, promoted me to full colonel. The Chinese celebrated and made me wear a set of eagles twelve inches wide they had made for the party. General Tiger Wong, chief of the Chinese Air Force, came down and pinned the eagles on me.

In Taiwan there were few family housing units available. I applied and was placed on the list for homes to be built.

Interminable delays in the program occurred so that Aldine and Jimmy, then nine, arrived only a few months before we were to depart. We flew to Tokyo in our unit cargo plane, where we visited old friends from my hometown, Howard and Dutie Goodall. Howard was in the army stationed there. They took us all over the island. For me one of the most interesting places were the Tokyo fish docks. There were mile after mile of them handling the bounty of the sea. It seemed every kind of creature of the ocean was there and used for food, from tiny half-inch-long fishes by the billions and sold by the bushel, to whale meat. The latter would probably represent, in bulk, several trillions of the former.

From Tokyo we caught an MSTS supply ship to San Francisco. En route Aldine and I discussed our faded relationship and decided to divorce.

With several weeks of leave built up, I flew down to Navojoa, Mexico, to visit an old friend who was working for the Morrison-Knudsen Construction Company, which was building a large dam for the Mexican government. The company had forty-five Quonset huts, and fourteen Western-style homes for their workmen. They also had a hard-surfaced airport.

I asked what they planned to do with all that when the dam was finished. They planned to bulldoze it down as it had been written off to taxes, was the reply. I asked if they would sell it. I visualized making sportsman and tourist quarters of the dwellings.

I reported to my next assignment at the Pentagon in the Missions and Attachés department, Operations Division, Headquarters, USAF.

Sometime later I heard from the head office of the Morrison-Knudsen Company that they would sell their property in Navojoa to me. They advised me that I would have to get title to the land elsewhere, however, as they did not own it and were only tenants of the Mexican government.

My offices in the Pentagon were in the subbasement, two floors below ground level. Three-fourths of the people working there smoked. I tried several times to get a transfer, as I was miserable because of the thick smoke I had to work in (I never smoked) and the gravelike atmosphere of the workplace. Although it was a choice assignment, and an opportunity to acquire a star on my shoulder, there was the opportunity to acquire a million dollars worth of real estate with great potential. Since I had enough National Guard time and regular service combined, I retired.

Epilogue

After leaving the Pentagon, I returned to California to be near my son. From there I negotiated with Morrison-Knudsen and the Mexican government to acquire the assets of the large dam construction site just twenty miles east of Navojoa, Mexico. I flew to Boise, Idaho, to talk with Mr. Morrison, and I made two trips to Mexico City, trying to obtain a long-term lease on the site. The latter was complicated by the fact that the land was on an Indian reservation, and ultimately the project failed as a result.

This was a disappointment, as the new international highway from the United States to South America was being completed that year, and I had planned to make a sports resort and motel-type tourist stop for Americans there beside the huge lake. It could have accommodated 104 families at a time.

In California there was no lack of investment opportunities at that time; the state was booming. I found a friend who had been my transportation officer at Chico AFB, who worked in a title insurance company. I joined a group of developers and took land development courses at night at the University of California. We invested in a shopping center site with plans to develop it. Time was necessary to acquire permits and satisfy city requirements, so I returned to Oklahoma to be with my mother and ailing father.

While in Oklahoma I met the assistant dean of women at the University of Oklahoma, at Norman, where my parents lived. Sometime later I changed her name from Miss Betty Angerman to my own, and after my father's death, we moved back to California.

The partnership developed the shopping center, which proved to be profitable. From that beginning I bought other strategic properties that I exchanged mostly for commercial property. Later I developed the North San Francisco Bay industrial park in Petaluma.

In 1965, when twenty-one years old and a senior at the University of California, my son died in an accident in Yosemite National Park. Following that disaster, Betty and I started a small family of girls, Melanie Ann and Myrna Leah.

In 1975, at an age when I was considering re-retiring, I exchanged some lots for a home and forty acres of land on Sonoma mountain, six miles east of Petaluma, and I began doing all the things I had always wanted to do.

I hunted and fished and traveled to different parts of the world. I went to Ecuador and the Amazon jungle to visit a missionary we supported there. I bagged black bears in Alaska, and a grizzly in British Columbia. I hunted leopard in Nepal and collected lion and hippo in Ethiopia. I shot a Cape buffalo in Botswana and fished tigerfish in the Okavango River. I fished the Orinoco River for peacock bass in Venezuela, and hunted the Majellan goose in Argentina. I fished for tarpon in Costa Rica and bonefish in Belize. I fished for Mahi-Mahi and tuna in Mexican waters and Arctic char in Iceland. I returned on a trip of nostalgia with remaining members of the 49th Fighter Group to Darwin, Australia, in 1977. I was honored by my induction into the Oklahoma Air Space Museum Hall of Fame at a ceremony in my home state in October 1994. We took the family to the Bahamas, through the inland passage to Alaska on cruises, and we toured Moscow, the Ukraine, and the Crimea. This year at fourscore years of age I bagged a musk-ox and a caribou sixty-three miles south of the magnetic north pole, failed to bag an elk on a pack trip in Wyoming, and bagged a Texas whitetail buck and four wild turkeys on the Wallace Fields range at Shamrock, Texas. I have maintained a hunting diary and a fishing diary since 1946, wherein I have documented the results of my trips and outings. I recently tallied some of the figures shown there. I had been fishing 1,992 times and hunting 1,888 times. I had bagged forty-two deer and forty wild boar. I had caught 2,264 fish of many kinds.

When I was in Java at a time when life appeared near terminal, I made myself a promise. There is a cartoon that shows the ever-suffering husband at Christmastime with an armload of gifts for a large family, enumerating the gift for each member. The last was a tiny box that he held closely and proclaimed, "And this one is for myself." I resolved that if I managed to live through the war, I would devote some time and effort on the things *I* would like to do. My dear wife has supported me in that resolve and has never uttered one word about being a hunting or fishing widow, or raised a finger at one of those junkets.

We live on a hill overlooking one of California's coastal valleys, where I keep a large number of pheasants, jungle fowl, partridge, quail, guinea fowl, turkeys, chickens, peacocks, ducks, Canadian honkers, and the like. We take our trips, and attend the reunions of the Fighter Aces Association, the Legion of Valor, and old military units, as no friends can match those made as comrades-in-arms.

Editors note: Colonel Morehead remained active in the reserve forces after retiring from the active service and was nominated for promotion to brigadier general. He retired from all military activity in 1967.